CEO
Lifelines

CLIMB ON

Exceptional Habits of Elite Companies

Salvatore D. Fazzolari

Insight into the top 102 proven habits
for achieving and sustaining coveted elite status

SMART BUSINESS® BOOKS
An Imprint of Smart Business® Network Inc.

CEO Lifelines—Climb On: Exceptional Habits of Elite Companies
COPYRIGHT © 2017 Salvatore Fazzolari Advisors LLC

Published by:
Smart Business Network
835 Sharon Drive, Suite 200
Westlake, OH 44145

Printed in the United States of America
Editor: Dustin S. Klein
Cover design: Josephine Francis
Interior design: Tori L. Whitacre

ISBN: 978-1-945389-80-1
Library of Congress Control Number: 2017949978

CONTENTS

PREFACE

Do not go where the path may lead, go instead where
there is no path and leave a trail.
Ralph Waldo Emerson

The idea for this book emanated from two very distinct needs. First, to provide the necessary building blocks for my clients and readers to help them successfully implement the lifelines leadership framework outlined in my first book, *CEO Lifelines: Nine Commitments Every Leader Must Make*, published in April 2014. These building blocks, or exceptional habits, are fully explored in this book. The second is to answer an elusive question that, I believe, goes unanswered in current business and leadership books and is not addressed in the guidance provided by popular management frameworks. The question: What specifically makes a company elite, and, importantly, how do you build and sustain such an organization?

Leadership Books

Amazon.com currently lists more than 150,000 books on leadership. If you are a newly appointed leader, a young aspiring leader, or someone just starting a business, finding the most appropriate book to read for your needs is quite a challenge. The reason so many leadership books are published each year is because a strong need exists for guidance on the topic. But perhaps a reason just as compelling is the fact that no one book can possibly provide all the answers needed by every leader. Although I have diligently read dozens, if not scores, of business books over the past four decades searching for such an all-inclusive book, I have yet to find this "holy grail" business leadership book.

Usually, the books that do exist choose to focus on a few key characteristics of business success such as special or extraordinary leadership, innovation, superior culture or strategic plan execution, or the existence of great teams. What's missing from the existing business and leadership management frameworks is that none offers a comprehensive guide that readers can use to build a truly elite enterprise. Still, it should be noted that some extraordinary business books do exist, and these resources absolutely deserve their place in the pantheon of best business books of the current generation.

Of note is the work of three amazing business book authors: Jim Collins, Michael Porter, and Phil Rosenzweig. Their books and writings, among a few others, have influenced the leadership and management practices of thousands of high performing companies around the world and directly influenced my business and management philosophy and the conclusions and methodology documented in both this book and in my previous book, *CEO Lifelines: Nine Commitments Every Leader Must Make.*

The "One" Book

The question of whether I have succeeded in creating the "holy grail" book I have been seeking for so long is, of course, up to my readers to determine. However, this book does offer what, I believe, is a strong contender for an inclusive, innovative, and comprehensive management framework that will guide today's leaders towards answering the elusive question: What makes a company elite? As you will learn in the pages that follow, I believe elite companies are built and sustained by following the comprehensive management framework outlined in this book, which includes three specific parts.

The first part includes the framework's four high-level foundational pillars. These pillars include the following: an exceptional strategy; superb execution capabilities; an extraordinary leadership team; and, importantly, being on the right side of the luck spread. These foundational pillars metaphorically speaking are simply at the summit level, at the twenty-nine-thousand-foot level. These four high level principles are then significantly expanded into the second part, the *lifelines leadership framework*—which is reviewed in *CEO Lifelines: Nine Commitments Every Leader Must Make.*

This second part is at the fifteen-thousand-foot level; this part includes the nine lifelines principles, along with the luck spread. The third part is at base camp level and includes the essential building blocks that are expressed in the form of exceptional habits, which are detailed in this book. This framework is all you need to get your mind focused on ascending the ultimate summit, where the air is thin and where only the elite can successfully climb. It's important for the reader to understand that the foundational pillars along with the lifelines leadership framework represent high level principles that must be implemented through the exceptional habits, which are the building blocks and mechanisms necessary to effectively build and sustain an elite company.

This book is intended as a practical guide, reference book, and workbook focused on helping leaders build and maintain the exceptional habits required of elite leaders, enterprises, and boards. Its principal audience is small-to-medium-sized businesses and their leaders, not necessarily CEOs of Fortune 500 companies (although the book could serve as a useful resource). If you are a professional manager, business leader, newly appointed CEO, CEO of a family or privately-owned company, or even an MBA student, this book is for you. Leaders who believe their company is on the way towards elite status will also find this book highly useful as a benchmark and guide to keep their own initiatives and goals on track.

Unexpected Descent from the Summit – Climb On

As I explained in my first book, *CEO Lifelines: Nine Commitments Every Leader Must Make*, in February 2012, I was separated from my company—a large multinational—where I had served as its chairman, president, and CEO. At the time, I had no idea what I was going to do next. Luckily, I had a deep reservoir of indispensable experiences and skills I knew I could draw on, and I quickly set to work.

My first goal was to obtain at least three board seats at great companies. I landed four: one with a large elite public company, one with a technology company that recently went public, and two with excellent private companies. My second goal was to write a book and start a consulting practice. I wrote two books and successfully launched my advisory practice, Salvatore Fazzolari Advisors LLC. My third goal was to get engaged with private equity. I'm currently on the advisory board of one private equity firm and serve on the senior advisory council of another, and I am in an ongoing professional relationship with several other top-tier private equity firms.

Finally, my fourth goal was to engage in more public speaking and pursue my passion of cooking, which I did. Over the past five years, I have given numerous speeches at various events, and I attended cooking classes in Italy. I'm in the process now of writing a book on the Italian food culture, which includes family recipes dating back a century.

This book represents a distillation of all the successful company management knowledge I have gained over the past forty years. It is my unique experience as a CEO and CFO for a multinational corporation, as a board member of highly successful companies, and as an advisor and consultant to a wide variety of businesses that underpins the confidence I have in the advice and guidance offered in this book. It is this experience that also gives me the confidence to assure my readers that they can also climb the highest leadership summit (following the mountaineering metaphor used in this book and previous one) to achieve truly elite status.

Climb on!

ACKNOWLEDGMENTS

The tale of their teamwork is important because we don't often focus on how central that skill is to innovation.

Walter Isaacson[i]

I'm blessed to have such a loving wife, family, and supportive friends. This book would not have been possible without their insight, perspective, and wisdom. I am honored and humbled to have had my small focus group of talented family members and friends contribute so much to its pages.

A special thank-you goes to my exceptional editor and friend, Mark Morrow, who made such an extraordinary contribution. His counsel, editing skills, and amazing insight helped bring my idea for this book to reality. I'm deeply appreciative for not only his friendship, but also his ongoing commitment to helping me create it. Without his encouragement and precocious skills, this book would not have been possible.

Thank you to Michael Feuer, an elite CEO and friend, who made a significant contribution to the book. I am honored and humbled that he devoted so much time to my project. Michael co-founded OfficeMax and in sixteen years, as CEO, grew the retailer to sales of $5 billion and 1,000 stores worldwide. Today, as Founder and CEO of Max-Ventures, his firm invests in and consults for retail businesses. Serving on a number of boards, Michael is a frequent national speaker, and author of the business books, *The Benevolent Dictator* and *Tips from the Top*. His long running nationally syndicated *Smart Business* magazine column has received more than ten awards for excellence.

A special thank-you goes to my two wonderful sons, Salvatore Fazzolari and Michael Fazzolari, who both contributed to the book. Finally, I would like to also thank my long-time friend and entrepreneur, Sage Newman, for his contribution.

INTRODUCTION

*The main thing that has caused companies to fail, in my
view, is that they missed the future.*
Larry Page[ii]

C omplacency often follows success. If the
complacency continues
unchecked, it can easily
lead any company to fall from
the summit as an elite
enterprise. Complacency can

> *Good is the enemy of great.*
> Jim Collins

also be a condition that already exists and has become
deeply rooted in a company's underlying culture—and it is
this pre-existing condition that prevents non-elite
enterprises from ever achieving elite status. Usually,
complacency occurs when three conditions exist in an
enterprise.

First, there's a notable absence of A-players to build
and sustain an enterprise's elite status. This A-player gap
can include its CEO, the leadership team, or the board of
directors.

Second, there is a lack of discipline, a condition that can destroy even the best companies, best leaders, and best boards. Lack of disciplined action can also prevent good companies from achieving elite status. And, third, arrogance among both company leaders and the board. Outsized hubris prevents leaders and boards from recognizing important trends and events and usually results in bad decisions that cumulatively impair an organization. These three conditions, more either cause an enterprise to fall from the summit or are the root cause of a company failing to achieve elite status. To put this point as succinctly as Jim Collins does in his book *Good to Great*, "complacency is the enemy of elite."

Mountaineering Metaphor

Mountaineering is an important metaphor in this book and in the previous one, *CEO Lifelines*, since its principles and practices align nicely with the concept of elite enterprises.

Elite mountaineers know the importance of having the right team of climbers (even if it's just one partner). They know how critical discipline is on the ascent and descent, and they know how vital it is to not let arrogance cloud or even blind their judgment and impair their ability to adapt. This need is particularly true when mountaineers need to make that critical final decision of whether to push for the summit or return to the camp below.

Making the right fact and circumstance decision can sometimes mean the difference between life and death on the mountain. Taking that so-called last step is something that needs to be decided through clear thinking and the use of sound, disciplined judgment.

Elite Simply Means the Best

This book, as noted, is a follow on to *CEO Lifelines: Nine Commitments Every Leader Must Make,* and, as such, draws on its concepts. Chapter 1 provides the context you'll need. It explains again the exceptional habits required to create and sustain an elite enterprise and provides the foundation companies must have in place to implement the *lifelines leadership framework.*

Clearly, the best companies achieve elite status because they consistently outperform merely good companies. The positive news is that the path is open for any company to achieve elite status through a laser focus on the exceptional habits outlined in this book and by learning and implementing the management framework described here. Thus, excellence or elite status can be achieved and sustained with the right leadership team and with an extraordinary strategy built on a solid foundation underpinned by superb execution capabilities.

Chance or luck can sometimes be a factor as well. The mechanisms necessary to build and sustain an elite company are derived from the consistent practice of what I call "exceptional habits" (which are the required building blocks needed to implement the lifelines leadership framework that I outlined in *CEO Lifelines).* Almost all organizations have the potential to reach the highest summit of elite organizations by implementing this innovative management framework.

How This Book Is Organized
Elite companies are focused on the habits and practices that create exceptional leaders, enterprises, and boards, as shown in Figure 1. It is important to note that these key habits are linked and do not exist on their own. If any of the major elements are disconnected from the other, then

achieving elite status will not be possible. It's a symbiotic relationship.

The cumulative effect of flawlessly executing all the relevant exceptional habits is what transforms a good or strong company into an elite enterprise. It's important to note that most of the habits are timeless and have endured for generations. There are, however, some habits that are more focused on today's environment and, thus, will evolve and change over time. In total, 102 of these habits are outlined in this book.

Figure 1:

The essential relationship among the habits also drives the arrangement of the chapters in this book. Chapter 1 provides an overview and review of what raises a company to elite status. Sections 1, 2 and 3 cover each of the exceptional habits in detail for leaders, enterprises, and boards. These habits are also examined in relation to the foundational pillars of leadership, strategy, and execution, as well as the luck spread and the nine lifelines principles of the lifelines leadership framework. Section 4 offers a crucial implementation tool kit. This tool kit includes checklists (important in both business and mountaineering) that will help enterprises prepare for the ascent to the summit of elite status. Finally, the book offers detailed answers to key questions relative to both the lifelines leadership framework and the exceptional habits of elite enterprises.

Chapter Overview

Chapter 1: What Makes Companies Elite? The first chapter answers that elusive question: What makes companies elite? Elite companies are built and sustained through key foundational pillars. These include an exceptional strategy; best-of class execution capabilities; extraordinary leadership team; and, being on the right side of the luck spread. These four principles then need to be expanded into the lifelines leadership framework and the exceptional habits, which are the high-level principles and the detailed building blocks, respectively. This is the formula for building and sustaining an elite company. It's important to note that the lifelines are segmented into nine specific principles along with an acute awareness to the luck spread. The habits are then segmented into three integrated and interconnected parts. They include exceptional habits of elite CEOs, exceptional habits of elite enterprises, and exceptional habits of elite boards.

This chapter demonstrates that there's a clear relationship between the lifelines leadership framework—as outlined in *CEO Lifelines*—and the exceptional habits of elite companies outlined in this book. *CEO Lifelines* is an innovative leadership framework that includes both personal and enterprise lifelines, as well as essential elements of the luck spread. The lifelines leadership framework represents high-level principles; the habits translate the principles or unique activities into specific building blocks necessary for building and sustaining an elite organization.

Section 1: Exceptional Habits of Elite Leaders. All great leaders possess incredible instincts. These leaders have developed and rely on a deep pool of exceptional habits to climb their respective summits. We can learn a great deal from these extraordinary and talented individuals by carefully studying and adopting their habits. In this chapter, we will review the most important exceptional habits of elite leaders that—if implemented with discipline and focus—can provide a leader with the skills needed to climb any summit. We will review thirty-eight exceptional habits in this section, and they are detailed in chapters 2, 3, and 4 under the foundational pillars of leadership, strategy, and execution, respectively.

Section 2: Exceptional Habits of Elite Enterprises. All great organizations have developed exceptional habits. These exceptional habits, built over time, provide these organizations with ample lifelines. The prodigious number of lifelines developed by elite companies allow these entities to not only survive and withstand any unexpected storm or global shock while climbing the summit, but these lifelines also provide the enterprise with a distinct competitive advantage. As leaders, we can learn so much from these elite organizations by vigorously adopting their habits. We will review forty-three exceptional habits in this section, and they are detailed in chapters 5, 6, and 7 under the foundational pillars of leadership, strategy, and execution, respectively.

Section 3: Exceptional Habits of Elite Boards. Just like leaders and organizations, elite boards of directors have also developed exceptional habits that differentiate them from the good and the average. Elite boards know how to add value through exceptional habits. Again, boards of directors can learn a great deal by adopting these exceptional habits, and they apply to both private and public companies. Many of the habits can also be adopted by advisory boards and non-profit organizations. We will review twenty-one exceptional habits in this section, which are detailed in chapters 8, 9, and 10 under the foundational pillars of leadership, strategy, and execution, respectively.

Section 4: Implementation Tool Kit. This section provides all the exceptional habits of elite leaders, exceptional habits of elite enterprises, and exceptional habits of elite boards. The information is summarized in checklist format as they appear in the book with key salient points added as well. The checklists are included in chapters 11, 12, and 13. Another key implementation tool included in Section 4 is a series of frequently asked questions from both the lifelines leadership framework and the exceptional habits. The detailed answers to questions arising from implementing the lifelines leadership framework principles and the building blocks, which are the exceptional habits, are included in Chapter 14. This chapter connects and combines the first book, *CEO Lifelines*, with this book by melding them into one larger book through *Questions and Answers.* The questions are all derived from my leadership experiences, advisory practice, board experiences, and research of elite companies.

Chapter 15: Conclusion—The Journey Never Ends. This chapter outlines key conclusions about the journey to achieve elite status.

Mountaineering Metaphors

I use mountaineering metaphors throughout the book to capture the essence of challenges that CEOs, enterprises, and boards face in today's fast paced and turbulent environment. What highly skilled mountaineers must do is very much like what CEOs, enterprises, and boards of directors must do as they plan and execute a successful strategy (summiting of a mountain). There are no shortcuts to the top, including the last step, which is often most challenging and dangerous.

The Death Zone

One of the most effective mountaineering metaphors as it relates to this book is the "Death Zone." In the book *The Climb: Tragic Ambitions on Everest*, authors Anatoli Boukreev and G. Weston DeWalt define the Death Zone as, "any elevation above 8,000 meters where extended exposure to sub-zero temperatures and oxygen deprivation combine and kill, quickly."[iii]

In the world, only fourteen mountains rise above 8,000 meters high; all of which are in Asia (East Asia, Central Asia, and South Asia). The highest peak in the world is Mount Everest at 8,848 meters (29,029 feet). It is in the Mahalangur Himalaya range. The second highest is K2, located in The Karakoram mountain range. It rises 8,611 meters (28,251 feet) above sea level and is considered to be the most difficult and dangerous mountain to climb in the world. Companies, like mountaineers, don't exist with guarantees that they will succeed (or they can be scaled); both mountaineers and CEOs are always in danger of perishing (or failing) on their climb to the summit. The best prepared and most skilled climbers (and companies) have the best chance to safely reach the summit.

Company Death Zones
The Death Zone in business can be a sudden change in the marketplace due to a disruptive new technology; for example, the impact of Apple's iPod on the music industry or Uber's devastating impact on the transportation industry. It can also be an external global financial or socioeconomic shock or a series of such shocks that have a material adverse impact on a company. The disruption might be the so-called commodity trap, when a company's products or services become rapidly commoditized, or made effectively indistinguishable from similar products or services. In all these cases, organizations and leaders unprepared for a sudden change can find themselves with little oxygen and little hope of making it safely down the mountain. It is vital for companies to adopt the exceptional practices of elite enterprises and to build an abundant number of lifelines so that they can withstand any unexpected major storm or calamity.

The need to prepare for the Death Zone is more important today than at any time since the Great Depression of 1929. In the last ten years, we've had (and continue to have) a series of global disruptions that include the 2008 Great Recession, the European Sovereign Debt Crisis, the ever-escalating geopolitical conflicts throughout the Middle East, in addition to the rise of terrorism. More recently, beginning in early 2016, the business environment began dealing with what I call the Global Chaos Crisis.

This latest crisis was driven by a series of extreme events, including the dramatic slowdown in the Chinese economy; the collapse of oil and commodity prices; the sharp rise in the U.S. dollar; Brexit (United Kingdom's exit from the European Union); anemic economic growth across the world; tremendous volatility in the equity markets; depleted options for central bankers to effect and boost major economies; significantly elevated debt levels in emerging economies; and ongoing conflicts in the Middle East that have caused a massive migration of refugees to Europe. This Global Chaos Crisis is having a dramatic effect on many companies, particularly ones that have not built adequate lifelines to sustain them. Now, more than ever and before it's too late, companies need to adopt the nine lifelines principles and implement the exceptional habits of elite companies outlined in this book. It is an essential move if today's organizations expect to survive in this new norm of world chaos.

CHAPTER 1

WHAT MAKES COMPANIES ELITE?

Greatness is not primarily a matter of circumstance;
greatness is first and foremost a matter
of conscious choice and discipline.
Jim Collins[iv]

In early morning hours of August 1, 2008, ten different groups of climbers set out from their high camp to climb the summit of K2, the world's second tallest mountain and arguably its most dangerous. The events from that day and what followed were masterfully captured by Ed Viesturs, with David Roberts, in their book, *Life and Death on the World's Most Dangerous Mountain*. This is how the authors described what happened that day:

> *Thirty climbers climbing up the same route on the*
> *same day would have been business as usual on*
> *Mount Everest. On K2—a far more serious*
> *mountain, and one that has seen far fewer*
> *attempts—such a crowd was unprecedented ...*
> *thanks to the perfect weather for which they had*
> *waited so long, the climbers were awash in*

optimism. The summit was within their grasp. And then things started to go subtly wrong. Small mistakes were made. Yet the single event that turned an awkward day into a catastrophe was nobody's fault. Within the next thirty-six hours, eleven of those mountaineers would die high on the Abruzzi Ridge. The disaster that unfolded ... would end up as the worst single-event tragedy in the mountain's history ... And nobody saw it coming. [v]

So, what exactly happened on that fateful day, and how can the lessons learned be useful to both mountaineers and business leaders?

Viesturs and Roberts make it abundantly clear that many mistakes were made that might seem fundamental, including climbers getting a late start; allowing too many people on the same route at the same time, which created congestion; a decision to reposition fixed ropes causing further delays; and allowing panic to set in after the serac (cliff of solid ice) collapsed during the night.

The authors connect all these events as a typical perfect storm of circumstance. "...people didn't die because of the serac collapse. They died because of what the serac collapse created, after all the other ominous conditions surrounding the ascent had come into play." Unfortunately, this 2008 accident mirrored a 1996 "killer storm" accident on Mount Everest that resulted from similar tragic circumstances and decisions: too many climbers, starting late, slower than anticipated progress, a refusal to turn around, and using up precious energy and oxygen bottles. Eight mountaineers died in that accident.

What lessons can we glean from these tragic climbing accidents? First, there are no shortcuts or easy paths to the top. Steady discipline is paramount to success. And, importantly, luck (either good or bad) is an undeniable factor. For businesses, facing a storm at the summit of a mountain is very much like the facing of a major economic shock like a financial crisis (take your pick: the 2008 financial meltdown, the dotcom bust of 1995 to 2001, or the financial downturn during the 1980s). When these events happen, panic often sets in, and mistakes are made. Enterprises find themselves inadequately prepared for these economic events because they have not established critical lifelines to prevent their fall. It's a mistake mountaineers— and businesses—usually only get to make once.

In this context, mountaineers like to say that "getting up the mountain is optional; getting down the mountain is mandatory." What they mean is that getting off the mountain safely is perhaps a bigger challenge than going up because the climber's natural tendency is to relax at the top. That loss of edge—along with weariness—is when mistakes, sometimes fatal, occur. In business, once an enterprise achieves elite status, our natural tendency is to relax (perhaps even develop a certain measure of hubris along the way) and be less consistently disciplined. Like the mountaineer who survives to climb another day, enterprise leaders must be vigilant to avoid making this mistake.

Ascending the Elite Summit

The definition of the term elite— as used in this book— simply means the best! In more quantifiable terms, here are enterprise results, I believe, qualifies a company as elite:

Proven superior shareholder value over at least a ten-year period as measured by stock price and the dividends paid to shareholders, and as compared with a reliable benchmark (usually the S&P 500 or the comparable results found in a peer group's proxy statement). My list of the top twenty-five elite large enterprises is listed in the appendix.

Superior value creation is ultimately what climbing to the summit of a mountain (or running an enterprise) is all about. As Greek philosopher Aristotle pointed out, "We are what we repeatedly do. Excellence, then, is not an act, but a habit."[vi] Enterprises that learn and adopt the elite practices outlined in this book, and do so with fanatical discipline and focus, greatly increase their chances of reaching the highest possible summit. Further, I firmly believe that such organizational achievement is available to any enterprise if the right building block enterprise, leadership, and board habits are in place.

What Makes Companies Elite?

The innovative management framework outlined in this book offers enterprises a comprehensive formula that will guide company leaders toward achieving and sustaining elite status. Enterprises that commit to this difficult goal must first start with the four foundational pillars that form the supporting base to build and sustain an elite company. These pillars are supported and sustained through both the nine principles in the lifelines leadership framework and the exceptional habits of elite leaders, enterprises, and boards outlined in detail in this book.

Elite enterprises are firmly anchored to the four foundational pillars, including:

- an exceptional strategy
- best-of class execution capabilities
- extraordinary leadership team
- being on the right side of the luck spread

All organizations have the potential to reach the highest summit in their business if they focus on all these key elements and fully recognize that getting any of these pillars wrong—wrong strategy, poor execution, wrong leaders, or ignoring the influence of luck—can lead to mediocrity or irrelevance. Here's a brief description of each pillar and how they correlate and are interconnected to the nine lifeline principles:

- *Strategy.* A company must have an innovative and unique (exceptional) business model captured in the way the core purpose or mission of the company is articulated. This model must be clearly underpinned by the core values that drive the company's culture. These elements are part of an enterprise's business model lifeline principle and core philosophy lifeline principle.
- *Execution.* A company must have a distinctive, highly skilled, capable and adaptive culture that drives excellence and high performance. The highest performing companies are continuous learning organizations. These elements are part of

the learning entity lifeline principle, exceptional
capabilities lifeline principle, and the distinctive
culture lifeline principle.

- *Leadership.* Great teams are built by elite leaders,
  and great teams build elite companies. As you'll
  learn in this book, this pillar correlates with the
  people excellence lifeline principle, precocious
  characteristics lifeline principle, indispensable
  experiences lifeline principle, and proactive actions
  lifeline principle.

- *Luck.* Companies must anticipate being on the
  wrong side of the *luck spread*, which can have an
  outsized negative impact on performance of the
  company, particularly when a series of bad luck
  events occur. We'll explore this concept in greater
  detail later in this book.

While these foundational pillars clearly represent
excellent business principles, elite companies connect these
practices to the nine personal and enterprise lifelines that
together form what I call the lifelines leadership
framework. As explained below, the nine lifelines are
segmented into three personal and six enterprise principles
that are essential to building and sustaining an elite
company.

**Lifelines Leadership Framework—High Level
Principles**

*CEO Lifelines: Nine Commitments Every Leader Must
Make* positions the lifelines leadership framework as high
level principles that organizations can use to build and
sustain an elite enterprise. These nine lifeline principles

outlined below are essential in guiding a company in the execution of the exceptional habits. It's important to note that within each of the nine lifeline principles, the exceptional habits detailed in this book neatly fit into the various principles and, thus, the nexus. Note also that some exceptional habits naturally apply to several different lifeline principles. However, when executed superbly, these habits form the building blocks that lead to building and sustaining an elite enterprise.

Here is a recap of the nine lifeline principles arranged by category:

Three Personal Lifelines: These three lifelines encourage personal growth and improved individual performance. Although these personal lifelines apply to everyone in the organization, it is imperative that the CEO, the board of directors, the key seats leadership team, and the global leadership team excel in these habits.

1. *Precocious Characteristics.* CEOs, board members, and the leadership team of the enterprise must possess thirty key precocious leadership characteristics that are necessary to achieve elite status. Some of these characteristics are innate while others must be developed, but leadership strength and suitability are defined by these precocious characteristics and a focus on them is essential.

2. *Indispensable Experiences.* Since experience is everything, leaders and board members must be able to learn through indispensable experiences.

Having the right collection of experiences, skills, and perspective among these leaders is essential.

3. ***Proactive Actions.*** Leaders and board members must have a fearless and proactive mind-set in carrying out and executing the fiduciary and shareholder value creation responsibilities of their job.

Six Enterprise Lifelines: These interdependent lifelines represent the six practices of healthy, thriving, and elite enterprises.

1. ***Business Model.*** All stakeholders, including the enterprise leaders and the board of directors, must have a tenacious focus on an innovative business model that provides a distinctive competitive advantage. The business model is the key driver of strategy and drives the creation of economic value; that's why creating the business model is the most complex task of leadership.

2. ***Learning Entity.*** Enterprises must learn from both success and failure, a concept that is the cornerstone of building a learning entity. Leadership requires the creation of efficient corporate mechanisms and processes to gain this essential knowledge.

3. ***Exceptional Capabilities.*** Achieving and maintaining elite status requires enterprise leaders and their boards to possess exceptional operating capabilities that provide a sustainable competitive advantage through consistent execution.

4. ***People Excellence.*** A team of A-players (including the leadership and the board) is essential to

achieving the summit of business success. As such, an enterprise must have a powerful internal talent-management and leadership-development process focused on elite status creation.

5. *Distinctive Culture.* Strong cultures are built by focusing on six characteristics including: (a) a value-based leader and leadership team; (b) team members that demonstrate an infectious passion for the core purpose, values, and business model of the enterprise; (c) respectful, authentic connections between enterprise members; (d) shared standards of enterprise behavior; (e) how leadership communicates to members of the enterprise; (f) the success of the governance framework functions. Boards should also develop and build their own distinctive and healthy culture.

6. *Core Philosophy.* Greatness must be underpinned and driven by a clear and effective core purpose and core values. Everyone in the organization needs to be aligned and passionate about the core philosophy.

Luck Spread

Luck impacts all leaders and enterprises whether they admit it or not—no one is inviolable from the potential adverse effect of the serendipity of chance. In my first book, I explained in detail the concept of luck spread; simply put, luck spread is a continuum of how chance can impact an enterprise, from positive (good luck) to negative (bad luck). Enterprise leaders and the board must understand and account for the potential impact of the luck spread on the strategic decisions they make.

As I pointed out in *CEO Lifelines: Nine Commitments Every Leader Must Make*, Jim Collins provides the most compelling view on luck in his insightful book *Great by Choice* when he notes: "We observed an asymmetry between good luck and bad. A single stroke of good fortune, no matter how big, cannot by itself make a great company. But a single stroke of extremely bad luck, or an extended sequence of bad luck events that create a catastrophic outcome, can terminate the quest. There's only one truly definitive form of luck, and that's the luck that ends the game."[vii] Author Phil Rosenzweig in his book *The Halo Effect* (Free Press, February 2007) makes the following cogent point about luck, "... acknowledge that luck often plays a role in company success. Successful companies aren't "just lucky"—high performance is *not* purely random—but good fortune does play a role, and sometimes a pivotal one."[viii]

Building Blocks to Elite—Exceptional Habits
All nine lifeline principles are interdependent and important for the success of the leader, the board, and the enterprise. These high-level principles must be implemented and sustained through the exceptional habits of elite leaders, exceptional habits of elite enterprises, and exceptional habits of elite boards. Insight into the top 102 proven habits for achieving and sustaining coveted elite status are covered in the pages that follow.

The exceptional habits are the unique activities that essentially drive the execution of the nine principles. Each habit is a building block that can cumulatively put a company on the path to greatness and, ultimately, sustain it.

Hence, the natural connection between the lifelines leadership framework and the exceptional habits.

Attaining and Sustaining Elite Status

In Walt Rostow's 1960 book, *The Five Stages of Economic Growth*, the MIT professor showed how undeveloped economies typically go through on what he called the five stages of development. The book brilliantly outlines each stage of development and demonstrates how critical each stage of the process contributes to the building of a developed economy. In many ways, enterprises follow a similar development path, and, as such, Rostow's work is a good background model for both the mountaineering metaphor used in this book and the crucial steps companies need to make on the way to the elite status summit.

Stage 1: Base Camp—Establishing a Strong Foundation

While at base camp, enterprises must build their teams and establish other important foundational elements as suggested by the lifelines leadership framework. Creating this foundation means building the executive leadership group as well as the global leadership team required to prepare for the climb to the summit. In addition to the team, the enterprise must develop its core purpose and core values, and clearly define, through its business model, an overall business strategy—including an organizational structure. It also needs to sharpen and develop execution capabilities and ensure that the enterprise is a learning entity. Creating these lifelines provides the foundation for the exceptional culture needed for the organization's climb to the summit.

Stage 2: Advance Base Camp 1—Building to the Summit

As the enterprise successfully transitions from stage one to stage two, it places itself in a better strategic position to ultimately ascend the summit of elite. During this critical phase of development, enterprises must demonstrate the exceptional execution capabilities of all the habits outlined in this book. It's not possible for an organization to advance to stage three without consistently mastering the crucial building blocks that are necessary to achieve and sustain elite status. During this stage, enterprises need to also develop an acute awareness of how to manage the luck spread while simultaneously building a prodigious number of "lifelines" that will help the enterprise survive any unexpected storms while climbing in the dangerous territory mountaineers call the Death Zone.

Stage 3: Advance Base Camp 2—Transition and Breakthrough

During this vital phase of development, the enterprise reaps the rewards of an extraordinary execution of both its business model and the elite habits. It is the transition point from an average or even good company to something greater. Clearly evident at this stage is a strong leadership team, brilliant strategy, superb execution capabilities, and, most importantly, consistent strong performance. In short, an enterprise's breakthrough moment is when it is clear the company is well positioned to take that last and most important step to reach the summit.

Stage 4: Ascending the Summit of Elite

One of my key criteria for elite status is a ten-year record of consistent year-over-year exceptional performance. Once this milestone has been achieved, a company is ready to climb the summit to elite status. The key indicators are when operational excellence and best-of-class performance is the norm; the leadership team consists of A-players; a healthy and strong organizational culture exists; and its business model and core purpose are integrated into its strategy to provide a competitive advantage. The enterprise is also highly optimized and scaled with an enormous number of critical lifelines to safeguard against a fall from the summit. The air is thin above 8,000 meters so only the most prepared, disciplined, and strong companies will make it to the top.

Stage 5: Sustaining Elite Status on the Summit

Being recognized as an elite mountaineer or an elite company is an extraordinary accomplishment that most can only dream about. What makes the truly elite stand out, however, are the companies that can sustain their superior performance over a long horizon as measured in decades. Achieving and sustaining an elite status is difficult and even dangerous, so there is no time to relax. To stay at the top requires vision, teamwork, discipline, exceptional execution, innovative business model, and all the lifelines that an enterprise has built over time. As demonstrated in both Collin's *Good to Great* and Rosenzweig's *The Halo Effect*, it is difficult to stay on the summit. A significant portion of the high-achieving companies highlighted by the authors were unable to maintain their high-flying status.

As proof of just how difficult it is to sustain elite status, one only must examine examples of companies that have fallen from the summit. First, let's start with the *Good to Great* companies identified by Jim Collins. Although this is covered in more detail in Chapter 3, we will briefly cover it here. Of the eleven companies identified as great by Collins, three—or 27 percent—of the enterprises fell from the summit for various reasons. That's a striking number. Second, Rosenzweig, in *The Halo Effect*, studied elite companies that were identified in some of the most successful business books in history and came to some interesting conclusions.

Rosenzweig studied the market performance of seventeen so-called visionary companies identified in the Jim Collins and Jerry Porras book, *Built to Last.* He discovered that only eight of the seventeen companies outperformed the S&P 500 market average for the five years after the authors' study ended. Likewise, Rosenzweig found that of thirty-five so-called excellent companies studied in the book, *In Search of Excellence*, thirty declined in profitability over the five years after the authors' study ended. In both cases, the percent of companies that underperformed is remarkable.[ix]

Elite Management Framework—Summary
The integrated elite management framework outlined in this chapter can provide an organization with a path forward to successfully ascend to the coveted summit of elite. The path forward to the summit is summarized in Figure 2 and answers the elusive question: What makes companies elite?

To achieve elite status, all enterprises must start with the foundational pillars. These pillars include assembling an extraordinary leadership team with the ability to develop an exceptional strategy, execute at the highest level, maintain awareness of the need to stay on the positive side of the luck spread. Once clearly understood, these foundational pillars—which can also be viewed as principles—must then be expanded into the lifelines leadership framework that includes nine lifelines principles outlined in this chapter. The lifelines leadership framework functions as high-level principles for the enterprise that must be implemented through the building blocks, which come in the form of exceptional habits of elite leaders, enterprises, and boards.

Figure 2.

On the Summit: Elite Status

| Foundational pillars include: leadership, strategy, execution, and luck | High level principles - lifelines leadership framework - include: nine lifelines and an acute awareness of luck spread | Building blocks include: exceptional habits of elite leaders, enterprises, and boards |

Section 1

Exceptional Habits of Elite Leaders

The only source of knowledge is experience.
Albert Einstein[x]

G erlinde Kaltenbrunner was the first woman to summit the fourteen highest mountain peaks in the world above 8,000 meters (26,247 feet) without the assistance of supplemental oxygen. To be sure, what the Austrian-born Kaltenbrunner accomplished is amazing, but the most significant factor supporting her success is the set of exceptional habits she developed over the years. These habits absolutely include her regime of physical endurance training, but also the mental training she did, such as learning to keep her focus on the task at hand, the disciplined way she made near-term and long-term decisions, and the courage she displayed built on unwavering faith in her abilities.

During the summer of 2010, Kaltenbrunner was perched directly below K2 summit, preparing to make a final push to the peak, when her climbing partner, who was climbing above her, slipped and tumbled past her to his death. Even though K2 was the last summit Kaltenbrunner had to climb to achieve her long mountaineering quest, she did not hesitate to abort the summit attempt to look for her fellow mountaineer. Although it was her sixth failed attempt to summit the world's most deadly peak, she had the discipline to turn around once again. A year later, in the summer of 2011, Kaltenbrunner returned to K2. This time, on her seventh attempt, she reached the summit.[xi] Elite business leaders exhibit many of the same exceptional habits that Kaltenbrunner drew on to succeed where others fail.

Leaders Are Not All Created Equal

Great leaders use their superior instinctive habits to have both an outsized impact on their organization; they also are extremely disciplined about choosing other leaders who show equally strong potential. Steve Jobs is, of course, the obvious example here. Not only was he an outsized elite leader, but he brought exceptional talent to Apple, who themselves had a disproportional positive effect on the company's performance. Nothing is more important than building a coterie of high-performing teams throughout an organization. In fact, strong teams are the cornerstone of building an elite enterprise with a healthy, distinctive culture.

In this section, we explore the most important habits of elite leaders (both those that are instinctive and those leaders develop) that provide an enterprise with the energy, vision, and creativity to build and sustain an enduring elite company. Towards the end of the section, I'll review specific habits of arguably two of the greatest business leaders of all time, Warren Buffett and Steve Jobs, and one relatively unknown but effective leader, Stefano Pessina.

Habits of Elite Leaders
Exceptional habits support three essential foundational pillars: leadership, strategy, and execution. Leaders, enterprises, and boards that focus on these three areas (in addition to an awareness of luck spread—another foundational pillar) have a clear path to achieving elite status. Here are the three sets of exceptional habits required of leaders that will be covered in Section 1:

Chapter 2: Twenty Leadership Habits of Elite
            Leaders
Chapter 3: Eight Strategy Habits of Elite Leaders
Chapter 4: Ten Execution Habits of Elite Leaders

CHAPTER 2

20 LEADERSHIP HABITS
OF ELITE LEADERS

Leadership is the capacity to translate vision into reality.
Warren Bennis[xii]

E lite leaders exhibit twenty essential leadership habits:

Habit 1: Manifest Integrity in Every Action, Every
    Word, and Every Deed
Habit 2: Build Your Brand of One
Habit 3: Go with Your Instinct—It Will Never Fail You
Habit 4: Treat All People Equally and with Respect
Habit 5: Allow for a Period of Inner Reflection and
    Growth
Habit 6: Be Inquisitive and Develop Critical Thinking
    Capabilities

Habit 7: Display a Proactive Mind-Set and Bias for
      Action

Habit 8: Deliver on Your Commitments

Habit 9: Maintain an Unwavering Faith and Exhibit
      Equanimity

Habit 10: Learn to Listen and Learn to Stop Doing

Habit 11: Master the Art of Communication

Habit 12: Deal Effectively with Adversity

Habit 13: Know What to Do and What Not to Do

Habit 14: Think Before You Speak

Habit 15: Show That You Are Interested

Habit 16: Be Passionate About Learning and
      Development

Habit 17: Demonstrate Gratitude

Habit 18: Adopt the "Buffett" Management Approach

Habit 19: Adopt the "Jobs" Management Approach

Habit 20: Adopt the "Pessina" Management Approach

Habit 1: Manifest Integrity in Every Action, Every Word, and Every Deed

An elite company cannot be built without the supremely important twin moral fibers of integrity and ethical behavior. Both are vital to building your enterprise's "brand of one," and both are essential qualities of an elite leader. Integrity is ultimately the cornerstone of a leader's reputation and legacy.

As the author M. H. McKee once said, "Integrity is one of several paths—it distinguishes itself from others because it is the right path ... and the only one upon which you will never get lost."[xiii] Integrity above all else defines a leader.

Integrity means doing the right things, for the right reasons, in the right way. In other words, integrity is manifested in everything you do and everything you say. Elite leaders possess the moral courage to always do the right thing. Without integrity, you really have nothing! Most companies make integrity one of their core values and enforce it through a robust code of ethical business conduct.

Integrity is also crucial in establishing relationships and building teams. In the book, *The Architecture of Leadership*, authors Donald T. Phillips and Adm. James M. Loy, USCG (Ret.) captured this concept perfectly when they wrote, "...honesty provides credibility for a leader; without credibility, there are no followers. Honesty is also critical in building relationships and forging teamwork. A leader's bond with other people is only as good as the leader's word." [xiv]

Habit 2: Build Your Brand of One

Build your brand of one and differentiate yourself from everyone else. Most importantly, be authentic, and don't try to be something that you are not; people easily see through the fakery. The same principles that organizations use to build a great brand can also be applied to individuals. Great, differentiated brands are usually built through vision, innovation, creativity, remarkable execution, reputation, and hard work. Be reflective and creative, and develop a long-term plan for building your brand. Execute it with discipline and passion.

You can build your brand by embracing and developing all thirty precocious characteristics outlined in *CEO*

Lifelines. You should also deliberately obtain indispensable experiences, by manifesting a proactive mind-set, and by living daily the exceptional, effective habits of elite leaders. As much as possible, work with and learn from the best. Being proactive can also mean engaging a public relations firm, just like an enterprise, to protect your reputation and brand.

Manifest a deep passion for everything you do. Such engagement can be infectious, and it will inspire others. Blend all these things with humility and together these elements can be a powerful force in building your career and elite status.

Habit 3: Go with Your Instinct—It Will Never Fail You
Your innate ability or so-called sixth sense should never be ignored. On the contrary, it should always be trusted and relied upon! Most of the negative lessons learned over my long career are directly linked to not trusting my instinct. Experience has taught me that both discipline and critical thinking capabilities are essential precocious characteristics, and that both can help you rely more consistently on your instinct.

A very powerful example of this precocious characteristic is Apple's Steve Jobs, who built a world-changing organization on the strength of his extraordinary innate intuition. Another example is Warren Buffett, who is viewed as the most successful investor of our time. His instinct about when and where to invest are truly precocious and inimitable. Of course, most leaders do not possess the outsized innate instincts of Jobs or Buffett, but everyone has a certain level of instinctual abilities. What's important is that you understand how to use your own level of instinct to take proactive action.

Habit 4: Treat All People Equally and with Respect

Maya Angelou said, "I've learned that people will forget what you said, people will forget what you did, but people will never forget how you made them feel."[xv] Treat everyone you meet equally and with respect, no matter their position or their social standing. To me, this rule came naturally. My Italian parents taught me well. I was always amazed over my lengthy career at how many people struggled with such a common sense approach. One important caveat and warning—your behavior must be authentic, and it must come from the heart—otherwise, people will see right through it.

The fact is, as a leader you'll be remembered more for this personal characteristic than any other aspect of your career. It is absolutely a critical component in building your brand of one. President Abraham Lincoln captured this better than anyone when he said, "In the end, it's not the years in your life that count. It's the life in your years."[xvi]

Habit 5: Allow for a Period of Inner Reflection and Growth

Take the time—at least annually—for a sustained period of inner reflection and make it your personal mission statement to continuously improve. The period you allocate for inner reflection needs to be meaningful, usually measured in days or perhaps weeks. It's important to step back and see the bigger picture through a different lens (using your best common sense and critical thinking capabilities) and then to use the insight gained to take crucial next steps. The result of this inner reflection should be new perspectives and immediately actionable decisions.

Here's a personal example of what I mean by this inner reflection: When I was separating from my company in 2012, I took time for a period of inner reflection and settled on a set of start and stop decisions. I decided to stop working for large organizations and start focusing more on personally fulfilling advisory work. Consequently, I developed a plan that included serving on boards, working with private equity, and pursuing my own consulting practice.

You also need to clearly embrace the discipline of self-renewal and continuous self-improvement. Just as companies need to grow, renew and practice continuous improvement, leaders must pursue a life-long mission to never stop learning. Take additional college classes, attend internal company-sponsored university programs that are part of the leadership-development program, read high quality books on leadership and business models, and read relevant business articles daily on specific areas of interests. Even watching interviews of successful entrepreneurs, including TED talks, help leaders remain curious, involved, and build your brand of one.

Habit 6: Be Inquisitive and Develop Critical Thinking Capabilities

As a leader, it's important to always ask why, why, why? You should not assume or take anything for granted. Learn to value facts that are unimpeachable. Do not make decisions based on emotion, rumors, or attribution because they will usually result in bad outcomes. Live by the old southern Italian proverb, "Don't believe anything you hear and only believe half of what you see." Personally validate and live by the facts.

What do I mean by critical thinking? Critical thinking is purposeful, reflective, and involves a careful evaluation of information; it also improves one's judgment. If you improve your judgment, you will have better career outcomes. The cumulative effect over time of the decisions you make help determine your ability to reach the summit. Do not doubt the importance of not treating decisions in isolation. Inquisitiveness and critical thinking often provide the ability to see things that others can't see, and this ability to "connect the dots" will be very helpful to your quest of climbing the summit.

Habit 7: Display a Proactive Mind-Set and Bias for Action

Elite leaders consistently manifest a proactive approach and a clear bias for action in everything they do. This habit is also underpinned by a disciplined focus on doing the right things at the right time. Discipline, along with integrity, are two cornerstones of building a successful career and your brand of one. *CEO Lifelines: Nine Commitments Every Leader Must Make* outlines a nine-step process (or recipe) through a proactive mind-set and a bias for action that you can use your entire career no matter what position you hold or what professional path you choose.

Here is a personal example of proactive actions: When I separated from my previous company, I outlined four broad objectives that I wanted to achieve and then took extremely proactive action to make them happen. I contacted private equity firms, began networking with those people I knew sitting on boards, wrote a book, and started a business. I reached all these objectives with fanatical focus, a proactive mind-set, and a bias for action that got the job done.

Habit 8: Deliver on Your Commitments
Elite leaders clearly understand the need to consistently deliver results—they embrace this necessity. Elite leaders truly appreciate what the great race car driver Mario Andretti once said, "Desire is the key to motivation, but it's determination and commitment to an unrelenting pursuit of your goal—a commitment to excellence—that will enable you to attain the success you seek."[xvii] Elite leaders also know that consistently delivering on commitments requires both tremendous discipline and skillful management of expectations. Disciplined people consistently deliver on their promises through strong execution abilities that are underpinned by an unrelenting focus on their stated objective. This proclivity is what separates elite leaders from the rest.

Disciplined people also grasp the importance of taking full responsibility for results. They understand the true meaning of accountability. Accountability means having the courage to admit mistakes. Accountability means you do not point fingers at others, and it means you look in the mirror and accept total responsibility for what happened.

Moreover, disciplined people have an unshakeable faith in their abilities to consistently deliver on their promises. They are not arrogant. They are focused and methodical in their approach and practice extreme commitment to ensure their word is sacrosanct. However, these disciplined people are mature and pragmatic enough to understand that no one is perfect. When failure does occur, these leaders have the courage to apologize, learn from failure, and to put mechanisms in place to ensure that this disappointment does not happen again.

Habit 9: Maintain an Unwavering Faith and Exhibit Equanimity

You will certainly encounter many obstacles on your personal climb to the summit, but elite leaders always maintain an unwavering faith in their abilities, no matter the circumstance. As a leader, you must be resolute in your conviction that you will prevail. This habit was captured best by William H. McRaven, a Navy SEAL, who said, "If you want to change the world, you must be your very best in the darkest moment."[xviii]

Elite leaders consistently manifest equanimity and are cool, calm, and collected, no matter what transpires. This habit goes together with unwavering faith. Such displays of clear thinking and quiet confidence are essential to leaders as they encounter unexpected turbulence on their climb to the summit.

Habit 10: Learn to Listen and Learn to Stop Doing

Stop talking, and start listening. It is often hard for a leader to stop being directive. After all, leaders are supposed to direct, but listening is also an essential skill for a successful leader.

Highly successful elite leaders have an uncanny ability to know what to do and what not to do, and, importantly, how to unplug the many "doing" habits that naturally form over time. Before obsessing over your "to do list," instead focus on your "stop doing list". This simple change can benefit your career and your organization in ways you can hardly imagine right now. Cutting out extraneous things that do not add value can unleash substantial resources you can use to build an elite company.

Habit 11: Master the Art of Communication
The art of communication is indispensable for a leader since one of their key roles is to compellingly articulate a vision and strategy so that their team will embrace and execute it. Therefore, the message must be delivered with passion and authenticity, and it must be concise. Elite leaders who articulate their message in this way are more likely to gain support in the organization and be highly effective. If you examine great leaders—Ronald Reagan, Winston Churchill, or Steve Jobs, for example—you'll realize they are all incredible storytellers. They share life lessons that are meaningful and add lasting impact with at least one pearl of wisdom as a takeaway.

Communicating effectively takes years of practice and focus. Very few leaders are natural speakers. Great communicators learn and fine tune their approach and use storytelling as an effective tool. Can you think of a speech that used storytelling to completely captivate and engage? Was it a story that resonated with your life?

Leaders are also conscious about using effective presentation techniques, such as scanning the audience to ensure they are engaged and interested. Also, when preparing for any type of speech they imagine themselves in the audience and consider how to make their speech relevant, concise, and impactful.

The *Wall Street Journal* reported on a speech by Adm. William H. McRaven, who was sharing the life lessons he had learned from his Navy SEAL training with a graduating class at the University of Texas. His speech consisted of ten lessons. As he recounted each lesson (after noting that the lessons applied regardless of background, gender, social status, ethnicity, or religious background), he connected each one to a takeaway message for the students, so that they could easily understand and remember them. He brilliantly made the speech powerful, authentic, and, most importantly, unforgettable.

Another great communicator is Apple's Steve Jobs. In Walter Isaacson's book, *Steve Jobs*, he recounts how Jobs—who had always written his own presentations, but never had done a commencement speech—began his Stanford commencement address by saying, "Today, I want to tell you three stories from my life... ." He then went on tell the graduates about dropping out of college, getting fired from Apple, and being diagnosed with cancer. His speech captured the attention of the students. Isaacson said of the speech, "The artful minimalism of the speech gave it simplicity, purity, and charm. Search where you will ... you won't find a better commencement address."[xix]

Of the numerous effective ways you can use to improve communications within your organization, particularly with the people you interact with frequently, it's important to follow a few practical common sense guidelines. To start with, don't be too reliant on emails. Use more face-to-face meetings with direct reports when possible, and if not, then call or use video technology instead of sending an email. Send a handwritten or typed note when the occasion fits. Sometimes such personalization is the most effective way to communicate. Finally, hold a weekly call (if an in-person meeting is not possible) with your direct reports, which provides an excellent forum for communicating and having a robust dialogue.

Habit 12: Deal Effectively with Adversity
Just as mountaineers face incredible adversity from unexpected storms in their climb to the summit— particularly when they are climbing in the Death Zone— leaders must be equally adept at confronting unexpected storms and turbulence facing their enterprise.

Adversity in business comes in many different forms and can be segmented into essentially seven major categories: (1) a direct threat to the survival of the enterprise due to a disruptive innovation; (2) a series of management missteps—usually over a long period of time— that cumulatively have a significant adverse effect on the organization; (3) an aggressive elite activist investor who challenges even the most successful elite companies; (4) a major product recall that presents a clear and present danger to the survival of the company; (5) a major global shock, or worse, a series of severe shocks that can dramatically weaken or even possibly destroy an enterprise; (6) a sudden and unexpected change in the market that causes the company to fall deeply into the commodity trap with little room to maneuver; and (7) an unexpected illness or even death of the incumbent CEO, which can dramatically alter the path of the company (this is particularly difficult when no clear successor is in place).

Here are some examples of exceptional, elite female CEOs and two exceptional male CEOs who faced down difficult situations using the precocious habits described in this book.

1) **Mary Barra (General Motors).** In her first year as CEO of GM in 2014, Barra spent most of her time dealing with a decade-old scandal involving the company's failure to address ignition switch defects. Not only did she inherit the deadly ignition-switch matter, she also inherited the company's legendary difficult culture. She set forth her philosophy on how the company would be managed in the future while at the same time dealing with this crisis. Her approach to changing the GM culture was quite simple. As outlined in an October 6, 2014 *Fortune* article: "Her approach to changing the culture is highly un-GM-like ... She proposes to alter the mind-set by behaving differently every day than any GM CEO has behaved in decades, and through her example and a CEO's influence, to change the way everyone else behaves every day."

In another September 30, 2014 article in the *Wall Street Journal*, the author, Joseph B. White, added the following insight based on a meeting with the top 300 GM executives: "Ms. Barra told managers they could no longer confuse steady progress with winning. GM, she said, must do what it takes to be the world's most valued automotive company, a measure that includes customer satisfaction, quality, and financial results. Ms. Barra told her leadership group that, if you're not in line with this vision, you don't need to be here."

Barra is an elite leader, but her abilities will be tested since changing a long-established culture like GM's is exceedingly difficult. Geoff Colvin, in an October 6, 2014 *Fortune* article, summed up the difficulty this way:

> GM's way of behaving is the kind that's hardest to change: embedded in a big, old company that utterly dominated its industry for decades. Cultures like that have occasionally been altered. Jack Welch did it at General Electric in the 1980s; Lou Gerstner did it at IBM in the 1990s; Doug Conant did it at Campbell Soup in the 2000s. But more often the transformations fail, as they did at Kodak, Sears, Westinghouse, Pan Am, and many other storied colossi that succumbed largely to their own weaknesses. The odds are against GM, and another factor makes the challenge even harder. Employees have seen it all before. Over the past 30 years, they've learned that CEOs come and go, but the way we do things around here is invulnerable. At GM, trying and failing to change the culture is part of the culture.

Barra has an enormous summit to climb. However, if anyone can reach her goals, I believe that Barra can because she is truly an elite CEO. The early evidence—from strong operating results to excellent strategic moves—shows that she has a strong chance to succeed.

2) **Ellen Kullman, (former CEO of DuPont).** During Kullman's tenure at DuPont, she skillfully and successfully transformed the company. However, probably her greatest challenge came from a prominent and highly successful activist investor through a proxy fight. The proxy contest between the activist and the company went to a shareholder vote in May 2015, and was at the time the largest proxy fight in U.S. corporate history to go to a shareholder vote. According to the company's proxy information, if you had invested $100 in DuPont when Kullman became CEO in 2008, it would have grown to $366 by the end of 2014, which is a 266 percent return (including stock price and dividends).

This performance exceeded both the S&P 500 and the proxy peer group. Many CEOs can only dream of a performance achieved by Kullman. Irrespective of her extraordinary performance, Kullman was confronted with a fierce activist campaign that tested both her resolve and skills. Initially, she prevailed with major shareholders supporting the position that she and board put forth. Kullman made winning over major shareholders her primary focus by articulating well all the accomplishments, performance, and future direction of the company. It worked, but for only a short while. Unfortunately, her victory was ephemeral and pyrrhic because months later, in early October of 2015, Kullman unexpectedly announced she was stepping down as CEO.

This unfortunate and abrupt change in her circumstance does not diminish the amazing work that she accomplished during her tenure. Kullman clearly is an elite leader, and she successfully climbed many difficult summits during her tenure and throughout she consistently manifested remarkable habits. Kullman exemplifies well all the characteristics of an elite leader. Shortly after Kullman's separation from DuPont, it was announced that venerable company would merge with Dow.

3) **Meg Whitman (CEO of Hewlett-Packard before company split into two separate public companies; now CEO of Hewlett-Packard Enterprise Co.).** The former H-P (before it split into Hewlett-Packard Enterprise Co. and H-P Inc.) had its share of challenges over the past decade, including the $11 billion 2011 acquisition of British software company, Autonomy Corp. The acquisition of the British company was consummated during the tenure of a former CEO, and it was part of a reinvention strategy that was being pursued at the time. The acquisition, however,

did not go well, and H-P later took an $8.8 billion write-down, or 80 percent of the value.

Whitman took over as CEO in late 2011 during a very challenging period for the company. In addition to the acquisition write-down, she inherited a company that had gone through its share of management and board turmoil. Simultaneously, the company faced significant market challenges with the accelerating growth of mobile computing, cloud computing, big data, and other key emerging technologies. Since H-P generated a substantial part (approximately two-thirds) of its revenues from mature hardware markets—such as personal computers, printers, servers, and storage devices— the new, fast growing technologies undermined the future of these market segments.

So, what did Whitman do? First, she stabilized the company and developed a turnaround plan. As part of her plan, she streamlined the company and made it nimbler. Cost savings, innovation, and talent-management were some of her key priorities. Ultimately, in October 2014, Whitman announced that H-P would be broken into two companies of similar size. The new HP Inc. would focus on printers and personal computers, while Hewlett-Packard Enterprises would focus on an ecosystem of products and services, including servers, data-storage devices, software, and consulting. Whitman said that the breakup of the company would result in a nimbler organization.

On November 1, 2015, the separation became a reality. However, the market challenges for both companies remain and they now face these market forces separately. It will be interesting to see how the two separate companies perform over the next five to ten years. Obviously, many new chapters will need to be written on this story, but Whitman is, no doubt, an elite leader. She has proven over and over in her long and successful career that she possesses all the exceptional habits of elite leaders.

4) **Ana Botín (Executive Chairman of Banco Santander SA).** Botín assumed the executive chairman position in September 2014, when her father passed away. She acted quickly and decisively upon being swiftly approved as successor to her father. Her grandfather, as well as her great-grandfather, also served in the past as chairman of the bank. In an article by Jeannette Neumann in the *Wall Street Journal* on June 9, 2015, she writes, "Since taking charge ... has overhauled the giant bank's strategy and shaken up the executive team assembled by ... her late father ... she has replaced Santander's chief executive ... and moved about half of the management team into new chairs."

The article goes on to say how Botin focused immediately on shoring up the balance sheet by selling shares, how she stopped doing large acquisitions, and how she wanted to shift the focus on improving customer service. The article also quotes Botín as saying that "We need to change the culture. If we get it right, we can have a huge impact." Finally, the article states, "Ms. Botín's aptitude to lead is rarely questioned among investors and analysts ... Her grooming as the eldest of six children, they say, was unrivaled ... as a Santander board member since 1989 and as head of its U.K. bank."

As we have seen with many of the stories in this section, many new chapters will need to be written in the future on the bank and Botin's stellar career. However, Botín is no doubt in that elite class of leaders as she has clearly and consistently manifested exceptional habits over a long and successful career.

5) **Lou Gerstner (Chairman of the Board and Chief Executive Officer of IBM).** Gerstner's penetrating book, *Who Says Elephants Can't Dance?*[xx] is a powerful account of how he reinvented and transformed IBM in the early 1990s and established the foundation for sustainable and profitable growth. Gerstner's extraordinary rescue and transformation of IBM lands him a spot on the list of top CEOs in history. It's an instructive case study on how to manage in a crisis.

So, how did Gerstner do it? He focused on transforming IBM's culture and its competitive position. These changes are the most difficult to effect when taking over as a new CEO. At a very high level, here are some of the key actions that he took: He rebuilt his leadership team and gave the organization a renewed sense of purpose. Gerstner demanded that managers work together. He made a bold decision to keep the company together. He slashed prices on core products.

However, what impressed me most reading his book was Gerstner's decisiveness and all the well-reasoned decisions that he made. Also, how he so effectively utilized in an extraordinary manner all the indispensable experiences he gained from prior positions that he held with various elite institutions.

6) **Steve Job's return to lead Apple.** After being ousted from his own company by the board of directors in 1985, Steve Jobs came back to Apple in 1997. When Jobs returned after a twelve-year absence, the company had fallen on difficult times, and its return to elite status was truly in doubt. In probably the greatest turnaround in business history, Jobs did his magic and restored Apple to not only elite status, but he also took it to even a higher level, making Apple the most valuable and admired company in the world. So, what did Jobs do that others couldn't?

The story of what Jobs did at Apple has been recounted many times by incredible authors and in films, so the story won't be repeated here. However, my favorite account of what Jobs did was captured best by Jim Collins in his amazing book, *Great by Choice*, which I highly recommend. There's obviously no argument that Jobs was an elite leader, and a strong argument can be made that he should be viewed as probably the greatest CEO of our generation. Jobs' phenomenal habits are worth summarizing as a separate habit, and they can be found later in this chapter.

It is highly instructive to study the habits of elite leaders, particularly ones that have dealt with tremendous adversity. Their exceptional habits provide a roadmap to success and thus should be carefully analyzed and adopted by leaders aspiring to climb the summit.

Habit 13: Know What to Do and What Not to Do
Knowing what to do and what not to do are equally important. CEOs are constantly being faced with choices. It is imperative that CEOs choose wisely because bad choices—either regarding people or personal habits—can take a leader down a dangerous path that can ultimately have dire and irreversible consequences. As the story of mountaineer Gerlinde Kaltenbrunner demonstrates, knowing when to turn back is vital to survival and ultimately to your success.

Elite leaders learn to rely on their precocious characteristics, such as instinct, perspective, experience, critical thinking and, of course, facts, as they make decisions impacting the enterprise. Developing a stop doing list that clearly identifies ineffective or non-value-creating activities is also important to have in your elite leader tool kit.

Habit 14: Think Before You Speak

Communication aligns unity of purpose. It is imperative that leaders carefully craft their words, no matter the environment or circumstance to ensure consistency of message. A consistent message inspires the global leadership team and instills an important discipline in the organization. Elite leaders understand that when they speak, members of the enterprise carefully listen and act based on what is communicated. Conflicting and confusing messages can cause confusion and even paralyze an organization.

To ensure flawless communication, elite leaders often retain an outside professional communication and public-relations team to develop a communication plan. Such professional help is indispensable and can be a true lifeline for a leader.

Habit 15: Show That You Are Interested

Elite leaders are inclusive and communicate to everyone in the organization that each individual plays an important role in the success of the enterprise, and that his/her work is important. Whether visiting a plant site, distribution center, or corporate center, elite leaders engage with everyone they meet, asking about their families, their jobs, and making a point to remember names and important events.

Recognize important events or a notable contribution to the organization by sending a personal note or even sponsoring a special celebration. A personal, handwritten note is always appreciated, but even an email carries a powerful message. Sometimes a leader can be empathetic with employees—for example, a personal tragedy such as a family member's death. If appropriate, a leader should engage with employees in this way as long as the communication is authentic and respectful.

Habit 16: Be Passionate About Learning and Development

Elite leaders have a deep passion for learning and for improving their personal leadership skills. They passionately believe in continuous self-improvement and are consistently disciplined in their approach to learning. The best way to demonstrate this habit is by using an elite leader as an example. One of the best-of-class examples can be found in how Airbnb's CEO Brian Chesky approaches this habit.

According to a July 1, 2015 article in *Fortune* magazine by Leigh Gallagher titled, "The Education of Brian Chesky," Chesky was passionate about wanting to improve his management skills, even as a young 31-year-old leader. He proactively sought elite leaders and asked for their counsel. He augmented their advice with targeted reading. As *Fortune* explains, "Rather than trying to learn every single aspect of a particular topic, Chesky found that it was more efficient to spend his time researching and identifying the single best source in that area, then going straight to that person." The article went on to say, "As the company became more prominent, so did Chesky's sources. Soon

came meetings with Facebook's Mark Zuckerberg,
Amazon's Jeff Bezos, and eBay CEO John Donahoe. He
went to Bob Iger and Marc Benioff to ask how they push
their executive teams to do more. From Facebook's Sheryl
Sandberg, he picked up tips about efficiency in scaling
internationally ... Chesky reached out to [George] Tenet
[former director of the CIA] not for tips on global security,
but for corporate culture ... Chesky's biggest source
triumphs was his audience with [Warren] Buffett."

Obviously, not every newly appointed CEO is going to
be as fortunate as Chesky to visit and engage with so many
elite leaders. Nonetheless, his approach or habit is
instructive, and it's a powerful recipe for newly appointed
CEOs (or for that matter anyone in a leadership position) to
follow. I truly believe that if you use the building blocks
employed by Chesky, you will have success in your career.
What's important is to be proactive, disciplined, focused,
and consistent.

Habit 17: Demonstrate Gratitude
Elite leaders show authentic gratitude for their teams.
President John F. Kennedy captured this attribute in his
famous quote, "As we express our gratitude, we must never
forget that the highest appreciation is not to utter words, but
to live by them."[xxi]

The willingness to express gratitude on a regular basis is
truly an exceptional habit of an elite leader. Alphabet's elite
leader Larry Page, one of the founders of Google, is a good
example of authentic gratitude. As reported by Janice
Kaplan in the *Wall Street Journal* on August 8-9, 2015, "...
Google's Larry Page got the highest approval ratings of any

chief executive on the job-review site Glassdoor.com. His likable, low-key style accounts for much of his popularity—but so does his willingness to express gratitude to the people who work for him ... Google and a few other companies are setting a new trend—because expressions of gratitude around the workplace tend to be scarce ... Being appreciated is one of the great motivators on the job, even better than money."

Habit 18: Adopt the "Buffett" Management Approach
Warren Buffett, the leader of Berkshire Hathaway, has had an outsized impact on business. All leaders can learn from his management approach. His impeccable and nearly inimitable track record speaks for itself, but I will provide my own thoughts on his recipe for success below. Note that my assessment was influenced by a May 1, 2015 *Fortune* magazine article by Roger Lowenstein that really captured the essence of Buffett's success.

First, Buffett has a laser focus on capital allocation. Organizations that focus less on this aspect of business can run into problems over the long haul. Buffett's disciplined and focused approach always generates long-term shareholder value. Another elite CEO, Jack Welch, also believed passionately that capital allocation was one of the two most important jobs of a CEO. A *Fortune* magazine article on February 28, 2011, summarized well Welch's philosophy, "Welch used to say that GE's CEO has only two jobs: allocating capital—deciding where and how much to invest—and evaluating people." It's hard to argue with that view given what Welch achieved during his tenure as an elite CEO.

The second ingredient for Buffett's success is his
acquisition holding philosophy. Once acquired for his
portfolio, he rarely sells. Unlike most private equity firms
that hold on to acquisitions for a specific maximum holding
period, Buffett's objective is the creation of an enduring
and value creating enterprise. Because of this long-term
view, critical decisions can be made with the overall
objective of building an elite and enduring enterprise.

The third element of success is creating a framework of
freedom and responsibility. Buffett provides his business
unit CEOs with the freedom to do what they believe is right
for the business for the long-term. This freedom,
underpinned by responsibility and accountability, usually
results in a loyal team that performs and delivers on their
commitments.

The fourth element of success is Buffett's dislike of
bureaucracy; a typical characteristic of elite entrepreneurial
leaders. Buffett ensures that his business units are not
burdened with layers of bureaucracy that can suffocate an
organization.

The final element of success is that Buffett does not
spike stock price in the short term by providing earnings
guidance or announcing a stock split or announcing a spin-
off of a business unit. Buffett also shuns stock options or
using stock for acquisitions.

Habit 19: Adopt the "Jobs" Management Approach
What Steve Jobs accomplished in his relative short tenure
as CEO of Apple is something that will be studied by
business students for a long time. Although the world lost
this marvelous and creative leader much too soon, his

legacy as an elite CEO will live on for generations. So, what was Jobs' recipe for success? Walter Isaacson captured best the essence of Steve Jobs in his amazing book by the same name. I will outline key elements that I believe made Jobs such a business legend.

First, Jobs had an incredible passion for everything he did with an inimitable innate ability to see things that others couldn't see. His instinct is legendary. He was a creative and innovative leader. He was a great storyteller. His passion, instinct, creativity and ability to tell stories offer many lessons for leaders.

Jobs believed in product simplicity and design. Anyone who has purchased an Apple product understands the beauty and simplicity of the design. He also had a laser focus on the global supply chain because he understood how critical it was to Apple's success. As a matter of fact, it was so important to him that Jobs appointed current CEO Tim Cook to lead the global supply chain initiative.

Jobs built an innovative business model in both how he organized the company and the recipe he developed for doing business. He controlled his team and pushed them to work together as one cohesive group. He organized the company with one income statement, so teams would not be distracted from the true mission of the enterprise. He designed the office buildings to promote encounters and unplanned collaborations, which now is a standard practice across many creative and innovative enterprises.

Jobs held weekly meetings with executives that were robust dialogue sessions focused on the future. Meetings were also used to enforce a great sense of mission or purpose. He kept his team focused on just two or three priorities at a time. He challenged his team to identify the top ten projects that the company should be working on. Then, he would reduce the list down to about three. He had uncanny ability to select the right projects to work on and which to stop doing.

Jobs established the top 100 retreat. He would hand pick the top 100 people in the organization regardless of position. Finally, he would push his engineers to deliver the impossible. He had an amazing ability to get people to perform at the highest level possible.

Habit 20: Adopt the "Pessina" Management Approach
Unlike Buffett and Jobs, Stefano Pessina is not a household name. Even in the business world he is not as well-known as other CEOs more frequently mentioned in the news. Pessina is the CEO of Walgreens, and he is also an Italian billionaire.

In 1977, Pessina took over his family's pharmaceutical wholesale business in Naples, Italy, and ultimately—through hard work, great instinct, and precocious characteristics—built a world-class company called Alliance Boots. He negotiated a smart transaction with Walgreens that positioned him in the leadership role when Walgreens acquired his company. In a February 1, 2016 article by Jennifer Reingold (with Marty Jones) for *Fortune* magazine, the journalist captured Pessina's rise to the top by noting, "Billionaire Stefano Pessina cannily took control of Walgreens using the chain's own money."

Metaphorically speaking, Pessina has ascended to the top of all the 8,000-plus meter summits during his long and brilliant career, and he is clearly an elite CEO. So, what are

Pessina's precocious characteristics that other leaders should emulate? I could list many, but here are some salient ones:

The first element is a decades-long unblemished and consistent track record that speaks for itself.

The second element is an unrivaled vision and an ability to bring it to fruition. Pessina has demonstrated tremendous vision over the decades, seeing opportunities others don't see. This ability along with superior execution skills makes him elite—he simply gets things done!

The third element is focus and discipline. Pessina has consistently demonstrated an ability to focus on the task at hand in a disciplined manner. He does not allow emotion to cloud his objectivity.

The fourth element is an exceptional playbook. Pessina has demonstrated his uncanny ability to successfully complete acquisitions and improve the acquiring company's performance and value creation ability.

The final element is that Pessina enthusiastically embraces change and approaches it in a proactive way. He believes those enterprises and leaders with the ability to change and adapt will likely be the ones to survive.

CHAPTER 3

8 STRATEGY HABITS OF ELITE LEADERS

The best CEOs I know are teachers,
and at the core of what they teach is strategy.
Michael Porter[xxii]

E lite Leaders exhibit eight essential strategy habits:

Habit 1: Embed an Entrepreneurial Spirit in the
          Organization
Habit 2: Create and Sustain a Startup Mind-Set
Habit 3: Exhibit a War Mind-Set
Habit 4: Ensure Your Successor is a Success
Habit 5: Create an Environment that Fosters Creativity
          and Innovation
Habit 6: Learn Leadership Habits from The Military
Habit 7: Develop an Audacious Turnaround Plan
Habit 8: Build an Enduring Enterprise

Habit 1: Embed an Entrepreneurial Spirit in the Organization

Tory Burch, the successful fashion designer, captured well the essence of entrepreneurial management when she said, "Entrepreneurs have a great ability to create change, be flexible, build companies and cultivate the kind of work environment in which they want to work."[xxiii]An entrepreneurial spirit provides elite organizations with a distinct competitive advantage, and it's often a key recipe element for an innovative business model. Elite leaders are particularly effective at building the exceptional habit of creating, retaining, and motivating entrepreneurial management teams.

To have exceptional teams, it's essential that both internally developed teams as well as teams acquired through acquisitions are equally motivated and inspired to operate in this supportive culture. Creating and retaining an entrepreneurial management team that is either home grown or acquired is no easy feat! It's difficult enough to create an entrepreneurial environment with internally developed teams; it's even more difficult to do with teams acquired through acquisitions.

To achieve this difficult feat, elite enterprises typically focus on several important elements. They provide the acquired teams with the exceptional capabilities to scale their businesses and accelerate innovation, while simultaneously allowing the retained management team to continue to operate the business. Elite companies smartly retain acquired management teams by creating a light governance framework that is both effective and motivational. They provide them with the right tools and resources, and welcome them into the larger family of the organization. The ability of elite companies to attract family businesses and retain and motivate them under a new structure and culture is a highly effective component to building and sustaining an enduring enterprise.

Habit 2: Create and Sustain a Startup Mind-Set
A startup mind-set or mentality simply means that the enterprise must be highly nimble, must be in a continuous state of innovation, and must be flexible. Meg Whitman, CEO of H-P Enterprises, captured this well when she said, "Being nimble is the only path to winning."[xxiv]

A startup mind-set also means that the people in the enterprise connect well with each other by ensuring they operate in a framework of transparency and accountability. Most importantly, team members must trust each other. Startups empower teams to do great things, and members usually practice extreme commitment to the cause.

Startups create a culture of innovation. Everyone in the organization brings a deep passion for the company's core purpose and its business model to their jobs. A flat organizational structure is also a common aspect of startups as is an open floor plan that allows for collaboration, creativity, and connectivity.

Leaders wishing to create and sustain a startup mind-set need to follow a simple recipe with the team members they hire following these key elements: (1) hiring creative and innovative people. Google (Alphabet) is extremely fanatical about recruiting and hiring the right people, "Smart Creatives"; (2) hiring collaborative people who are able to work in a team environment; (3) hiring disciplined, passionate team members with a proactive mind-set; (4) setting up a framework of accountability and responsibility with an effective governance framework that frees people from suffocating bureaucracy; and (5) establishing a clear mission, sound values, and an innovative business model.

Habit 3: Exhibit a War Mind-Set

A four-star general once said to me, "In battle, we do not want a fair fight. We want overwhelming power that provides a significant competitive advantage."[xxv] This well-focused and compelling statement is easily translated to the business environment. Companies that possess superior power through exceptional capabilities, an innovative business model, people excellence, and other habits outlined in this book, will most likely prevail in any battle with their competition. All companies should take this advice to heart.

One of the best business examples of this superior power is Disney. Under elite leader Robert Iger, Disney has been transformed into a high-performing global brand that is unmatched in its industry. During his tenure, Iger has accumulated and developed the most enviable stable of brands. Such franchise names as Marvel, Star Wars, Pixar, and, of course, all the original Disney brands. The power of these brands is unrivaled, and they provide Disney with overwhelming power in the marketplace.

This supremacy was captured well by the Wall Street Journal on June 9, 2015, by Ben Fritz: "Disney's collection of successful intellectual property is so vast that a senior executive at one Disney rival complained recently: It's almost unfair given the amalgamation of resources they have." Clearly, Disney has done great work in building their vast power base. The article goes on to note: "Some on Wall Street no longer see Disney as a media company and see it more as a global consumer-products company ..." Iger has accomplished this change by transforming and refocusing Disney around brands and franchises, such as Marvel. The result of this refocus, plus its ongoing strong performance, is that Disney has managed to outperform its media peers over a ten-year period, ending December 2015. Disney's total shareholder return or TSR was an impressive 350 percent, compared with its media peers, who turned in a 222 percent TSR.[xxvi]

Habit 4: Ensure Your Successor is a Success
As I wrote in *CEO Lifelines: Nine Commitments Every Leader Must Make*, it's the obligation of a departing leader and the board of directors to take substantive and measurable action to ensure that the incoming CEO is a success. I outlined five basic and minimal lifelines a company needs to provide a new CEO to ensure success: (1) an experienced and talented mentor; (2) unwavering board of directors and executive team support; (3) appropriate training and leadership-development; (4) assistance in establishing an outside relationship with a trusted confidant; and, (5) assistance in obtaining a seat on the board of directors at another company. Boards that fall short of providing these five essential lifelines to a new CEO should reassess their internal succession planning process.

Elite CEOs, however, go way beyond the five basic lifelines provided by an effective board. First and foremost, elite leaders devote their entire career to building an enduring and high-performing organization. They begin by building a distinctive culture, one that is deeply ingrained in the organization. A strong culture is built on the foundation of a clear mission or purpose and embedded core values. Nothing is more important for a leader than ensuring that a healthy culture permeates the enterprise.

A recent *Fortune* magazine article outlined the findings of a Deloitte's annual survey of 3,300 executives in 106 countries that found, "... top managers say culture is the most important issue they face, more important than leadership, workforce capability, performance management, or anything else."[xxvii] Newly elected CEOs who inherit a healthy and vibrant culture will no doubt start their tenure on a much stronger footing that significantly increases the probability of their success.

In addition to culture, elite leaders assemble an exceptional team, develop an innovative business model, develop exceptional capabilities, create a learning entity, and build multiple lifelines during their tenure. With all these elements in place, successors have a clear and substantive advantage over other newly appointed CEOs. The best example of an elite leader providing their successor with exceptional elements for success is Steve Jobs. Jobs' successor, Tim Cook, inherited a company that was extraordinarily strong and unequalled. It is not surprising that Cook has been a tremendous success and that Apple continues its extraordinary and unmatched climb. They are in an elite class of enterprises that operate in the thin air of the summit with extraordinary strength and flexibility.

Apple is clearly an example of the work done by the former leader to prepare for a new leader. It has reached new heights and continues to climb summits that most organizations only dream about. *Fortune*'s Adam Lashinsky cataloged Cook's first 3 1/2 years of success in the April 1, 2015 issue. Here are some salient points: "... there's little debate that the state of Apple under Cook is fundamentally sound. Its stock has soared ... translating into a market capitalization well north of $700 billion, the first company to cross that level." The article goes on to say, "At the same time, Apple's cash hoard has tripled since 2010 ... he largely has held together the long-tenured management team he inherited from Jobs, augmenting it with a few key players ... ."

Habit 5: Create an Environment that Fosters Creativity and Innovation

Elite CEOs first and foremost understand their role as the creativity and innovation officer chief. This ability to create an environment that fosters and rewards creativity and innovation is paramount to the long-term value creation equation.

Elite leaders understand the importance of hiring the best, most creative people and providing the right organizational framework and workplace environment that allows their creativity to flourish. So, who are some of greatest elite leaders of our time that have created such an environment? My list will not surprise anyone: Steve Jobs (Apple), Robert Iger (Disney), Larry Page and Sergey Brin (Google), Mark Zuckerberg (Facebook), Bill Gates (Microsoft), Brian Chesky (Airbnb), Jack Dorsey (Twitter and Square), and Reed Hastings (Netflix). Of course, there are many more highly creative and innovative leaders, not just in the tech sector but throughout the global economy. The author, Walter Isaacson, captured the essence of the importance of a leader fostering creativity and innovation in his book *The Innovators*, and in the foreword, he wrote to General Stanley McChrystal's book *Team of Teams*. "In today's world," Isaacson wrote, "creativity is a collaborative endeavor. Innovation is a team effort."

Creativity and innovation are fundamental for building and sustaining an elite enterprise. Great leaders clearly understand the connection between extraordinary teams and the right environment, the right culture, and the right leadership that fosters creativity and innovation. Unfortunately, no simple recipe exists for this task; however, it's instructive to study how other elite enterprises have created this environment that allows creativity and innovation to flourish. This habit will be viewed from multiple lenses throughout this book in the form of specific examples that cumulatively help explain this essential capability that is imperative for the long-term health of the enterprise.

Habit 6: Learn Leadership Habits from the Military
The U.S. military is elite and unmatched in the world. Therefore, it offers business leaders and CEOs many lessons on developing effective habits. A wonderful mechanism for assessing and developing this habit is an executive leadership training program called "Staff Ride." The objective of the staff ride is to learn valuable leadership lessons from historic battles as taught by

generals and other high level military personnel, and then applying the lessons to the business environment. Here is how the program is conducted:

An enterprise partners with the U.S. Army War College in Carlisle, Pennsylvania, to design an effective leadership program for their company. Usually, a group of about fifteen to twenty executives, along with military personnel, travel to a famous battle site—such as Normandy or Gettysburg— to learn what happened on the battlefield and the connections that can be made to business. Battle plans and the decisions made (both right and wrong on all levels) are viewed and discussed through the lens of experts, who discuss critical factors that greatly influenced the outcome of the battle. Participants complete assigned reading before attending so that they fully understand the historical context.

I attended a staff ride in both Normandy, France and Gettysburg, PA. Here are my key takeaways from this outstanding and life-changing experience:

- **Don't fight a fair battle.** Overwhelming power puts the enemy in a significant competitive disadvantage. Companies need to adopt this mind-set and position themselves to dominate their market and the competition.

- **Importance of being a learning entity and engaging in after-action review**. The military operates in a learning culture that values lessons learned. After-action reviews or debriefs is a formal process to thoroughly review what happened with the sole objective of learning and improving processes going forward. After-action reviews are performed for actions that succeed and fail. The military clearly understands human behavior and the purpose of the post-event debrief is to eliminate attribution and hindsight biases.

- **Communicate Commander's intent**. One of the key reasons that the military is elite—particularly Special Forces—is because team members have total clarity on commander's intent. Everyone on the team knows the mission with no ambiguity or confusion on what must be done. In business, companies with a clearly understood powerful mission or purpose that is embraced by everyone in the organization will, over time, outperform enterprises that lack such clarity of purpose.

- **Distinctive lines of command.** No confusion exists in the military as to whom the decision makers are. Regardless if it's an army division or a small special operations team, such clarity is vital to the success of the mission. In organizations, clearly understood lines of command and decision-making responsibility is essential.

- **Succession planning and leadership-development**. Before going into battle, every team member is keenly aware of the chain of command at least two levels down. The military understands well the importance of succession planning and the importance of developing leaders who can assume a leadership position whenever necessary. Elite enterprises also devote significant resources to ensure that succession planning and leadership-development are a high priority and is executed with excellence.

- **Training.** The military spends incredible resources on training. They understand the correlation between extensive training and success on the battlefield. This disciplined focus on training is an effective habit that all enterprises need to vigorously embrace and implement.

- **Planning and strategy.** Detailed planning and strategic thinking along with the development of a long-term strategy are cornerstones in the building of an elite institution. The military's elite status can be traced to this focus. For example, consider the amount of planning and strategic thinking necessary for the D-Day invasion during World War II. Consider also the military adage about planning that once the first bullet is fired, all plans go out the window.

- **Innovation.** The military understands the connection between innovation and the impact of emerging disruptive technologies. Cybersecurity, stealth technology, drones, cutting-edge weapons systems, and numerous other innovations all underpin U.S. military elite status. As demonstrated throughout this book, elite enterprises likewise understand how important innovation is to achieve sustained success.

- **Small unit capability.** The military has discovered that small teams, such as special operation forces, are highly effective. They attribute this high success rate to a simple recipe that includes four elements: trust, commander's intent, a shared consciousness, and empowerment. A shared consciousness is simply having a holistic understanding of the environment and high levels of connectivity. In other words, everyone on the team is on the same page. Finally, empowerment means that everyone on the team is empowered to make decisions.

- **Speed of trust**. Military units operate effectively because of the speed of trust, meaning a high level of trust exists within each unit, which results in high-speed decision making. In battle, high trust and speed of decision making, along with resolve and execution, are vital to success.

Habit 7: Develop an Audacious Turnaround Plan

Even elite companies stumble. In Jim Collins' seminal work, *Good to Great*, eleven companies were identified in the book as being great. Of the eleven, three of the enterprises have experienced significant change: one completely disappeared (Circuit City), one was acquired (Gillette), and the third was highly stressed and needed a government bailout due to the 2008 Great Recession (Fannie Mae). The fact that three of the eleven companies experienced varying difficulties does not negate that they were once great. It only demonstrates that it is very difficult to sustain greatness for long periods of time. In the book, *The Halo Effect*, Phil Rosenzweig states, "... getting to the top is hard ... staying at the top is even harder, because success attracts imitators ..."[xxviii]

Provided it is not too late, the antidote to this illness is to develop an audacious and sustainable turnaround plan. Sometimes companies fail to think big when planning their turnaround plan and consequently end up with a series of plans over a long horizon that are small in scope and have a minimal impact on the performance of the company.

Whenever boards are confronted with sudden performance issues, the usual path they follow is to first appoint a new CEO to develop and execute a turnaround plan. When this change occurs, the newly appointed CEO will usually develop and execute a robust turnaround plan—often known as the "First 100-Days Plan." I believe that boards should insist that such a plan be audacious in scope; otherwise, the turnaround may be more difficult to achieve and could actually make matters worse.

This timeframe for creating an audacious turnaround plan is usually perfect because newly appointed leaders are generally given a honeymoon period to develop a strategic plan or road map on how he or she will revive the company. The blueprint usually hinges on a broad array of elements that include both immediate changes as well as long-term items. During this honeymoon period, the board of directors and the management team are usually highly supportive and will back the new leader because everyone wants him or her to be successful.

While the personnel of the company are initially supportive, it is critical for the newly appointed leader to develop an effective and audacious plan that is executed flawlessly with some immediate and demonstrable achievements. Elite leaders understand the importance of communicating a substantive and audacious plan to both the board and the shareholders, followed by some meaningful and tangible results in the first 100 days. Elite leaders also understand that it's unlikely that they will get a second opportunity at another plan, and, thus, it is doubly important that the plan be audacious.

Habit 8: Build an Enduring Enterprise

Elite enterprises must be built over time. Visionary elite leaders consistently focus on building a company that will endure and transcend their leadership. Elite leaders know how to skillfully balance a long-term perspective with short-term needs. They build not only a prodigious number of lifelines to ensure that the enterprise can withstand any form of turbulence, but they also position the company in such way that they have distinctive competitive advantage that allows the company to perform at a high level. This positioning is no easy feat. Some key lifelines that are built by elite leaders include:

- A strong balance sheet with ample cash reserves and very manageable debt

- A long-term commitment to innovation including an innovative business model
- Consistently investing, in a disciplined manner, in innovation, people, business processes, and the business model—no matter the economic environment
- Making a long-term commitment to leadership-development and talent-management, including hiring and retaining the best and brightest
- Investing over a long horizon in exceptional capabilities so that the organization performs at the highest level possible
- Ensuring that a value-creating board of directors is appointed and that all directors are held accountable
- Ensuring that capital is invested effectively and efficiently
- Ensuring that the focus of the company is on free cash flow, the ultimate metric for measuring long-term success
- Identifying the most mission critical processes to the enterprise and investing through such mechanisms as Lean and Six-Sigma continuous improvement capabilities
- Investing in learning at the individual level, enterprise level, and board level
- Focus on simplifying and eliminating as much complexity as possible out of the organizational structure and key processes
- Building an adaptive and resilient organization that is underpinned by teams that win

CHAPTER 4

10 EXECUTION HABITS OF ELITE LEADERS

Success doesn't necessarily come from breakthrough innovation but from flawless execution. A great strategy alone won't win a game or a battle; the win comes from basic blocking and tackling.

Naveen Jain[xxix]

E lite Leaders exhibit ten essential execution habits including:

Habit 1: Act Quickly and Decisively
Habit 2: Stand Your Ground When Challenged
Habit 3: Live the Inverted Pyramid
Habit 4: Be the Top Salesperson in the Organization
Habit 5: Focus on Indispensable CEO Metrics
Habit 6: Guard Against Attribution

Habit 7:   Be Intolerant of Mediocrity
Habit 8:   Utilize the Quarterly State of the Business
           Report
Habit 9:   Empower Your Employees
Habit 10: Develop an Obsessive Focus on Survival

Habit 1: Act Quickly and Decisively

The business world continues to change quickly and
unpredictably as the weather changes on the summits of all
the world's highest mountain peaks. Speed, more than ever,
provides either a competitive advantage for enterprises, or a
disadvantage when a company is adversely impacted by a
shifting business climate.

I see the impact of rapid change firsthand as both a
climber and through my work as an advisor to enterprises,
the work I do as a board member, and through my
association with private equity firms. The speed of change
will only accelerate as we move forward due, in part, to
activism.

A Fortune 500 survey conducted in 2015 discovered that
most CEOs (94 percent) agree with the statement, "My
company will change more in the next five years than it has
in the last five years."[xxx] Therefore, elite CEOs act quickly
and decisively. Instinct, cumulative business knowledge,
and overall perspective are essential characteristics that can
assist a CEO in choosing wisely. An excellent example of a
CEO acting quickly and decisively in response to change is
Virginia Rometty, IBM's CEO.

Reporter Monica Langley captured the essence of this
extraordinary habit in a *Wall Street Journal* article on April
21, 2015. According to the article, Rometty made the
following statement when confronted by her team, who

pressed for more money and more time to jump-start their cloud computing strategy: "The market is moving too fast. I can't give you more time." Instead, the article pointed out that, "... she spent $2 billion on a cloud-technology company ... and made a $1.2 billion investment in additional data centers." Clearly, Rometty acted quickly and decisively, and manifested many crucial characteristics of an elite leader.

Acting quickly and decisively is even more important when there's a crisis. It's imperative to understand that elite leaders do not lead by consensus in a crisis; they act quickly because time is of the essence; they have no time for extended debates or to study different scenarios. An elite business associate related such an example recently while reflecting on the impact of the Great Recession. The CEO said he went with his instinct and cut heavily the company's cost structure, including laying off a significant number of employees. He did not wait to see how things played out. He did not spend an endless amount of time analyzing numerous scenarios. Due to his proactive, instinctive, and audacious action, his organization recovered more quickly than competitors from the recession. As a result, the company took market share while the competition was still reacting to the economic shock. This decisiveness is what leadership is all about, going with your instinct that is underpinned by many decades of experience and making quick and conclusive decisions.

Habit 2: Stand Your Ground When Challenged

Leaders are constantly being challenged by subordinates, peers, their supervisors, and by customers. At times, these challenges are unrelenting. It's important for leaders to stand their ground, particularly when their position is backed by facts or their instinct. It is doubly important when it involves customer challenges that impact shareholder value. During my many decades of experience, I have witnessed how to properly handle these types of situations and how not to.

It is not unusual for large customers to put tremendous pressure on suppliers to reduce costs. A request for a price reduction can occur even when there is a legally binding contract. The threat of losing such an important customer often results in a leader and an organization caving and granting the price reduction. This is a dangerous path which should not be followed because invariably there will be another or perhaps many more requests from other customers as well.

If a leader believes that they have no other alternative, they should still hold their ground. If they feel absolutely backed to the wall and must capitulate, then at a minimum a *quid pro quo* must be part of the deal. When capitulation occurs, a leader cannot accept a one-sided deal. A *quid pro quo* scenario can be achieved with creativity and hard work so that the result is a win-win for both parties.

Numerous elements can be brought into the dialogue as the offset to a possible temporary price discount or permanent price reduction. One of these elements can include the customer granting a contract extension without putting the work out for bid, which often can be a lengthy and expensive process. The customer could also agree to provide additional work which can be incorporated and added to an existing contract. A win-win might also mean working collaboratively with the customer to reengineer a process with the objective of lowering the overall cost for both parties.

Let's now examine how it should be done. In an April 14, 2015 *Wall Street Journal* article, (former) DuPont CEO Ellen Kullman exemplified such an approach when "... she held her ground with customers who occasionally threatened to take their business elsewhere. She listened but at the end of the day she had to be firm for the DuPont shareholders ... She's extremely calm under pressure." The exceptional habit that Kullman manifested is critically important and should be carefully studied and emulated by leaders. My view aligns well with Kullman's—hold firm because if you don't you will be taken down a path that you will most likely regret and, at worst, be unable to undo or control.

Habit 3: Live the Inverted Pyramid
The inverted pyramid is an upside-down triangle. The concept is simple, yet powerful. It puts the frontline troops first and the C-level executives at the lowest level. This grounded view is practiced very effectively by an elite company, Home Depot. In a November 17, 2014 *Fortune* article on Home Depot CEO Frank Blake, the magazine quotes him as follows, "The right way to look at this is me on the bottom ... My job here is to clear away the things that get in your way."

Elite leaders understand the importance of the inverted pyramid. They possess the right mind-set and humility that drive the behavior of the many customer-facing employees, including shop employees, those selling or servicing or making the product, and the customer service professionals. Elite CEOs focus on the frontline troops and clear unnecessary obstacles so they can perform their jobs efficiently and effectively. In addition, this mind-set has the added benefit of building a strong organizational culture.

Habit 4: Be the Top Salesperson in the Organization
CEOs have broad responsibilities that include interacting with customers, investors, the board, and their employees and, as such, should be the top salesperson for their organization. Let's examine each of these constituents a little closer starting with the customer.

Customer visits are an integral part of an elite leader's playbook. A leader can never visit too many customers. It's a habit that needs to be well developed and consistently used in a focused manner. Elite CEOs know when to visit key customers or prospective customers; they are highly skilled in closing deals. However, elite leaders, understand that they need to listen and learn from their customers. Elite leaders also know the importance of keeping promises and to deliver on them with excellence and passion that amazes the customer.

CEOs must also sell their organization to prospective and current investors. These gifted leaders know that they must carry the burden of being the face and voice of the company. Just as important as selling the company and its products and services to the outside world, an elite CEO must sell his or her vision to the board, the senior management team, and all employees. As part of the vision, a leader must clearly articulate and sell the purpose and business model of the enterprise. Leaders are also the key driver of the company's culture, and their ability to sell effectively to the organization the components to build a distinctive culture is paramount.

Habit 5: Focus on Indispensable CEO Metrics

CEOs are awash in financial metrics and the challenge is always to select the ones for their dashboard that are most effective for managing the enterprise. So, what are these key financial metrics for an effective dashboard? Elite CEOs will likely focus on growth in revenues, margins, and free cash flow. In addition, they monitor the health of their balance sheet because it is a critical lifeline. A full list of the dashboard metrics is summarized below. The metrics are segmented into operating performance and business valuation.

CEO Dashboard—Operating Performance Metrics:
- Return on Invested Capital
- Gross Margin
- Operating Margin
- Earnings Growth
- Sales or Revenue Growth
- Backlog/Sales Cadence
- Free Cash Flow
- Cash Realization Ratio
- Net Debt-To-Equity Ratio
- Effective Tax Rate

CEO Dashboard—Business Valuation Metrics:
- Price/Earnings Ratio
- Price/Book Value
- Dividend Yield
- Free Cash Flow Yield
- Enterprise Value/EBITDA

Here are some additional notes on these important metrics:

Revenue growth—CEOs focus on three elements to determine growth revenue, sales cadence, backlog, and revenue mix. The sales cadence is important to know daily (if possible) since this is the flow of orders in dollars and as a percent compared with prior periods and plan or forecast. The backlog should also be known in real time. The detail of the backlog can vary— just like the sales cadence—but it's important to at least know the dollars and the percent of change. The revenue mix includes two major elements: product mix and source. The product mix is simply which products and business units are generating the revenues, and the source is made up of organic revenue growth, foreign exchange impact, and the effect of acquisitions and divestitures.

Margins—The focus should be on gross margins (or gross profit), operating margins, and net margins. Each is important because it allows the leader to focus on different influences. All margins are, of course, highly impacted by the sales price and pricing leverage. But it's just as important to focus on the cost side as well because a great deal of variability and flexibility can be built into the cost model. When examining the cost side of the equation as opposed to pricing leverage, gross margins are usually most influenced by raw material and labor costs along with depreciation. On the operating margins line, the selling, general, and administrative expenses drive that margin percentage. On the net margins, it's the effective tax rate and interest expense.

Free cash flow—This is ultimately the most important number because in the end, cash flow is what drives valuations. Free cash flow is calculated by taking cash flow from operations less capital expenditures and less dividends. However, the more traditional method of calculating free cash flow is to take cash flow from operations less capital expenditures, meaning that dividends are excluded from the calculation. There are many instances when dividends should be deducted in calculating the free cash flow number. If the company has a long history of paying an increasing dividend, the dividend then is not discretionary because negative ramifications to the company's stock price would result if the dividend was reduced significantly or stopped altogether. However, if the dividend has a highly discretionary element to it, it should then be excluded from the free cash flow calculation.

Habit 6: Guard Against Attribution
CEOs have a responsibility to guard against blind attribution, which emanates from cognitive bias. This natural human bias can be counteracted by implementing effective mechanisms. It's imperative that these mechanisms be enforced by the leader so that they will guard the facts and dispense with the attribution, with the sole objective of accurately capturing history.

The concept of cognitive bias is something that leaders need to understand. In Phil Rosenzweig's *The Halo Effect*, the author captures the concept well in the following excerpt: "The tendency is to look at a company's overall performance and make attributions about its culture, leadership, values and more. In fact, many things we commonly claim drive company performance are simply attributions based on prior performance." Rosenzweig further explains that "... people attribute one set of characteristics to groups they believe are effective, and a very different set of characteristics to groups who are ineffective."

"When times are good," the author points out, "we lavish praise and create heroes. When things go bad, we lay blame and create villains."[xxxi]

Elite enterprises embed mechanisms that provide unfiltered and unbiased feedback on both success and failure as they occur. This feedback is vital because human memory tends to be, at times, selectively poor. Consequently, sometimes we tend to attribute results differently from the facts. This powerful editing tool can attribute success and failure either disproportionally or completely inaccurately. Worst of all, this unreliable credit can result in flawed decision making by leaders and boards, which is why after-action reviews are a powerful mechanism that prevents history from being re-written. Companies that are exceptional at learning through post-event debriefs will most likely not suffer from attribution bias.

Habit 7: Be Intolerant of Mediocrity

Great leaders are totally intolerant of mediocrity—it's an anathema to them. In the book, *Steve Jobs*, by Walter Isaacson, and in Eric Schmidt & Jonathan Rosenberg's book, *How Google Works*, numerous examples show how both enterprises focus intensely on hiring the best and brightest people. Steve Jobs was utterly intolerant of mediocrity, and he would only accept A-players. He believed that if you compromise on these standards of excellence, it would ultimately harm the company. In the Google book, the authors provide incredible detail and insight on how the company focuses on hiring what they call the "Smart Creative," and why it's so important in creating an elite enterprise. Given the success of Apple and Google—arguably the two most elite technology organizations—it's difficult to disagree with their approach. We can learn a great deal from their intense focus on the best and brightest and how they execute on this most important lifeline.

So, how do you go about creating a world class team that wins consistently? I believe that four elements need to be part of talent-management and leadership-development framework. The first element is identifying internally people who have an innate ability to assess talent. These are the individuals who should be making the hiring decisions and the ones who should recommend internal promotions. It's amazing how many companies delegate hiring and internal identification to incredibly ineffective and untrained people in their organization.

In addition to being able to assess talent, the second element is using a third-party firm that utilizes behavioral assessment tools. Predictive and behavioral tools are indispensable in the overall equation of building a great team.

The third element is a robust internal succession planning process. The succession planning process must include a comprehensive plan that effectively develops and prepares the future leaders of the company.

The fourth and final element is a series of robust metrics that measure such elements as the number of key seats filled with the right people, success of external hires, and performance of hiring team(s).

Habit 8: Utilize the Quarterly State of the Business Report

Sometimes the most basic habits are the most important. One that stands out is the quarterly state of the business report to the board prepared by the CEO. This report should capture succinctly the state of the company as seen through the eyes of the CEO and the senior leadership. It is essential that the CEO provides his perspective and insight.

Ideally, the report should be in two parts: a written section that summarizes all salient points augmented by a charts and graphics section. Some CEOs prefer reports that have both parts combined into a single report. They believe that the financial information is self-evident in all the various reports provided to the board. No matter which format is adopted, what is important is that the CEO captures accurately the essence of the current and future state of the enterprise.

Some of the elements typically covered by CEOs in the written section of the report include major wins, disappointments, failures, products and services performance, what went well and what didn't go so well, emerging risks and issues, and expectations for the near term and longer term. From the board perspective, this critical document can assist them in better assessing the performance of the CEO and senior team. Sometimes boards can obtain incredible insight on how the CEO approaches the job and how he or she thinks by simply reading the report.

When I was CEO, I put together a comprehensive quarterly report on the state of the business. I used a combination of written part, which I called the board letter, that was augmented by a second section filled with key financial charts. I found this to be an effective habit because it puts together in one place everything that matters, and, importantly, the words provided are those of the CEO.

An excellent example of this habit that I have discovered in my research is how *Google* views its quarterly state of the business report. In the book, *How Google Works*, the authors Schmidt and Rosenberg emphasize just how vital the quarterly report is to the management, the board, and to employees. Here are some salient comments:

> "Each quarter the team creates an in-depth report ... to be presented to the board. There is a written section ... which is crammed with data and insights on the business and the products, and slides with data and charts that product leads ... use to guide the board meeting. Not surprisingly, much of this information is not for public consumption. But after the board meeting we do something that is

surprising. We take the material that we presented to our board and share it with all of our employees."

The authors go on to say how the exact slides are presented at company-wide meetings and how most the board letter is communicated in a company-wide email. This amazing and healthy habit must get results when reviewing Google's (Alphabet) success.

Habit 9: Empower Your Employees

Empowerment is one of the four key elements in General McChrystal's recipe for building effective Team of Teams. Empowerment is widely practiced in the tech sector, and it's one of the reasons that so many companies thrive and are so successful.

Established CEOs understand the potential of empowerment and its importance to building a healthy and vibrant culture in the organization. Elite leaders focus intensely on embedding empowerment in the DNA of the organization through effective mechanisms. In fact, ensuring that appropriate mechanisms are implemented and have teeth are two of the most important CEO responsibilities. However, for empowerment to be effective, it is critical that these established mechanisms free people from bureaucratic policies and practices. Leaders need to ensure that decision making is pushed down to individuals and small teams. This knowledge-sharing means the CEO must not only support and live this empowerment every day, it also means the CEO needs to ensure that the implemented mechanisms are functioning as designed.

Habit 10: Develop an Obsessive Focus on Survival
Elite mountaineers must be focused (obsessed) on surviving the Death Zone when ascending and descending the top summits of the world. They know that they must be in top physical condition. They also know that they must plan and execute both the ascent and descent with exceptional skills. This healthy obsessive focus can be the difference between surviving or dying in the Death Zone.

It's no different in business. Elite leaders must also obsess about survival and preparing for unexpected events before they happen. As we have seen, global shocks and bad luck events occur with some frequency. Elite leaders know these occasions happen, and they are deeply focused on preparing for the worst by building an abundance of lifelines, as discussed earlier. Also, elite leaders skillfully manage risks and uncertainties, and they effectively scan the environment for brewing storms. This healthy obsession about survival, no matter the environment, separates the successful elite leaders from all the others. Elite leaders clearly understand that the preparation for severe economic turbulence and unforeseen global shocks needs to occur during good times.

SECTION 2

EXCEPTIONAL HABITS OF ELITE
ENTERPRISES

After climbing a great hill, one only finds that
there are many more hills to climb.
Nelson Mandela[xxxii]

Companies that do not adequately prepare for future shocks and are unable to adapt to the ever-changing business landscape do so at their own peril. If you examine the entire history of the Fortune 500 list (1955 to 2015) you'd probably be surprised to learn that an astonishing 88 percent of the company names on the 1955 list don't appear in the 2015 list. Mark J. Perry of the American Enterprise Institute, recently blogged about this surprising fact:

"Comparing the Fortune 500 companies in 1955 to the Fortune 500 in 2015, there are only sixty-one companies that appear in both lists ... In other words, only 12.2 percent of the Fortune 500 companies in 1955 were still on the list sixty years later in 2015, and nearly 88 percent of the companies from 1955 have either gone bankrupt, merged with (or were acquired by) another company, or still exist but have fallen from the top Fortune 500 companies ... ." Perry goes on to say, "The fact that nearly nine of every ten Fortune 500 companies in 1955 are gone, merged, or contracted demonstrates that there's been a lot market disruption, churning ... ."[xxxiii] Such statistics are both shocking and compelling and clearly support the need for companies to focus on the elite guidelines offered in this book.

Companies typically fall primarily for two reasons: First, they have not built enough of the enterprise lifelines discussed in this book that adequately prepare them for any circumstance. Second, because circumstances are always changing, they may be too slow to adapt to a change or, worse, may not even recognize that change is needed. It is almost impossible to list all the events and elements that could adversely affect an organization and make it irrelevant, but the underlying reasons a company falls from the summit can usually be traced to a shortage or absence of A-players, a lack of discipline, and an outsized hubris about their business. Specifically, these three elements often are manifested in the following ways:

- An elite leader retires, and the successor does not have equal skills; remember not all leaders are created equally.

- The business model is no longer innovative because competitors have copied their recipe for success, and the company has been slow to adapt to the changing environment.
- A disruptive technology completely changes the competitive landscape.
- The enterprise takes outsized risks in growth, investment, and/or in contractual obligations.
- A significant fraud or scandal engulfs the organization.
- A major global shock or a series of shocks evaporates a substantial portion of a vital end-market.
- The company suffers a series of catastrophic bad luck events that end the journey.
- The company lets it hubris get out of control. Yes, arrogance can be the true enemy of elite. In his insightful book, *How the Mighty Fall*, Jim Collins provides a highly effective framework that he refers to as the five stages of decline. He points out that the first stage of decline is "Hubris Born of Success." Here is what Collins says about Stage 1: "Great enterprises can become insulated by success; accumulated momentum can carry an enterprise forward, for a while, even if its leaders make poor decisions or lose discipline. Stage 1 kicks in when people become arrogant, regarding success virtually as an entitlement, and they lose sight of the true underlying factors that created success in the first place. When rhetoric of success ... replaces penetrating understanding and insight ...

decline will very likely follow. Luck and chance
play a role in many successful outcomes, and those
who fail to acknowledge the role luck may have
played in their success ... have succumbed to
hubris." [xxxiv]

Mountaineers, like companies, also face many obstacles
that can slow or even terminate the ascent to the summit.
Avalanches, which tend to be the deadliest, are at the top of
the list. Unexpected storms, high winds, equipment
malfunction, and team members making bad choices are
some of the more common obstacles. However, great
mountaineers know how to adapt to the situation.

It's no different in business. Companies face formidable
obstacles that can slow their ascent to the summit. A great
recession, a disruptive technology, a geopolitical event, or
even a cyber breach can dramatically and adversely impact
the climb. Businesses, like mountaineers, need to be able to
adapt to any circumstance. The best way to prepare an
enterprise to deal with any challenge is to adopt the
exceptional habits outlined in this book along with the nine
lifelines.

Exceptional Habits of Elite Enterprises
In this section, we will review the exceptional habits of
elite enterprises. As we did in the first section, the
exceptional habits are segmented and discussed under three
essential foundational pillars: leadership, strategy, and
execution. Enterprises that focus on these three areas, along
with an overall awareness of the luck spread foundational
pillar, should enjoy success through sustained high
performance that will ultimately lead a company to elite

status. The exceptional habits discussed in this section include:

Chapter 5: 12 Leadership Habits of Elite Enterprises

Chapter 6: 14 Strategy Habits of Elite Enterprises

Chapter 7: 17 Execution Habits of Elite Enterprises

CHAPTER 5

12 LEADERSHIP HABITS OF ELITE ENTERPRISES

The price of greatness is responsibility.
Winston Churchill[xxxv]

E lite Enterprises exhibit twelve essential leadership habits including:

Habit 1: Appoint a Digital Advisory Board
Habit 2: Don't Make One Large Bet; Make Small Targeted Investments
Habit 3: Create a High Energy Annual Shareholders' Meeting
Habit 4: Do Not Be Afraid to Fail, But Fail Fast and Well
Habit 5: Appoint a Strong Number Two
Habit 6: Excel at Communication
Habit 7: Stop Providing Earnings Guidance

Habit 8: Elevate the Chief Information Officer Position
(CIO)
Habit 9: Focus on Diversity
Habit 10: Appoint and Empower a Global Leadership
Team
Habit 11: Stop with the Serial "Adjusted" Earnings
Habit 12: Go Private

Habit 1: Appoint a Digital Advisory Board
Elite companies recognize the value of having an effective
digital strategy—it's truly indispensable in today's
hypercompetitive global e-commerce marketplace, the rise
of cloud computing, and the essential need to develop
robust cybersecurity measures. Some of the biggest names
in corporate America (and at least fifty of the Fortune 500
companies, according to a June 10, 2015 *Wall Street
Journal* article) have appointed a digital advisory board,
including GE, American Express, and Target. It is difficult
to imagine how a major company can operate without at
least a digital advisory committee.

In addition to an advisory committee, elite companies
recruit digital directors and establish alliances with key
technology partners. When establishing a digital advisory
board, some key elements should be considered by an
organization to ensure the committee is effective. The
advisory board should:

- Have a clearly stated mission or core purpose
- Set forth the responsibilities of all parties including
  those persons retained to serve

- Be informal, providing maximum flexibility to the company
- Not have authority to vote on corporate matters
- Not bear legal fiduciary responsibility
- Provide non-binding advice, insight, and perspective on digital matters
- Be a key resource to the CEO, management team and the board, and it should be respected and highly valued
- Appoint members to one year terms; re-appointment of each member should be at the sole discretion of the CEO
- Be collaborative, engaged, and promote a healthy, distinctive culture
- Be assessed annually with key metrics established

Habit 2: Don't Make One Large Bet; Make Small Targeted Investments

When enterprises make significant strategic investments—such as expansion in new territories, introducing new products, or developing new products through innovation—the elite companies usually approach these projects with laser-like focus. Moreover, they do not make one large bet. Many examples of elite companies that have taken this approach exist. Apple, again, offers a good leadership example in the launching of Apple retail stores. Apple first did a significant amount of preparatory work, and when they did finally launch, they only opened one store instead of opening multiple stores. As they gained more experience with the concept and the format, they expanded slowly, store by store, until broad network of shops was in place.

JC Penney and Target took the opposite approach. JC Penney decided to radically transform their retail stores format across the entire company without testing the changes in a more focused way. The results from JC Penney's large bet were significantly different and the roll out sent revenues plunging as customers fled to the competition.

Target's expansion into Canada offers a similar lesson. As captured by a *Fortune* magazine article at the time;

> Rather than launching new stores in carefully selected spots and building slowly, Target acquired 124 locations in 2013 in one fell swoop by buying all the outlets from a defunct discounter called Zellers. Never mind that one of the causes of Zeller's demise was the poor location of its stores. Or that the spaces were designed to enable a different strategy from Target's. Throw in supply-chain problems that yielded empty shelves and high prices, and it added up to an unmitigated disaster.[xxxvi]

Google, on the other hand, completely understands the learning approach as articulated extremely well in an official August 10, 2015 blog concerning the reorganization of the company into Alphabet Inc. posted on by its co-founder and CEO Larry Page. He first reiterated what he and his co-founder Sergey Brin had previously said about the need to make smaller bets in areas that may seem very speculative. Then Page went on to say, "We did a lot things that seemed crazy at the time. Many of those crazy things now have over a billion users, like Google Maps, YouTube,

Chrome, and Android ... We've long believed that over time companies tend to get comfortable doing the same thing, just making incremental changes. But in the technology industry, where revolutionary ideas drive the next big growth areas, you need to be a bit uncomfortable to stay relevant."[xxxvii]

Habit 3: Create a High Energy Annual Shareholders' Meeting

Elite companies are re-examining how their annual meetings are conducted. The range of options currently on the table include: simplified meetings, virtual meetings, meetings moved to the corporate office, or simply scaling back on all aspects of the meeting. Although the trend is certainly away from old style large meetings with elaborate meals and gifts for members, I believe that creating a high-energy, celebratory meeting, a model practiced by several elite companies including Berkshire Hathaway, is a better model.

According to an April 28, 2015 article in the *Wall Street Journal* by Anupreeta Das, "Berkshire's annual meeting stands alone. Part question-and-answer session and part trade show, it offers attendees not just a chance to listen to Buffett ... but also to browse and buy products from Berkshire's ever-expanding collection of businesses ... This year's meeting is a grander-than-usual show ... expect more than 40,000 people ... ."

Admittedly, Buffett draws crowds anywhere in the world, but the concept of making the annual meeting more than a perfunctory exercise is something to consider. Another well-known company, Wal-Mart, also holds an uplifting event. Lindsay Frost wrote in the June 15, 2015, issue of *Agenda*, "Wal-Mart spent nearly $1.2 million at the University of Arkansas to house its shareholders for the annual meeting ... its celebrity-filled agenda included performances and employee testimonials."

I have attended such annual meetings of elite companies that celebrated the shareholders, the leadership team, and the board of directors. The high level of energy and enthusiasm that I experienced at these meetings was contagious. Choirs from local schools sang gospel music and the national anthem, products were on display (like what Berkshire does, but on a much smaller scale), products were given to attendees (this, of course, depending on what the company produces), a great question-and-answer format was used that engaged the shareholders, testimonials, and, of course, plenty of food and refreshments. However, in order to be successful, all of these events must be carefully planned and scripted by professionals.

Habit 4: Do Not Be Afraid to Fail, But Fail Fast and Well

Edward Land, the famous American scientist and inventor once said, "An essential aspect of creativity is not being afraid to fail."[xxxviii] However, in today's hypercompetitive economy not fearing failure is no longer enough. Perhaps a modern version might be that it is vital to "fail fast and well."

Speed has always been a critical factor in business, but it has never been more important than today. Speed can provide a company with a distinct competitive advantage, and speed is essential to take advantage of creativity and innovation. Enterprises that are smart about creativity and innovation understand that if an idea is going ultimately to be unsuccessful, that failure needs to happen quickly. In addition to speed, failing well is equally as important, which means you learn from mistakes and utilize valuable parts from the project in future projects. The reasons for this are obvious. Less money and less intellectual capital is used on the failed project and valuable lessons and technology are harnessed and directed to the next idea. This practice instills indispensable discipline in the organization.

Google offers the best example of this mind-set. In the book *How Google Works*, authors Schmidt and Rosenberg call it "Fail Well." Here is how their approach works:

> To innovate, you must learn to fail well. Learn from your mistakes: Any failed project should yield valuable technical, user, and market insights that can help inform the next effort. Morph ideas, don't kill them: Most of the world's great innovations started out with entirely different applications ... The timing of failure is perhaps the trickiest element to get right. A good failure is a fast one: Once you see that the project will not succeed, you want to pull the plug as quickly as possible, to avoid further wasting resources and incurring opportunity costs.[xxxix]

Habit 5: Appoint a Strong Number Two
Creating a chief operating officer position is a question that periodically comes up in business articles and in board

meetings. The real question should be: Do we have a strong number two in the organization? For elite companies, the answer is yes; there is an exceptional number two in the organization.

Some examples of a strong number two team member include Tim Cook at Apple under Steve Jobs; and Sheryl Sandberg at Facebook under Mark Zuckerberg. General Electric has for decades ensured a strong number two is in the pipeline by continuously developing an elite group of potential successors to the CEO.

Mike Esterl of the *Wall Street Journal,* offer an example of how this process works was in an August 14, 2015 article about Coke's process: "Coca-Cola Co. elevated an insider to the No. 2 job amid board concern that Chairman and CEO Muhtar Kent needed a powerful deputy to help manage the far-flung business empire ... The board has been encouraging ... Mr. Kent to appoint a No. 2 for some time ... The company said it named James Quincey president and chief operating officer ... makes the 19-year Coke veteran the leading internal candidate to eventually succeed Mr. Kent." (Subsequently, the company announced that in May 2017 that Quincey would be elevated to CEO.)

The strong number two often come from one of three positions: the chief operating officer, the chief financial officer, or the head of a large business group. Often with the chief operating officer title will also have the title of president. Sometimes even chief financial officers will be appointed president. However, the titles are not important. What is most important is that the CEO has someone that they can trust to execute superbly and a true partner in climbing the summit.

In today's hypercompetitive environment, an exceptional number two is indispensable. I would argue if you look closely at high performing elite companies, you will find an exceptional number two that helps the CEO to build ample lifelines as they ascend the summit. For companies and boards that want to build an elite company, the succession planning should not be solely focused on the CEO, it needs to go deeper to identify and appoint an extraordinary number two.

Habit 6: Excel at Communication
An effective and focused communication plan is an essential habit for an organization, its leader, and the board of directors. A well-crafted communication plan needs to be a top priority and it needs to be professionally managed. This is doubly important when a company faces tremendous headwinds and challenges, such as during times of great financial upheaval, or during a product recall, or when a key executive has been dismissed. Such a plan is also important when undertaking a business transformation initiative.

A professionally managed communication plan is not only indispensable, but it can sometimes be the difference between success and failure. Here are some of the key elements necessary for an effective communication plan:

- An outside public relations team should be retained to assist with the most difficult challenges. Do not delegate this to an internal communication professional.
- The leader of the organization must personally champion the communication plan.

- The leader must be adept at delivering a consistent message.
- The communication plan must be comprehensive. It must target all key stakeholders and must be reinforced.
- Social media, other appropriate technologies, as well as traditional media outlets should be used to effectively communicate.
- Appropriate mechanisms need to be implemented so that feedback and key data are analyzed in real-time.

Habit 7: Stop Providing Earnings Guidance

Companies that currently provide quarterly earnings guidance should add this ineffective habit to their stop doing list. They should either stop providing guidance all together or least move to a habit of just providing annual guidance. Do not give in to the temptation that it may improve communication with the analyst community.

In an article published in the March 2006 issue of *McKinsey on Finance*, the authors Peggy Hsieh, S. R. Rajan, and Tim Koller, made a compelling case for not issuing quarterly guidance. Here are some salient points from their article:

> Most companies view the quarterly ritual of issuing earnings guidance as a necessary, if sometimes onerous, part of investor relations. The benefits, they hope, are improved communications with financial markets, lower share price volatility, and higher valuations. At the least, companies expect frequent earnings guidance to boost their stock's liquidity. We believe that they are

misguided. Our analysis of the perceived benefits of issuing frequent earnings guidance found no evidence that it affects valuation multiples, improves shareholder returns, or reduces share price volatility ... Our recent survey found ... that providing quarterly guidance has real costs, chief among them the time senior management must spend preparing the reports and an excessive focus on short-term results ... Our conclusion: to maintain good communications with analysts and investors, companies that currently provide quarterly earnings guidance should shift their focus away from short-term performance and toward the drivers of long-term company health as well as their expectations of future business conditions and their long-range goals. Companies that don't currently issue guidance should avoid the temptation to start providing it and instead focus on disclosures about business fundamentals and long-range goals.[xl]

Providing only annual guidance is an exceptional habit of many elite companies. The only major risk to not providing quarterly guidance is the possibility of a large expectation gap between what the analyst community expects during a quarter compared with what the company expects. If there is a major gap in expectations—no matter the cause from misunderstanding to mistakes to weather issues—there's a mechanism for correcting the record. A company should simply issue an 8-K explaining the variance while at the same time reaffirming annual guidance. If possible, the 8-K should be timed around an

investor meeting or investor presentation so that more
insight can be provided.

Habit 8: Elevate the Chief Information Officer Position (CIO)

Elite enterprises are elevating the CIO position to the same
level of importance as the CFO. Elite enterprise recognize
that the hypercompetitive marketplace requires a new
mind-set to deal with the digital age. CIOs are increasingly
commanding substantial responsibilities and, along with
that, higher financial rewards for performance and a direct
line to the CEO.

Elite CIOs make a significant contribution to the
performance of the enterprise by bringing in more revenues
and improving overall productivity and efficiency through
innovation. Elite CIOs make the enterprise more
competitive and, in some instances, provide a competitive
advantage. Clearly, the stature and pay of these talented
individuals will most likely continue to rise and become
increasingly prevalent in elite organizations.

Habit 9: Focus on Diversity

Elite companies understand the power of building an
enterprise that embraces diversity. Sheryl Sandberg in an
article in the *Wall Street Journal* on September 30, 2015,
captured the power and competitive advantage of diversity
in an enterprise, "There is a wealth of evidence that
diversity helps teams and organizations perform better in
terms of innovation, creativity, revenue and profits."
Sandberg goes on to say, "Using the talents of our full

population is critical to our economic growth, corporate productivity and individual happiness."

Irene Rosenfeld, Carol Meyrowitz, Ellen Kullman, Indra Nooyi, Marissa Mayer, Mary Barra, Ginni Rometty, and Regina Dugan are just a few examples of diversity in the C-suite. And although not in business, one of my favorite elite leaders is Condoleezza Rice, who at one time was provost of one of the top universities of the world, Stanford, and later served as U.S. Secretary of State.

Another *Wall Street Journal* article by Rachel Feintzeig discusses the importance of metrics in building a diverse team, "Realizing that simply voicing support for diversity initiatives won't lead to meaningful change, big companies are setting discrete goals for hiring and retaining women." She goes on to say, "J&J, Intel Corp., BASF SE and many others say putting hard numbers around diversity and tying those numbers to pay and performance helps ensure real progress... ."

Habit 10: Appoint and Empower a Global Leadership Team

An enterprise can have the most innovative business model and the clearest and most powerful vision statement, but without a superior management team that excels at execution, it's impossible to build an elite company. Elite companies understand that greatness is achieved with elite people that have an outsized impact on the performance of the organization. Besides the appointment of the CEO, which is obviously the most important, a superior and high performing global leadership team needs to be built and developed. So, how do the elite companies go about achieving this? The framework for building and developing an elite global leadership usually includes the elements outlined below.

Define the leadership group. Many companies simply refer to their management leadership as either the Top 100 or the Global Leadership Team. No matter what it's called, the most important step is to define the group. Give the team a purpose and create connections throughout the year so that they interact effectively with each other. The Top 100 annual meeting must be meaningful through a well-conceived agenda that strengthens and perpetuates the culture of the company.

Build a best-of-class talent-management and leadership-development process. Great teams are built, developed, and sustained through a robust, results-oriented talent-management process. Leadership-development and succession planning are vital components of this. The board and the CEO should spend considerable amount of time on getting this right.

Key seats must be filled with the right people. Filling the right seats with the right people takes considerable skill and a robust process that has the full support and oversight from the board and the CEO. A key metric here is that more than 90 percent of the key seats (Top 100) are filled with the right people in the right seats. Companies that fail to achieve this metric on a consistent basis will ultimately encounter setbacks and make its journey to the summit even more arduous and, I would argue, impossible.

Habit 11: Stop with the Serial "Adjusted" Earnings
The number of adjusted earnings reports appears to be an epidemic among enterprises. Although there is a place for a "one-time" adjustment, it seems that these adjustments have become routine and even somewhat perfunctory. Generally accepted accounting principles exist for a reason, and the routine nature of adjusted earnings is slowly undermining these principles. Only true one-time adjustments should be accepted by investors, the board, and management itself. Although it's difficult to provide very specific rules or guidelines on what is a true one-time adjustment, here are some thoughts on what may be considered as a special item:

- A substantial restructuring charge that is truly transformative in nature. The charge must be material, unusual, and not repeatable. This should not include routine operating charges such as closing a plant, exiting a country, laying off a small group of employees, or terminating a contract.
- A substantial gain or loss on the sale of assets, particularly the sale of a business unit or segment or a valuable equity stake in another company
- A substantial impairment charge that is nonrecurring
- A substantial and unusual tax event that materially distorts the earnings per share number
- Generally, any so-called one-time events that are truly both unusual (non-recurring) and material that substantially distort a quarter and/or a fiscal year

Under these guidelines, I believe that most adjusted earnings would disappear from press releases, which would be a good thing.

Habit 12: Go Private
This habit may appear extreme but it's something that every public company should consider due to a growing hostility towards many public companies. They are often viewed as villains by government officials, the press, and the public in general. Also, suffocating regulations are significantly raising the cost of doing business. The cover of *Fortune's* June 1, 2016 issue supports this point of view: "So Long, Wall Street ... Why Companies Are Going and Staying Private." An article in the *Wall Street Journal* on January 5, 2017 states, "Investors' Lament: Fewer Public Listings."

In the *Fortune* article by Geoff Colvin, he notes that, "More and more companies are forgoing the pressure of public markets for a friendlier and less scrutinized form of ownership. The amazing part of the story is how damn easy it is to go—and stay—private."

The article is rich with reasons why companies should be private. Here is a sampling of some of more salient points made by Colvin against being a public company, "Public companies face additional rules ... Economists figure the costs may be enough to tip the balance against going public for smaller companies ... many disclosures required of public companies are rich with information for competitors to study ... there's all the time managers spend dealing with Wall Street analysts and potentially thousands of shareholders ... Being public can become a wild, uncontrollable ride for a young company ... ."

The *Fortune* article is also rich on reasons why being a private company can be attractive. Here are some other reasons offered in the article to support why going private can be so attractive for a company:

"A PE firm can also bring broad managerial wisdom that many companies lack ... Private ownership can be powerfully attractive to managers on another dimension: pay. At public companies, top executive pay is publicly reported ... Few executives like the attention ... None of that matters at private companies, where pay plans can offer a CEO far greater rewards if he or she is willing to accept more risks."

Clearly, many companies are making this change, at least according to a *Wall Street Journal* article by Maureen Farrell. The article points out that, "The number of U.S.-listed companies has declined by more than 3,000 since peaking at 9,113 in 1997."

If a company is thinking about going private, the best and most effective route is to connect with private equity. I have a great deal of experience with private equity, and I believe they have a business model that is superior to many public companies. Here are some of the numerous advantages of going private:

- Private equity is very astute at allocating capital
- Private equity brings a tremendous skill set that can benefit a public company on many levels
- Going private eliminates the distractions that come with being public, particularly the unrelenting pressures for short-term stock gains

- Going private allows management to focus intensely on execution, strategy, and building an exceptional team

CHAPTER 6

14 STRATEGY HABITS OF ELITE ENTERPRISES

Strategy is about making choices, trade-offs; it's about deliberately choosing to be different.
Michael Porter [xli]

E lite Enterprises exhibit fourteen essential strategy habits including:

Habit 1: Build a Value-Creating Corporate Center
Habit 2: Create a Unique and Sustainable Competitive Position
Habit 3: Build Formidable Intangible Assets
Habit 4: Be Audacious with Transformations and Restructurings
Habit 5: Differentiate with Disruptive Innovation
Habit 6: Use a New Model for Creativity and Innovation

Habit 7: Properly Segment Platforms
Habit 8: Build an Internal Venture Group
Habit 9: Create the Future with a Powerful Vision
      Statement
Habit 10: Build an Enduring Culture that Wins
Habit 11: Develop a Strong Growth Engine
Habit 12: Build a Flat and Responsive Organization
Habit 13: Excel at Strategy and Execution
Habit 14: Re-imagine Your Business Model

Habit 1: Build a Value-Creating Corporate Center

Most CEOs grapple at some point with the age-old question
of how the corporate center can add value? In a white
paper, *The Boston Consulting Group*, captured the essence
of this dilemma as follows: "CEOs of multinational
corporations are under constant internal and external
pressure to add value to the portfolio of businesses so that
the whole is worth more than the sum of its parts. Many
CEOs, however, struggle to devise a strategy for the
corporate center and to translate that strategy into an
organizational design that actually adds value."[xlii]

Unfortunately, and too often it appears, corporate
centers fall short on this measure. A common mistake made
by senior leaders is believing they are better equipped to
make the most informed decisions. The good news is that
the corporate center can be designed to add value. Here is
how to create a value enhancing corporate center,
irrespective of the organizational structure the enterprise
adopts as part of the business model.

The value creation process begins with understanding
the true purpose of the center. First, it is completely the

wrong mind-set to have an arrogant view that the corporate center is the global headquarters. Along with hubris, the global headquarters mind-set usually manifests itself in many other value-destroying characteristics that include bureaucracy, high overhead costs (with costs allocated to individual business units), highly centralized decision making, additional staff costs, and office designs that offers little or no opportunity for interaction.

On the other hand, a value-creating center is completely different. It is characterized by numerous positive attributes: an entrepreneurial culture, lean staffing, minimal bureaucracy, highly decentralized decision making, and an office designed for maximum interaction that stimulates innovation and creativity.

Here are some specific key areas where the corporate center can add value:

- Establishing a clear and powerful vision framework, particularly the core purpose and the core values
- Developing a business model that positively drives the culture of the company
- Setting the tone for the enterprise relative to integrity and business conduct
- Providing a robust strategic planning process for the entire enterprise that is flexible and effective
- Working with the business unit leadership to develop a long-term strategy that is consistent with core purpose and business model
- Providing the business units with exceptional capabilities, such as the ability to successfully execute acquisitions and divestitures

- Establishing disciplined and sound capital allocation policies
- Ensuring that the enterprise capital structure is optimized
- Appointing a value creating board
- Keeping the governance framework nimble and effective
- Maintaining an optimized cost structure
- Establishing an entrepreneurial environment

Habit 2: Create a Unique and Sustainable Competitive Position

Elite companies create a unique position in their industry that sets them apart from the competition. This unique position should be captured in the business model. As detailed in *CEO Lifelines*, the business model includes two interconnected parts; the recipe and the organizational structure. The unique position of the company is clearly articulated in the Lifelines "recipe," and the organizational structure is built to execute on each crucial element of the recipe while aligning with the company's overall core purpose.

Your recipe should be limited to between eight and twelve elements. Most of these recipe elements can usually be identified by a careful reading of the CEO letters to shareholders (and CEO presentations at investor conferences), annual reports, and 10-K filings. Here are some examples of powerful recipes taken from exemplary companies that will help you fill out your own enterprise's recipe. These include two elite U.S. companies, Roper Technologies and Nucor, and a German company, Aldi, that has significantly changed the grocery store model in Europe and is determined to do the same in the U.S.

Roper

Roper's recipe is extraordinary and is clearly a "best-of-class" paragon for companies wishing to develop their own. It's also important to note that Roper changed its name to Roper Technologies, which better reflects their strategy and the current state of the company. Here is an excerpt from the CEO letter to shareholders that is included in the 2014 annual report. It provides great insight into the company's recipe:

> Roper's name change reflects a relentlessly consistent strategy. Our company is engaged in niche-focused, asset-light businesses with leading-edge technologies that create significant free cash flow, enabling future investments for sustainable growth. The consistent execution of this strategy has driven our company far beyond our industrial roots into a technology leader across many high-value end markets. We have created a culture that recognizes value is created from localized innovation and nimble decision making by highly engaged and accountable leadership teams at each of our businesses. Regardless of the niche market we serve, our growth strategies utilize intellectual capital, application engineering expertise, new product development, channel expansion and a high degree of customer intimacy to drive sustained growth. Our businesses are not dependent on significant investments in property, plant and

equipment or shifts in macroeconomic trends. United by common tools and metrics, Roper's governance process is our highly-scalable business system. We emphasize both accounting ratio and economic disciplines to continually improve financial performance. Our high performing businesses generate substantial free cash flow that we deploy to acquire additional high-performing businesses that generate additional free cash flow.

An examination of Roper's annual reports and investor presentations reveals nine key elements that make-up Roper's recipe. The company's innovative public recipe includes the following unique activities:

- Cash return discipline that delivers compelling free cash flow
- Niche-market leadership positions through a diverse set of businesses
- A focus on proprietary and differentiated solutions that generate high gross margins
- A culture that recognizes value is created from localized innovation and nimble decision making
- Exceptional, highly engaged operating managers who are accountable
- A nimble governance system
- Asset-light businesses, minimal capital expenditures, and efficient working capital
- Effective and efficient redeployment of free cash flow to drive growth
- Strong growth prospects for acquisitions

Roper's recipe is one of the key reasons the company continues to post superior results. As pointed out in 2014

CEO letter, Roper has posted a total return of 445 percent since 2004, which is simply incredible! Clearly, this extraordinary recipe can be used as a model on how to develop a recipe for your business.

Nucor

Nucor's success is anchored in its decades-long history of extraordinary CEO leadership. But first, let's examine the company's 2014 annual CEO letter to shareholders: Here is what CEO John Ferriola wrote:

> As I speak to groups across North America, I consistently emphasize that Nucor's teammates are our company's greatest asset and our greatest competitive advantage. That's the reason we list the name of each teammate on the cover of our annual report; 2014 is the 40th consecutive year for that important recognition. Our people, combined with our strong balance sheet, are two reasons why Nucor grows stronger during economic downturns. We did not lay off any teammates at our steelmaking operations during the recession. Instead, our teammates worked to deploy strategic capital that enhances our earnings during challenging cycles and accelerates growth when markets improve. We also make it a point to pay our teammates well for their hard work. Nucor teammates do not receive guaranteed incentives or retiree benefits. Instead, we have long embraced a pay-for-performance philosophy. Therefore, Nucor teammates only receive fully-funded profit sharing contributions when we deliver profitable results for our shareholders. This is a model where everyone

wins. Our customers get the high-quality steel products they need. Our shareholders get a profitable return on their investment. And our teammates have received $2 billion in profit sharing retirement savings since the program was established in 1966.

Just from this letter alone, it is possible to glean a few key unique recipe elements. Here is my list of ten recipe elements that I believe underpin Nucor's extraordinary performance:

- Teammates are both the company's greatest asset and competitive advantage
- A focus on profit per ton of finished steel
- A high-productivity, high-performance culture
- A flexible non-union workforce that is empowered to make decisions
- An unofficial no-layoff policy
- A commitment to pay well for high performance and a policy of no guaranteed incentives or retiree benefits
- Use of electric arc furnaces and a scrap-based process (mini-mill)
- A focus on plants located in the south
- A relentless focus on costs, safety, process improvement, and maintaining a strong balance sheet
- A focus on innovation and technology advancements

One reason I can speak with such confidence about Nucor is because I spent 32 years working in the steel industry as a key partner and provider of services to the global steel industry. The global steel industry in one of the most highly competitive industries in the world. It is prone to major swings in production, pricing, and on certain input costs, such as scrap metal prices. The global steel industry is dominated by China. The World Steel Association notes that in 2015 steel production in the world was 1,599 million tons, with China accounting for approximately 804 million tons or about half of the world's production. But production is only part of the story.

The global steel industry has a glut of steel production with most excess capacity residing in China. China exports a significant amount of steel to the U.S., as do several other countries which puts constant pressure on the price of steel. So, how is it that Nucor is an elite company in an industry characterized by overcapacity and highly volatile pricing while its many steel competitors across the world continue to struggle?

Nucor's success can be categorized into three distinctive areas: people, financial discipline, and competitive structure. First, the people. Nucor is truly focused and passionate about its people and has built a strong culture that drives the company. Amazing mechanisms have been established that truly work. Some of these include: an innovative no-layoff policy; pay-for-performance that offers no-guarantee payments or benefits; a strong safety culture; and, the company's practice of listing every employee or teammate on the cover of the annual report. Nucor is a company that works in every way.

Second, financial discipline. Nucor has a relentless focus on costs and process improvements, and the discipline of maintaining a strong balance sheet to ensure it can weather all storms. The company's key financial metric of profit-per-ton-of-steel-produced is also vital in its success story.

Third, competitive structure. What I mean by competitive structure is the company's focus on mini-mills as opposed to less flexible and more expensive integrated steel mills. Nucor's focus on locating plants mainly in the south with favorable non-union labor environments is another vital element of the competitive structure. And finally, the company's relentless focus on innovation and technology.

Nucor's recipe is probably the reason that the company was identified as a *Good to Great* firm in Jim Collins' seminal book by the same name. This is clearly another extraordinary recipe that can be used as a model on how to develop a recipe for your business.

Aldi

The German grocery chain Aldi has developed a disruptive business model which fits well with today's cost-conscious consumer. The *Wall Street Journal* wrote an article on how German discount grocers took the U. K. market by storm and are now expanding in the U.S. market. In the article by Saabira Chaudhuri in the September 11, 2015 issue, the author explains in detail how two German discounters, including Aldi, have shaken the U.K. grocery business to its core with its disruptive business model. The article goes on to say, " ... they have stolen away market share ... Those grocers, in turn, have seen their stock prices plummet, triggering executive ousters, layoffs and billion-dollar write downs."

I used the article and other research to compile ten key elements that make-up Aldi's innovative business model recipe:

- No-frills, affordable shopping
- High-quality items at low prices
- Prioritizing speed of deliveries
- A focus on operational efficiencies
- High turnover of inventory
- Charging for bags
- Separate packing areas to keep register lines moving
- Requiring every employee in the store to do every job
- Supply deliveries done at night to avoid traffic and to lower fuel costs
- Minimizing the number of offerings

Aldi demonstrates that even in the razor-thin margin grocery business, an innovative and disruptive recipe can cause significant damage to established giants and fuel the growth of an innovator.

Habit 3: Build Formidable Intangible Assets
Elite companies are keenly focused on building their most important intangible assets—superior brands, patents, knowledge-based solutions, and even trademarks and copyrights—because these assets will ultimately drive the culture and exceptional performance of the company. Of course, it is human capital that underpins the value of these assets, and it is these human assets that ultimately drives an enterprise's performance and supports its elite status. Let's

first examine a shining example of this habit before listing its key attributes.

Disney CEO Robert Iger is an elite leader. He has successfully transformed the venerable company during his tenure into a business that is focused around franchises and built it into an elite enterprise. In an article in the *Wall Street Journal* on June 9, 2015, Ben Fritz quoted a research analyst that accurately captures Disney's accomplishments and power in the marketplace. In the article, the analyst pointed out that "Disney's collection of successful intellectual property is so vast that" it's almost unfair to other players in the space. As noted earlier in this book, an unfair advantage is good both in the military and in business. The same article goes on to say that "Over the past decade, Disney has primarily fostered franchises in its own animation divisions and at companies it bought. The takeover of Marvel ... purchase of Lucasfilm ... Pixar Animation Studios ... delivered a jolt of energy to Walt Disney Animation Studios ..." And these are just a sample of the superior brands that Disney has accumulated.

Powerful and successful brands are built by people. So, the number one priority of elite leaders is building teams throughout the organization that know how to win. Building teams that win starts with hiring the right people. Google calls their A-players, "smart creative." No matter what you call them, I believe that the right people must possess the right character, they must possess certain key personal traits, they must have above average emotional and cognitive intelligence, and they must align well with the company's core ideology. More specifically, these four broad elements can be broken down to the following precocious characteristics that one should expect to find in A-players that know how to win. These players:

- have a significant amount of accumulated indispensable experiences;
- a high sense of purpose and urgency;
- consistently deliver on commitments;
- effectively rely on instinct;
- are creative and generative thinkers;
- align well with core purpose and core values of the enterprise;
- are team players and are naturally collaborative;
- consistently demonstrate depth of integrity, perspective, passion, humility, and courage;
- have an ability to learn and grow through personal and professional continuous improvement discipline;
- are highly adaptive and embrace change;
- know how to create value and are accountable and responsible;
- consistently demonstrate discipline and focus;
- have a bias for action and demonstrate a proactive mind-set with an ability to get things done; and
- consistently demonstrate emotional maturity, common sense, and sound judgment.

Habit 4: Be Audacious with Transformations and Restructurings

When undertaking a transformation, a major restructuring, or spin-off of a large enterprise segment, elite companies tend to be audacious. Enterprises that announce audacious restructuring and transformational plans are usually rewarded by investors. Conversely, less bold enterprises that take baby steps in the form of multiple plans executed over many years tend to be punished by investors. This serial approach also results in a constant stream of so-called adjusted earnings (as discussed in an earlier habit) and mostly feeling its way through the fog of market turbulence. This approach can distract the company and delay the realization of potential benefits, which can hurt the company's competitive position and reputation.

A strong example of an audacious transformation and restructuring action is General Electric (GE). In April 2015, GE announced a significant and transformational shift by announcing plans to exit the banking business and refocus the large conglomerate on its industrial assets. Specifically, GE announced that it would repurchase approximately $50 billion in stock and repatriate approximately $36 billion in cash from overseas. To put this strategic move in perspective, here are some of the more important impacts from the shift.

First, GE would no longer be one of the largest financial institutions in the world, and its industrial businesses would now have to contribute approximately 90 percent of future earnings, up from about 58 percent in 2014. The remaining 10 percent would be generated from the few financial businesses it kept, such as leasing operations that support its industrial businesses. GE plans also included a charge of approximately $16 billion for asset write-downs due to impairments and taxes. GE's effective tax rate was also expected to increase substantially as result of divesting the financial business.

GE's audacious transformation was covered in *Fortune* on September 1, 2015. Geoff Colvin sums up the plan as follows, "The world's biggest diversified conglomerates are finally realizing that combining entirely dissimilar businesses in one company almost never works. For the first time in living memory, GE is on the road to becoming a coherent whole, built around industrial infrastructure businesses ... ." Colvin goes on to write, "The corporate transformation is so pervasive that GE is even altering its famous culture ... They call the new ideal a culture of simplification ... The goals are speed, empowerment, and minimal bureaucracy, a tall order in a 137-year-old company with 305,000 employees, but necessary."

Another audacious transformation was undertaken by IBM. In a *Wall Street Journal* article by Monica Langley on April 21, 2015, the reporter points out that in January 2015, CEO Rometty unveiled, "IBM's most sweeping reorganization in three decades, moving it from units defined by hardware, software and services toward a structure of integrated businesses that focus on specific industries." More specifically, the article points out the boldness of Rometty's transformation action, "She wants more than 40 percent of IBM's revenues in 2018 to be from corporate markets in analytics, cloud computing, cybersecurity, social networking and mobile technologies. Those businesses were 27 percent of IBM's $92.8 billion in 2014 revenues ... ." Rometty captured perfectly the bold and sweeping move in the article, "I can only change a company this size by making big bets."

One of my favorite elite industrial companies is Danaher. They also announced a bold transformation in 2015. Here is what the *Wall Street Journal* wrote about the move in a May 14, 2015 by Bob Tita: "... Danaher Corp. intends to break itself in two next year, becoming the latest company to isolate units viewed as having strong growth potential from cyclical, slower-growing business lines. As part of the breakup, Danaher will acquire filtration-equipment maker ... to fortify a revamped business portfolio focused on science, health care and technology markets. Danaher plans to divest itself of its industrial units by assembling them in a new public company that will be spun off ... ."

Danaher is different from many other industrial companies because their audacious plan is being driven by proactive action, as opposed to being forced by an activist investor to make sweeping changes. Danaher's proactive nature is driven by internal visionary thinking, a healthy culture, and a long-term value creation mind-set.

Habit 5: Differentiate with Disruptive Innovation
Innovation is one of the most important lifelines for a company since it transcends all business models and all end-markets. Without innovation, an organization will eventually wither away.

Fortune magazine recently published an insightful article on Disney's focus on innovation. The article provides a wonderful example of how this elite company applies technology throughout its business to derive a competitive advantage. In the article, *Fortune* reveals a "killer app" that Disney developed for its parks' business, RFID-enabled MagicBands. Disney said that "75 percent of MagicBand users engage with the 'experience' ... before their visit to the park. Online, they can connect their wristband to a credit card, book fast passes ... and even order food ahead of time ... it can now better track visitors' purchasing habits ... MagicBands have led to increased spending at the park ... the plan is to expand to other locations, including the company's line of cruise ships."[xliii]

The Disney innovation is a wonderful example of how an app can have an outsized impact on a business. Another similar example can be found in Starbucks. The company attributed, in part, a reported sharp jump in quarterly sales and profit to digital initiatives. According to a *Wall Street Journal* article on July 24, 2015 reported by Julie Jargon, "... in December the company began testing an app that allows customers to order and pay for their drinks ahead of time so that they can bypass store lines ... 20 percent of the U.S. transactions now are made using mobile devices, up from 9 percent two years ago ... [Starbucks] expects the app to boost the average check size when a feature starts later this year that suggests additional purchases to users." Starbucks and Disney are not the only elite companies that are using digital initiatives. If you read annual reports and review analyst presentations, you will find numerous examples of how elite companies are using technology and innovation to strengthen their competitive position.

Uber, the car ride service, offers one of my favorite examples of the enormous potential of a disruptive technology. Using the customer's smartphone to match drivers and passengers is a transformative innovation that has utterly changed car and taxi services while creating tremendous shareholder value. The simplicity of the idea, the powerful app that drives it, and the company's focus on execution are what makes this company so special. Uber has essentially no physical infrastructure, which is the extreme and positive example of an asset-light business. Another technology company that is more in the Uber model is Airbnb which is transforming the hospitality industry. Both Uber and Airbnb are viewed as the poster children for what is referred to as the sharing economy.

Habit 6: Use a New Model for Creativity and Innovation

Creating a start-up environment within a larger organization that fosters creativity, collaboration, and innovation is extremely difficult. However, a new model has emerged, and its outlines were captured well in a May 1, 2015 *Fortune* magazine article titled, "Startups ... Inside Giant Companies" by Jennifer Alsever. The elite companies highlighted include MasterCard, Tyco International, GE, IBM, Mondelez, Coca-Cola, and Cisco.

Here is how *Fortune* summarized some of these programs, "Unlike special skunkworks projects of the past, intended to hive off a single project into its own unit, these efforts are intended not only to nurture profitable new entities, but also to infuse entrepreneurism into venerable operations filled with layers of middle managers."

Some of the specifics of how these elite enterprises have created their in-house startups is instructive, so here is a list of key mechanisms that support this innovative practice:

- Innovation workshops that promote creativity and help build exceptional capabilities,
- Internal venture capital groups that approve investment money to fund new ideas,
- Idea-pitch parties that stimulate creativity,
- Workshops designed to speed-up cycle time for developing prototypes of new ideas at minimal costs,
- Coaching and teaching entrepreneurial principles,
- Failure conferences as part of learning entity where people describe their largest mistakes with objective of not repeating them in the future

An additional mechanism being utilized by some elite enterprises in the heart of the U.S. tech sector in Silicon Valley is the creation of an innovation lab. The innovation lab is usually staffed with engineers that operates like other start-ups in the region. For these innovation labs to be successful, however, they need a clear purpose, and they need to be connected and aligned with overall enterprise mission and strategy.

Habit 7: Properly Segment Platforms
Elite companies constantly review their portfolio of businesses to fully understand the competitive position of each business unit in their portfolio. This deep dive approach usually includes a comprehensive review of end markets, competitors, its own competitive position, unique recipe elements, exceptional capabilities, and many other

key items. One approach followed by an elite CEO is to segment all the business units using a quadrant. The first step in this analysis is to determine the appropriate quadrant for each business unit. Here are the four quadrants the elite leader uses along with a brief description of each:

Elite brands. To be included in this category, a business unit must be both a great company and a great business (meaning the business environment in which the company operates is robust and not highly cyclical). The business unit is a consistent high performer with high gross and operating margins, as well as high return on invested capital and prolific growth in free cash flows.

Cherished jewels. Business units classified in this category are usually prodigious free cash flow companies that also have good—and sometimes great margins—and returns. Often, business units in this category lack any significant growth prospects. Another common trait is that the end markets may have some commodity exposure. These types of business units are usually maintained to generate steady free cash flows to feed the emerging stars and the elite brands.

Emerging stars. This category includes all high potential business units that need capital to fuel their growth. These units can potentially be the future elite brands of the company. These emerging stars usually have strong margins and free cash flow growth characteristics as well.

Flashing lights. Business units that fall into this category are usually one of the following three types: (1) does not fit with current portfolio, business model, and core purpose of the company, and, thus, should be divested; (2)

the business unit is a consistently poor performer with declining margins and declining free cash flows that can't be fixed and should likely be divested or possibly even shutdown; or (3) the business unit fits the company but has operational and leadership problems and simply needs to be fixed.

The quadrant analysis should be underpinned by a free cash flow analysis of each business unit—defined as cash from operations less capital expenditures. It is imperative the free cash flow growth over a long horizon be evaluated and be the primary focal point to determining which quadrant each business platform should be classified.

Habit 8: Build an Internal Venture Group
A powerful habit that is utilized very effectively by technology companies for growth and innovation is building an internal ventures group. Internal venture groups are highly effective in expanding the reach of the company, accelerating innovation, and growing revenues. They also provide the opportunity to learn new business models, and they can help accelerate bringing new products and services to market.

Some of the more prolific elite U.S. companies in this category include Google, Facebook, Microsoft, UPS, Campbell Soup, Coca-Cola, and General Mills. In China, these companies include Tencent, Alibaba, and Lenovo. Tencent is China's social networking giant, and Alibaba is the e-commerce giant. Lenovo is one of the largest personal computer companies in the world. Through their internal ventures group, elite companies invest in partnerships and, at times, even acquisitions.

Technology sector internal ventures model can be highly adaptive and utilized across most industries. Given the hypercompetitive global marketplace, developing this exceptional capability—particularly with a focus on accelerating innovation—can provide a company with distinctive competitive advantage.

Habit 9: Create the Future with a Powerful Vision Statement

When an enterprise strives to reach elite status, it's imperative that they develop a clear and powerful vision statement. The absence of a clear vision framework or the existence of a confused vision framework will most likely result in the company falling short of its goal of ascending the summit.

Without a clear vision statement—particularly the core ideology section—it's impossible to build a sustainable elite enterprise. So, what is a vision framework, and what are the vital elements necessary to create one? Jim Collins and Jerry Porras provide some of the best advice in their seminal book, *Built to Last.* Another good source is a powerful article in the *Harvard Business Review* published in September-October 1994, "Building Your Company's Vision."

The vision framework is actually a road map, and it's made up of two critical parts: the envisioned future and the core ideology. The envisioned future and the core ideology each have two distinctive parts. The two parts to the envisioned future include the BHAGs—Big, Hairy, Audacious Goals—and vivid description. The two parts to the core ideology, include the core purpose and the core values. Thus, there are four critical elements to a company's vision framework. Getting these four elements right—along with the business model—will put a company on a more solid, direct, and clearer path to the summit.

The vision typically looks to a time ten to thirty years in the future. The BHAGs "... are ambitious plans that rev up the entire organization. They typically require ten to thirty years' work to complete." I personally like twenty years which obviously falls in the middle of the guidelines. The vivid description should "... paint a picture of what it will be like to achieve the BHAGs. They make the goals vibrant, engaging—and tangible."

The core ideology also has two parts: the core purpose and the core values. Collins and Porras say that core values "... are the handful of guiding principles by which a company navigates. They require no external justification." The core purpose "... is an organization's most fundamental reason for being. It should not be confused with the company's current product lines or customer segments. Rather, it reflects people's idealistic motivations for doing the company's work."

In *CEO Lifelines: Nine Commitments Every Leader Must Make,* I cover the core ideology in detail, and it's identified as lifeline number nine. For details on the envisioned future, the *Harvard Business Review* (noted above), article is an excellent source as well and it offers a clear road map for its development. The article also provides all the necessary information on developing a core ideology as well.

Habit 10: Build an Enduring Culture that Wins

No matter how well a company performs, there's always a
risk that an enterprise can lose its way and fall from the
summit. Sometimes, the wounds are self-inflicted due to
complacency, which can breed arrogance or loss of
discipline or a combination of the two. The board can make
a mistake and oust a good CEO (think Apple and Steve
Jobs, as an example) or the company can lose some A-
Players due to various other reasons.

On the other hand, wounds can be inflicted by outside
forces such as global shocks or a disruptive innovation or
the loss of a great leader due to tragic events. Elite
companies find a way to immunize the enterprise against
these negative and adverse forces by creating a winning
and enduring culture. Building a distinctive culture is
arguably the most important lifeline for an organization.
So, how does an organization build a distinctive culture that
wins and endures for generations? Broadly viewed, culture
is simply:

- The way people connect with each other
- The way people behave and think
- The way people embrace the core purpose and core
  values of the company
- The way people commit to the business model of
  the company, particularly the recipe
- The way the leadership team behaves and
  communicates
- The way the governance system functions
- The way the board behaves, thinks, and acts

These elements are functioning well in elite companies, and they are all underpinned by effective support mechanisms. Let's examine each element in detail.

The way people connect with each other. In cultures that win, people are entrepreneurial, collaborative, creative, and need little supervision. They are motivated and disciplined. The strong connection that exists between people drives innovation, productivity, and value creation.

The way people behave and think. In a winning culture, the character of the people is most important. Developing and hiring the right people who have the highest integrity and are generative thinkers is the cornerstone to building an enduring enterprise and culture. People clearly understand that they accountable and responsible for their actions. They are passionate about doing things the right way while propelling the organization forward.

The way people embrace the core purpose and core values of the company. How people connect to and are passionate about the core purpose and the core values of the company forms the foundation for building a winning culture.

The way people commit to the business model of the company, particularly the recipe. The business model must allow for a free flow of exchange, interaction, and connectivity. The ability to connect and collaborate is paramount. People clearly understand all the recipe elements, and they are passionate and committed to them. The know what to do and what not to do. The organizational structure is optimized to support the implementation of the recipe.

The way the leadership team behaves and communicates. Leader excellence is paramount. Do leaders walk the talk? Do they manifest integrity in every action, every word, and every deed? Do their actions embrace and passionately demonstrate a commitment to integrity, teamwork, and connectivity? Do leaders communicate effectively, with clarity and consistency?

The way the governance system works. Does the governance framework eliminate unnecessary rules and bureaucracy? Is the governance framework nimble? Does it promote trust and accountability?

The way the board behaves, thinks, and acts. A board that is not collaborative or does not work well as team can have a significant adverse effect on a company. Also, boards sometimes make wrong decisions, such as the ouster of a good CEO, that can have long-term negative impact on the enterprise. Consequently, boards on their own can have an outsized impact on the culture and, ultimately, on the performance of the company.

Sometimes boards feel compelled to make a change, and they don't always get it right. Ample evidence of boards making mistakes exists, as mentioned above with Steve Jobs. *The Wall Street Journal* wrote about how boards fumble the changing of the guard in an article titled, "Boards Often Fumble CEO Changes." The article, which was published on June 9, 2016, by Joann S. Lublin and Theo Francis, points out that "Many corporate boards fumble the changing of the guard... Stock-market returns suffer when large public companies force out their CEOs..." This article was followed by an opinion piece titled, "The CEOs Who Didn't Deserve the Boot," in The

Wall Street Journal on July 13, 2017. Jeffrey A. Sonnenfeld wrote that "Board panic is a feature of the current environment." He went on to say that "Corporate boards need backbone... Without it, many more quality CEOs will fall victim to the terror of short-termism."

Habit 11: Develop a Strong Growth Engine
Elite companies know that growth is the lifeblood of any company. Elite enterprises develop and build their growth engine through two key building blocks: acquisitions and organic growth. Both inorganic and organic growth need to be balanced over a long horizon through discipline and exceptional execution.

Enterprises that can develop both exceptional capabilities are usually rewarded with a higher stock price and sustainable value creation. However, it's important to understand that each capability requires a very different skill set. Let's start with inorganic growth or acquisitions.

Companies that excel at acquisitions, such as Roper and Danaher, are usually rewarded with growing free cash flows, growing revenues and profitability, and a higher stock price. Also, properly targeted acquisitions can accelerate the development of technology and innovation. Developing a strong acquisition process is not easy. Here are some key attributes of a successful and robust acquisition process:

- Aligns well with vision statement of the enterprise, particularly its core purpose
- Process is managed and led by a highly skilled team of A-players

- Acquisition team is disciplined and follows a rigorous process
- All aspects of the process are highly effective, including sourcing transactions, valuation, negotiations, definitive agreement, due diligence, integration planning and execution, post-acquisition review, all underpinned by a stage-gate process
- Key performance metrics are used to monitor performance, synergy capture, and value creation
- Lessons learned mechanisms are in place so that the company learns from both success and failure

The responsibility for organic growth rests with the management team running each business unit, but it must be overseen by the senior management of the company and the board of directors. Although organic growth takes a different type of skill from inorganic growth, all the attributes identified for inorganic growth apply (with the exception of the fourth element, sourcing transactions, valuations, etc). Some of most effective ways to grow organically include the following: innovation, scaling the business, pricing leverage, taking market share from competitors, new markets, geographic expansion, developing adjacent markets, strong brand development, value selling, and, of course, a robust macro-economic environment.

An innovative approach to organic growth can be found at Facebook, with their "growth team" concept. This idea was highlighted in a *Fortune* article on December 1, 2016, by Adam Lashinsky. The article provides insight into Mark Zuckerberg's management style. Here is what the article states, "One of Facebook's key business innovations is a 'growth team' ... that designs tactics for various parts of the company, relying on a rigorous set of metrics to gauge success. The unit has broad latitude to weigh in on any aspect of Facebook's business." The article goes on to say that the growth team essentially is responsible for removing obstacles that prevent Facebook from growing. This growth concept is being replicated across Silicon Valley, and I believe it has broad applicability to most non-technology enterprises as well.

Habit 12: Build a Flat and Responsive Organization
Companies need to be nimble and resilient and driven by exceptional people to achieve elite status. A key component to building such a company is the way that the organization is structured. When designing how the enterprise will operate through its organizational structure, it is imperative that the leadership force a flat organization. This means that leaders have as many direct reports as possible. Typically, it should include a group of direct reports numbering between ten and fifteen (possibly even more).

If the best and brightest people are hired and they operate within a framework of accountability and responsibility, there's no need to micromanage them. To the contrary, they should be unshackled and allowed to perform at a high level. It's also crucial that each team be led by an exceptional leader that can have a disproportionate impact on the company and its long-term performance. Exceptional people—when not micromanaged and not stifled by bureaucratic procedures and processes—will most likely outperform. Elite companies know this truth, and they structure a flat organization that unleashes high performing and talented leaders and teams.

Habit 13: Excel at Strategy and Execution

Elite companies are exceptional at strategy and execution. Strategy, of course, is developed by the leadership team to implement the vision statement and the business model of the organization. Before the long-term vision and strategy of the company is implemented, there must be total alignment between the board and the management team. This alignment must include a comprehensive set of metrics that clearly define success.

In order to successfully execute its strategy, a company must first implement a highly effective strategic planning process. An effective strategic planning process requires the development of certain exceptional capabilities and a deep understanding of enterprise risk. Elite companies understand well the implications of overall strategic risk elements and how important it is to identify and mitigate them before they cause harm to the organization. This area is also where building a prodigious number of lifelines is instrumental to the long-term success of the company.

Execution means doing everything incredibly well on a consistent basis. It also means that operationally the company is a best-of-class performer, that is, doing things right all the time. This performance means that all tactical operational elements align perfectly and are slave to the strategy. There are no wasted operational actions that do not support the strategy. The ability to execute at a high level—where operational excellence is achieved—is the economic engine that propels an organization to elite status.

Execution also means building those prodigious lifelines necessary for a company to sustain superior performance over a long horizon.

Habit 14: Re-imagine Your Business Model

Elite companies excel at creating an innovative business model and successfully reinventing their organization. Many of these elite companies I have already mentioned in the book, including Roper, Disney, and Alphabet, Inc. (Google's parent company). Let's briefly examine how these elite companies have successfully reinvented themselves.

Roper transitioned from an industrial company to a technology company. Disney reinvented itself by building a collection of inimitable brands through brilliant acquisitions. Google transformed itself into Alphabet due to the growth outside its core search engine business. All enterprises need to have this mind-set to reach the summit of greatness. Truly visionary leaders and boards need to re-imagine what the company can become in order to successfully transform the organization to elite status.

So, how should an enterprise think critically and creatively about re-imaging their business for both the near and far future? Here is a framework to consider:

- First, leaders must be able to imagine a company that has the right people in the right positions, a leadership team that has developed a brilliant strategy, and a team that executes flawlessly in all undertakings. Imagine a company that is innovative in all respects, entrepreneurial in its approach, flexible and variable from a cost standpoint, and is nimble and fast in all aspects of the business.

- Second, leaders need to imagine that achieving this elite status will likely require a new mind-set, a new business model, and a laser focus on the core purpose of the company.
- Third, leaders need to imagine all the key exceptional capabilities that will be required. Some of these capabilities include incorporating effectively technologies such as cloud computing, data analytics, and mobile apps; building an innovative global supply chain that functions like a finely tuned orchestra; developing the ability to scale the business quickly and effectively; possessing the ability to build teams that win; and managing the enterprise with minimal fixed assets (Uber model).
- Finally, leaders need to imagine a new company that skillfully incorporates new rules for management, production, partnerships, innovation, marketing, and, most importantly, talent-management and leadership-development.

CHAPTER 7
17 EXECUTION HABITS OF ELITE ENTERPRISES

Perfection is not attainable, but if we chase perfection
we can catch excellence.
Vince Lombardi[xliv]

Elite Enterprises exhibit seventeen essential execution habits including:

Habit 1: Utilize Zero-Based Budgeting
Habit 2: Allocate Capital Effectively
Habit 3: Simplify the Business
Habit 4: Focus on Free Cash Flow
Habit 5: Manage Risks and Understand Unknowns
Habit 6: Implement Effective Mechanisms
Habit 7: Be Highly Adaptive
Habit 8: Scan the Environment in Real-Time
Habit 9: Form an Internal University with a Clear
          Purpose
Habit 10: Adopt Best Practices from Private Equity

Habit 11: Optimize the Tax and Legal Structure
Habit 12: Forecast Accurately
Habit 13: Understand Customer Profitability
          Management
Habit 14: Utilize Technology to Gain a Competitive
          Position
Habit 15: Adopt Habits of Elite Activists
Habit 16: Make Every Customer Touch Extraordinary
Habit 17: Know Your Customer Through Value Selling

Habit 1: Utilize Zero-Based Budgeting

Zero-based budgeting was the brainchild of Pete Pyhrr, a Texas Instruments Inc. accounting manager, who introduced the concept about five decades ago as a way to significantly reduce costs for his company. Recently, the concept has been re-energized by *3G Capital Partners LP*, a private equity group in Brazil. The firm has enthusiastically embraced the tool and has used it to both transform and significantly reduced the cost structure of the U.S. food industry.

In its simplest form, zero-based budgeting requires managers to plan each year's budget as if they were starting from scratch. This practice forces tremendous discipline in an organization. It requires managers to break-down spending to the lowest level of detail. Decisions are then made about proposed expenditures.

When I was CEO of a large public company and faced the onset of the U.S. financial crisis and later the European sovereign debt crisis, we implemented a simpler cost cutting approach; although, we did not call it zero-based budgeting. In our case, we examined major spend categories and then asked the following question: is it a nice-to-have expense or an absolutely necessary expense? If the expense was absolutely required, we had to justify it. Otherwise, the expense was eliminated from the budget.

Leaders can learn a great deal from 3G and how the company has smartly developed zero-based budgeting into an exceptional capability. Although it may not be possible to completely implement zero-based budgeting with the same focus, intensity, and skill that 3G has done, any company operating in today's transformative and hypercompetitive environment should not ignore this tool's potential exceptional capability. This fact is especially true for proactive companies seeking a vital mechanism to dramatically lower their break-even point and improve their competitive position.

An August 7, 2015 *Wall Street Journal* article titled "Big Food Sees Big Changes" offers the example of two competitors in the space, Mondelez and Heinz, and how one (Heinz) used 3G's tool to improve its profit margin by 700 basis points as compared to Mondelez's announced 300 basis point improvement. Plus, Heinz made their improvement goal in half the timeframe announced by its competitor. The Heinz example demonstrates the power of superb execution, and it is a lesson for all leaders to learn.

Habit 2: Allocate Capital Effectively

The most important concept to remember about capital allocation is this: if return on capital— i.e. economic value created—is greater than the cost of capital, shareholder value is being created. Problem arises when the cost of capital is greater than the economic value created. If this imbalance occurs, then shareholder value is destroyed. This problem is exacerbated even more if a company must invest a tremendous amount of capital.

If an enterprise faces high levels of capital investment through capital expenditures, then the effective and disciplined allocation of finite resources is an essential competency. So, what are some of key elements of this habit that separate elite companies from the mediocre ones? The habit begins with having a clearly defined business model that focuses on the right businesses (i.e. knowing what businesses to be in and which ones to exit.). These elite companies also know how to plan and forecast accurately over a reasonable time horizon, usually in the three to five years' range; and with some confidence over a ten-year horizon. Without this forecasting, the risks rise dramatically, and companies are taking an outsized risk by essentially "rolling the dice."

Capital allocation effectiveness is doubly important for acquisitions because these decisions are even riskier than capital expenditures due to the relative size and complexity of the acquisition process. Allocating capital to acquisitions requires a high level of skill to generate long-term positive economic value. Included in this skill is the ability to decide which companies to acquire (the ones that fit with the core purpose and business model of the enterprise) and which ones to leave behind. Deficiencies in this skill-set perhaps accounts for the high failure rate of acquisitions.

Habit 3: Simplify the Business
It's not uncommon to pick-up a business article and read about a leader who is trying to simplify their organization

because it has grown too complex and too bureaucratic. The concept of simplicity was captured perfectly by the outstanding author Walter Isaacson in his book, *The Innovators,* when he said, "Most true geniuses ... have an instinct to simplicity." [xlv] True geniuses like Steve Jobs recognized and harnessed the power of simplicity, from the way he organized Apple to the way he focused on the product design.

Simplicity usually wins over complexity. Simplicity applies to nearly everything, from your core purpose or mission, to core values, to product design, to your processes, to your systems and applications, and particularly to your organizational structure. Elite leaders focus relentlessly on simplifying the complex because they clearly understand the connection to a more adaptive, efficient, and flexible organization.

Habit 4: Focus on Free Cash Flow

Free cash flow should be the primary focus of the enterprise. Elite companies clearly understand the power of generating substantial, truly discretionary cash flow. Free cash flow is the most complete metric because it touches all key aspects of a business. Free cash flow as defined above includes the narrower, cash flow from operations, less capital expenditures. As explained in other parts of the book, free cash flow can be viewed more broadly by including dividends in the calculation when they are not truly discretionary. For purposes of this habit, dividends are excluded to get a more uniform view of free cash flow.

It's important to understand the substantial free cash flow that an innovative business model can create (for example, companies such as Apple, Google, and Roper). Elite companies measure this amount through what is known as growth in free cash flow. The growth in free cash flow metric is vital because it indicates that substantial economic value is being created.

Within each component of a business, multiple actions or levers can be pulled to enhance and generate free cash flow. Let's examine some of the most important levers. Breaking free cash flow down to the critical parts will reveal the following elements: net income, working capital, and capital expenditures. Although non-cash items such as depreciation and amortization (as well as changes in other assets and liabilities) also impact the calculation, the focus of this habit will be on these three major drivers:

Start with net income. Obviously, net income is composed of many parts. For example, on a typical income statement you'll find a gross profit line, which is derived from sales less cost of sales. There are many drivers for improving sales, which will ultimately impact net income. For example, incremental revenues can be driven by value selling, effective pricing strategies, and new products that command higher prices.

On the cost side is cost of sales. Cost of sales can be driven down by powerful global supply chain initiatives, by lean continuous improvement initiatives, and by an optimized organizational structure. These components can drive significant value by increasing the gross margin percentage.

The next major part of an income statement is operating profit. As with gross profit, you can use many levers to improve the operating profit as well. The major challenge of operating profit how to keep its main component—selling, general, and administrative costs—in check. Operating profit can be improved by having a highly optimized organizational cost structure in place. Such a structure is particularly powerful when incremental revenues—through scaling of the business—allow the majority of these revenue dollars to drop down to operating profit with minimal increase in costs.

The last component of the income statement is, of course, net income. This line item is determined by deducting interest expense and taxes from operating profit. Again, many levers can be pulled to optimize and lower both interest expense and income taxes.

Working Capital Working capital usually consists of four elements: inventory, accounts receivable, accounts payable, and advances. The objective in managing this line item should be to have working capital as a source of cash. Unfortunately, most businesses do not have this luxury because it's normally a use of cash. Many levers that can be pulled, however, to optimize working capital components, and companies focused intensely on this lever are usually rewarded. One of the most powerful examples of this lever is advances on orders. Using other people's money is always a plus in the free cash flow equation. Reducing both inventory and accounts receivable days is also another excellent strategy or lever to pull. Although many companies utilize the lever of increasing the accounts payable days, this approach can have numerous adverse consequences with suppliers.

Capital Expenditures The best way to minimize the capital expenditures is to have an "asset light" business model. You have a range of levers to pull when capital expenditures are necessary including the development or use of a robust global supply chain, a flexible operating model, lean continuous improvement principles, a standardized fleet of equipment, and effective maintenance practices. Southwest Airlines offers a notable example of these practices.

Habit 5: Manage Risks and Understand Unknowns
Businesses, like mountaineers, face a multitude of perils. These perils will normally range from clearly identifiable risks to those that are completely unknown. Unknowns—such as global shocks like the U.S. Great Recession and the European Sovereign Debt Crisis—can pose unmanageable threats to an enterprise.

On the other hand, risks—such as currencies, commodities, cyberattacks, compliance, and acquisitions—can be managed with the right strategy, focus, and execution. Some risks can also be transferred and managed through insurance. Some risks can be shared through joint ventures.

To manage and understand risks, businesses must first separate and segment manageable risks from unknown risks using a standard tool kit that includes transfer of risk, sharing of risk, acceptance of risk, and minimization of risk. Unknown risk requires monitoring closely external events—I call it scanning the environment in real-time. The ability to scan the environment is much easier today due to big data capabilities, effective use of outside experts, and developing strong internal capabilities.

Here are three effective tools for managing risk: First, the CEO must possess a risk mind-set. Proactive leaders focused on various risks and risk mitigation strategies force these habits down through their organization. Second, an enterprise should form a risk committee responsible for overseeing and managing risks. Third, enterprises should use an effective tool for managing risk such as Enterprise Risk Management or ERM. ERM has been around for years, and elite companies have a sophisticated ERM processes in place that are guided by highly integrated risk maps. A recent study showed that there's a direct correlation between managing risk well and value creation. *Agenda*, the weekly newsletter from the *Financial Times*, wrote in their August 3, 2015 letter that " ... companies that operate with a specific amount of executive and employee clarity on risk appetite and processes and those whose valuation is as much as 25 percent higher than other companies."

Habit 6: Implement Effective Mechanisms
Elite companies clearly understand that it is imperative to implement effective mechanisms designed to improve the enterprise, provide early warning signs, and keep the organization focused on the right path to excellence. Mechanisms are essential because they instill discipline and consistency. However, for mechanisms to be effective, they need to be simple, strictly adhered to, and enforced without exception.

Jim Collins, in his 1999 groundbreaking article, *Turning Goals into Results, The Power of Catalytic Mechanisms*, highlighted the critical importance of mechanisms. Here is how Collins describes catalytic mechanisms, "... I have observed and studied a simple yet extremely powerful managerial tool that helps organizations turn goals into results ... Catalytic mechanisms are the crucial link between objectives and performance; they are a galvanizing, nonbureaucratic means to turn one into the other."[xlvi] Numerous examples are highlighted in this book, but let's examine five effective mechanisms that elite companies have successfully utilized.

Code of ethical business conduct ("Code"). It's hard to imagine a company operating in today's global business environment without some type of business conduct policy. However, what separates the elite companies from perhaps all other enterprises is having an intense focus and real "teeth" behind this vital mechanism. There should be a zero tolerance for violations of the Code, regardless of position. Whenever a violation occurs, action is swift, and everyone in the organization is made aware of the action. Elite companies devote substantial time and resources to imbedding the Code in the DNA of the organization because it is the cornerstone of an effective governance framework and a healthy culture.

Military after-action reviews. Post-event debriefs or after-action reviews as they are called in the military, is an effective mechanism for learning, taking action, and guarding against attribution. The post-event debrief mechanism is a formal process whereby the enterprise thoroughly reviews all key initiatives with the sole objective of learning both positive and negative outcomes with the clear objective of simply discovering what happened, and then taking action to ensure lessons learned are implemented. Such a review ensure that failures are not repeated, and the factors that lead to success are sustained.

Google's 70/20/10 rule for resource allocation. In the wonderful book, *How Google Works*, Eric Schmidt and Jonathan Rosenberg explain their concept of their 70/20/10 rule: " ... 70/20/10 because our rule for resource allocation: 70 percent of resources dedicated to the core business, 20 percent on emerging, and 10 percent on new ... While the ... rule ensured that our core business would always get the bulk of the resources and that the promising, up-and-coming areas would also get investment, it also ensured that the crazy ideas got some support too, and were protected from the inevitable budget cuts." [xlvii] This mechanism is marvelous because it is both simple and powerful, and it instills discipline and focus in the organization.

Google's trusted-interviewer program. In *How Google Works*, Schmidt and Rosenberg also note that the company created a "trusted-interviewer program" made up of an "elite team of people who were actually skilled at interviewing and liked to do it." Google, like all elite companies, take substantive action to hire the very best and brightest. According to Schmidt and Rosenberg, "The most important skill any business person can develop is interviewing ... We want to hire the best minds available, because we believe there is a big difference between people who are great and those who are good, and we will do everything we can to separate the two ... Nothing is more important than the quality of hiring."[xlviii]

At least 90 percent of key seats filled with the right people metric. Google, Apple, and many other elite companies focus on hiring the best and brightest; likewise, the people hired also need to put in the right seat. A powerful mechanism mandating that at least 90 percent of the key seats in the organization are filled with the right people in the right seats requires discipline, focus, and execution.

Habit 7: Be Highly Adaptive

Elite enterprises are highly adaptive. Their culture is such that people in the organization think differently, and they adapt to change easily. Agility and problem-solving skills are also part of the DNA of an adaptive organization. Just as mountaineers need to be highly adaptive to a changing landscape, so must business leaders. Steve Hawkins, the legendary scientist, put this skill in perspective when he said, "Intelligence is the ability to adapt to change."[xlix]

No one is better at adapting to change and circumstance than the U.S. Military, particularly the small teams of the special forces. In his wonderful book, *Team of Teams*, General Stanley McCrystal provides useful and powerful insight into the importance of building highly effective and adaptive small teams. General McCrystal outlines a recipe for success for building adaptive teams that includes the following elements: trust, common purpose, shared consciousness, and empowered execution. Let's briefly examine each of these critical elements.

Trust and common purpose. This is what bonds great small teams. Each team member has absolute trust in the other. Each team member clearly knows the mission so there's no confusion about the common purpose. It is hard to imagine the power of an enterprise that fully possessed such clarity of purpose and absolute trust among all team members.

Shared consciousness. Transparency and communication can produce extraordinary outcomes across even large groups and team when they can read one another's intent and potential actions. Many start-up organizations, particularly technology companies, possess this shared consciousness.

Empowered execution. Pushing decision making, ownership, and action to the right level to team members who are fully empowered and understand the importance of accountability and responsibility is vital. Also, a culture that empowers its employees has a distinct advantage over their competitors.

Here are some further insights about adaptive teams expressed by General McCrystal: "teams whose members know one another deeply perform *better* ... A fighting force with good individual training, a solid handbook, and a sound strategy can execute a plan efficiently, and as long as the environment remains fairly static, odds of success are high. But a team fused by trust and purpose is much more potent. Such a group can improvise a coordinated response to dynamic, real-time developments ... team members cannot simply depend on orders; teamwork is a process of reevaluation, negotiation, and adjustment; players are constantly sending messages to, and taking cues from, their teammates, and those players *must* be able to read one another's every move and intent."

Finally, General McCrystal makes the important point that "Purpose affirms trust, trust affirms purpose, and together they forge individuals into a working team."[1]

Mountaineers will often ascend the major summits as a team (even if it's only one partner). Elite mountaineers clearly know that teams are essential to safely ascend and descend the summit. They trust their partner or other team members to make good decisions because it is a matter of survival. Elite mountaineering teams also have a shared consciousness. They know what the other team members are going to do under various scenarios. Each mountaineer knows the importance of making the right decisions. They also know how to improvise, be adaptive, and be resilient.

Habit 8: Scan the Environment in Real-Time
A key early warning mechanism utilized by adaptive enterprises is their ability to scan or sense the environment in real-time. This real-time insight is invaluable, but it must be connected to a bias for fast action. All this critical data is useless unless a culture of being proactive exists, it needs a sense of urgency.

Scanning the environment in real-time is an exceptional capability that all enterprises need to develop. It is extremely important because of the hypercompetitive nature of markets and ongoing global shocks. As we have seen since the 2008 financial crisis, turbulence is here to stay. The ability to scan the environment effectively is critical to allow proactive actions to be taken and to avoid—or at least minimize—the potential effect from major threats, risks, and uncertainties. Like mountaineers, enterprises must stay ahead of the storm to survive.

This capability must also be connected to fast acting mechanisms that result in these adaptive changes. These adaptive changes and the ability to make those changes quickly will usually provide the enterprise with a competitive advantage. So, what exactly does scanning the environment in real-time mean?

Every company has some form of real-time embedded mechanisms in place. What distinguishes the elite from other enterprises is that they have made this habit an exceptional capability. This exceptional capability is usually underpinned by robust processes that are highly effective and timely. And, most importantly, these processes are connected to other lifelines or practices such as the ability to learn (learning entity), their business model, and the core philosophy of the company (particularly the core purpose).

These connections are critical. As an enterprise scans the environment, it must learn effectively from the data including facts and trends that are being accumulated and analyzed. This ability to learn is essential to understanding what is transpiring in the worldwide marketplace and global economy, and the potential impact on the business model and the core purpose of the enterprise.

Data is prioritized and focused on using what is learned to create value. These enterprises tend to be agile, and they react quickly. They also build an abundant number of lifelines as an insurance policy, so that if a major storm does arrive unexpectedly, they can survive and even thrive because they are well prepared. So, what are some of the key mechanisms utilized by elite companies to scan the environment?

Big data is used by elite companies to better understand customer habits, trends, and market changes. Elite enterprises obsess over data. They delve deep into the multitude of economic, market, competitive, and general industry information that is released almost daily. They know how to analyze the data and then organize it in a meaningful fashion, so it can be utilized effectively throughout the enterprise. This proactive practice provides both the early warning signs as well as a mechanism to spot opportunities which allows the enterprise to adapt and stay ahead of any threat while simultaneously seizing any potential opportunities. Some companies have formed internal big data teams (staffed by specialized scientists and engineers) because they understand that data drives critical decision-making. In fact, data is increasingly an exceptional capability that can provide a competitive advantage.

Other useful elements for scanning the environment is the use of economic models and a team of economists— either internal or ones that are developed or outsourced to a third-party partner. It's essential that macroeconomic indicators are scanned for early warning signals. The economic models need to be underpinned by key financial metrics that are monitored, scrutinized, and obsessed over by the right people.

Finally, other critical elements to be scanned by the enterprise for early warning signals include innovation and technology trends, the competitive landscape, geopolitical events, and regulatory trends across the globe.

Habit 9: Form an Internal University with a Clear Purpose

Many elite companies have highly effective internal universities. These universities usually have a dedicated facility, either a separate building or online, and enterprise-specific curriculum built to conform to the company's strategy. A May 16, 2015 *Economist* article notes that the number of corporate universities continues to grow and that, " ... more than 4,000 companies around the world have invested in them." The article notes that "Corporate universities can be particularly useful when a firm is attempting to overhaul its culture."

Some organizations have good intentions with their internal universities, but unfortunately, they sometimes lose their way and become ineffective. The best way to avoid this trap is to have a clear core purpose for the university and never losing focus on the reason for its existence.

Corporate universities can be highly effective mechanisms for developing top management, for training entire organizations, and for either changing the culture or sustaining it. For companies spread across the globe, an online platform can also be effective. Local branches of an internal university can also work well in international locations if the enterprise's core purpose is strictly maintained. One of the risks often pointed out about internal universities is that managers are not exposed to outside ideas. This can be countered by simply using a mix of internal and external professors. Also, hiring someone from a prestigious university to organize and even oversee the university can mitigate this risk. For an internal

university to be successful, it is imperative that the
following elements be in place:

- Adhere to the core purpose of the university
- Use a combination of internal and external
  instructors
- Use a combination of physical facilities and online
  classes
- Use it to train future leaders and key employees
- Use it to sustain a healthy and vibrant culture or to
  even assist with changing the culture
- Use it to communicate the business model
- Use it to reinforce the core values and core purpose
  of the enterprise
- Use it to effect change that the company is striving
  to accomplish
- Develop key metrics to measure success

Habit 10 Adopt Best Practices from Private Equity

Enterprises can learn a great deal from how private equity
companies consistently improve the businesses they
acquire. Most private equity firms passionately believe they
can improve an acquired company by following their
internally developed recipe and utilizing their playbook.
So, what are some of key practices or habits that can be
adopted from private equity? Here are some of the most
important recipe elements:

- Implementation of clear business strategies for
  substantive value creation. Private equity firms have
  a laser-like focus on value creation. This focus is

underpinned by discipline and a passion for improving the business.

- Hands-on, engaged partnerships with management to drive change with a high sense of urgency. The benefit of the private equity model is its hands-on, deep-in-the-operations-of-the-business approach. Private equity groups partner with the management team to execute at a high level, and they instill a high sense of urgency to improve the business.

- Implementation of a clear governance model to secure the business. Private equity uses a common sense, non-bureaucratic governance model to oversee the business. This practice speeds up decision making, lowers costs, and provides accountability where it belongs—with management.

- Implementation and execution of operational excellence. An area that gets a great deal of attention with private equity ownership is operational excellence. Private equity groups usually implement their playbook that has been tested and proven over many transactions. They clearly understand that superior value creation comes from developing an exceptional operational capability. The extreme example of this operational excellence exceptional capability is *3G Capital Partners LP* that we reviewed earlier.

- Appointment of a management team that is focused on value creation and growth. It's not unusual for private equity to make substantive changes to the management team once they take ownership of a business. They appoint managers who clearly understand the need to improve results and grow the business.

- Assisting the company to grow and develop into an elite company. Private equity groups have the skills, resources, and vision to take a mediocre or underperforming business and develop it into an elite company. They clearly understand the need to develop a sustainable business model that creates value.

- Achievement of total alignment between management, board, and investor. A great advantage of the private equity business model is the total alignment of interests between management, the board, and the investor. This arrangement is invaluable because everyone is working towards specific goals and objectives.

- Holding management team totally accountable with clear goals and objectives. All enterprises talk about holding management teams accountable to very specific goals and objectives. The reality is that sometimes companies fall short. Under the private equity model, this rarely happens. Management teams are completely held to a high standard of accountability and responsibility.

- Fostering an entrepreneurial performance culture. The private equity business model is all about establishing and sustaining an entrepreneurial culture, which is done through the implementation of effective mechanisms, many of which are outlined in this habit.

- Building a stronger, more sustainable high return on capital business. Private equity believes in building a redoubtable company that is highly efficient in capital allocation. Under their model, enterprises have an inexorable focus on achieving a high return on invested capital.
- Defining a clear core purpose and core values. The elite private equity firms clearly understand the need to develop a core purpose and core values that everyone embraces.

Habit 11: Optimize the Tax and Legal Structure

An exceptional capability that elite companies possess is their ability to optimize their tax and legal structures. These structures can have a material impact on the company both in terms of economic success and risk management. With respect to the legal structure, it is vital that a company build a legal firewall to protect the enterprise from this risk. The devastation caused by asbestos litigation is only one of many examples. In its simplest form, a company should structure all its business units as separate, wholly owned subsidiaries.

From a tax standpoint, a company can utilize certain weapons, including inversions and tax planning strategies. As of this writing, President Trump is proposing substantial structural changes to the U.S. tax code to positively position the country with a lower corporate tax rate to put it on a more equal footing with the majority of developed economies of the world. However, the comments that follow below only reflect current tax law which could change dramatically in the future if the proposed changes are enacted.

Inversions are deals in which enterprises reincorporate overseas—they shift their domicile to another country. This change happens when a U.S. company merges with a foreign company and then moves its legal residency abroad, usually to the U.K., Ireland, or the Netherlands, which have become in recent years the most popular destinations due to language, ease of business, and form of government. Inversions can make sense for U.S. companies with substantial overseas operations.

Inversions have become popular because the U.S. has one of the highest corporate income-tax rates in the world. The U.S.—unlike most countries of the world—taxes businesses on a world-wide basis irrespective of where the money is earned. Most countries tax only the money earned in that country. This setup means that U.S. companies are taxed twice. First, they are taxed in the country in which they do business, and then a second time when they repatriate their earnings back to the U.S., which puts U.S. based businesses at competitive disadvantage.

Inversions have been around for a long time, since at least the 1980s, when inversions were much simpler to execute. Further, because of the loss of potential tax dollars, the U.S. has been trying to stem the flow of inversions since 1996 when the Treasury Department passed regulations in response to some high-profile inversions. The regulations did not have a major impact, and so in 2004, new regulations were enacted which had more enforcement teeth. Even with beefed up rules, the inversions continued.

In 2014, even more difficult regulations were adopted by the Treasury. Although the new rules have significantly slowed the number of inversions, they have not stopped them from occurring. Consequently, in 2016 even more stringent rules were unilaterally adopted by the Treasury Department. These new rules appear to be extremely onerous and have already impacted significantly some announced and planned transactions.

Nonetheless, the avalanche of new stricter rules has had some unintended consequences—mainly, it has made U.S. companies even more vulnerable to foreign takeover. This risk is because foreign companies can use their significantly lower tax rate to their advantage when buying U.S. businesses. They can pay a higher price for a U.S. business and then utilize their earnings, which will then be taxed at a much lower rate. This setup is, unfortunately, making U.S. based companies prey to aggressive overseas competitors who have a distinct competitive advantage.

In addition, foreign companies have a clear advantage over domestic companies in a bidding or auction process. Foreign companies can pay a higher price to acquire a U.S. company because they can effectively utilize the substantially lower tax rate to their advantage. This situation puts the U.S. bidder at a distinct disadvantage. Although this problem has been in existence for a while, it's more acute now because U.S. companies have been severely handcuffed from buying foreign rivals through an inversion process. The inversion process has historically put U.S. companies (headquartered overseas) in a better competitive position because they can bid on domestic assets on a more equal footing with foreign rivals.

For companies that cannot pursue an inversion, other strategic tax planning strategies are a must, but the options

continue to diminish with global governments taking a
more proactive and harsher views of some of the tax
planning strategies that have been employed by
multinationals. Nonetheless, not all is lost because some
effective tax efficiencies can still be realized, but it will
require putting together an exceptional team of tax experts.
Most elite companies currently possess this capability, but
they will also need to raise their level of competency given
the hostile tax environment.

Habit 12: Forecast Accurately
Our ability to predict the future—no matter how
sophisticated we are—is fraught with risk. Forecasting and
planning scenarios can differ dramatically due to the macro
global business and geopolitical environment. As a matter
of fact, if you extrapolate global economic data from the
past sixty years, you can develop a rough rule of thumb that
says that most likely there will be some form of major
economic disruption approximately once every decade.
This forecast is because no economic expansion since
World War II has lasted more than a decade.

During these past economic cycles, we have
experienced periods of relative calm, turbulence, and a mix
of the two. However, because of the recent rise of China as
an economic powerhouse, what happens in their economy
adds further complexity and turbulence to the overall global
economic environment. This impact was felt by global
equity markets in the summer of 2015 and early 2016, and
it triggered a significant amount of market turbulence. This
reality should be factored in and seriously considered in
future planning and forecasting systems.

If the global economy is relatively stable and we have no major global shocks or disruptions, our ability to project and forecast future financial results with some accuracy gets much easier. However, if the global economy is somewhat mixed with some growth, some detractors, and others showing anemic growth, then planning and forecasting is more difficult. Moreover, if the environment is tumultuous—as we have been experiencing since the 2008 U.S. financial crisis—then planning and forecasting gets even more difficult and highly problematic. Let's review some of the major events since the Great Recession of 2008 through 2016.

First, the markets were shaken by the general European sovereign debt crisis. Then the Greek bailout occurred. Then the shock of Brexit (United Kingdom's exit from the European Union) happened. The impact of all these events was exacerbated by Europe's inability to show any meaningful economic growth. Second, the period had significant foreign exchange volatility, especially the dramatic strengthening of the U.S. dollar. Next came the unexpected devaluation of the Chinese Yuan, the panic in their stock market, and a slowdown in their economy. Third, there was the precipitous drop in global oil prices.

These situations are a few of the recent major obstacles to planning and forecasting accurately. I do believe that this turbulence is the new norm that elite leaders, boards, and enterprises need to confront and accept. This new norm of tumult and unpredictable shocks demands a new way thinking when preparing the annual plan as well as the three or five-year strategic plan. I believe that many of the assumptions that were used in past planning cycles by some companies are, for the most part, invalid. So, what does the new mind-set for planning and forecasting look like?

Mountaineering rule number one states, "Hope for the best, but plan for the worst." Companies need to perform a scenario analysis as part of their planning process. A considerable amount of data and generative thinking needs to go into various scenarios. As part of this process, companies need to adopt planning and forecasting best practices. Here is a list of key elements that should be incorporated into an effective planning and forecasting system:

- Know your business, your markets, your customers, and your competitive position extremely well.
- All major assumptions need to be challenged. Learn to not trust assumptions, trust only facts and data that are substantiated and validated. Use Monte Carlo simulation scenarios to underpin the analysis of major projects.
- Implement an effective sales cadence and backlog reporting system.
- Organize a diverse team—including outside consultants—to come up with various scenarios including extreme worst-case scenarios.
- Use big data to glean vital information on customers, markets, and even competitors.
- Retain an economist to assist with developing various economic models.
- Build a resilient and adaptive organization.

- Scan the environment effectively and in real-time as an early warning mechanism; involve the risk committee.
- Build an abundance of lifelines to ensure that the organization survives any worst-case scenario. Also, an abundance of lifelines can provide a company with a significant opportunity to thrive during tumultuous times. Strong enterprises can position themselves to seize opportunities that inevitably present themselves during periods of extreme turmoil.
- Develop a plan B that has substance. This backup is because plans never play out as envisioned due to numerous variables involved. Both mountaineers and the military know this rule well. As a U.S. military general once told me, when that first bullet is fired, the plan pretty much goes out the window. The reality of the situation dramatically alters expectations, and it is why adaptability and resilience are so important.

Habit 13: Understand Customer Profitability Management

Elite companies focus intensely on all aspects of their customers. One of the most important focus areas is customer profitability management. The Institute of Management Accountants (IMA) in a 2010 publication provides great insight into this critical analysis that all companies need to perform.

Here is how IMA defines customer profitability management: "Managing profitability requires not only a customer-centric focus but also a thorough understanding and effective management of customer profitability. Customer profitability management (CPM) is a strategy-linked approach to identifying the relative profitability of different customers or customer segments to devise strategies that add value to most-profitable customers, make less-profitable customers more profitable, stop or reduce the erosion of profit by unprofitable customers, or otherwise focus on long-term customer profitability. Managers are often surprised to find out that a small percentage of customers generate substantially more than 100 percent of profits, and the remaining customers are either breakeven or unprofitable. Using a customer profitability management system replaces intuitive impressions of customer profitability with fact-based information and supporting analysis." [li] The IMA publication goes into some detail on how a CPM system functions.

Another excellent source on this topic is the groundbreaking research paper in *Harvard Business* published by Robert S. Kaplan and V.G. Narayanan in May 2001, titled "Customer Profitability Management." This paper is also a must read for anyone interested in developing this exceptional capability.

For CPM to operate properly, a costing system must be developed that accurately assigns and allocates costs to each customer, which is the major issue or challenge in accurately measuring customer profitability. Activity-based costing or ABC was developed to address and underpin a CPM system. ABC systems can range from highly complex to simple. It takes considerable time and resources to develop an effective ABC system that accurately captures customer profitability. No matter the level of sophistication, a CPM system is indispensable, particularly in the world's new norm of a tumultuous global economy.

Habit 14: Utilize Technology to Gain a Competitive Position

Elite companies smartly utilize technology to drive growth, provide a competitive advantage, and to secure confidential competitive information about customer habits. Elite companies are focused on some key technologies: artificial intelligence, cybersecurity, big data, cloud computing, mobile computing, and social media. Let's examine each one of these important technologies through the lens of an elite company.

Artificial Intelligence

Artificial intelligence or AI—in its simplest form—is the ability of machines to learn. This technology is already having a significant impact in such areas as human capital, medicine, robotics, and autonomous vehicles. A great deal of material has been recently produced on how AI is transforming the business environment and thus won't be repeated here. The important takeaway, however, is that elite companies are already incorporating AI technology in key processes with the objective of gaining a competitive advantage.

Cybersecurity

Before we examine cybersecurity, one needs to understand cyberspace. The best definition is found in the insightful and well-reasoned book, *Cybersecurity and Cyberwar*, by

P.W. Singer and Allan Friedman. The authors do a
wonderful job in defining cyberspace: "Cyberspace is first
and foremost an information environment. It is made up of
digitized data that is created, stored, and, most importantly,
shared ... It comprises the computers that store data plus the
systems and infrastructure that allow it to flow. This
includes the Internet of networked computers, closed
intranets, cellular technologies, fiber-optic cables, and
space-based communications." [lii]

During the period from 2014 to 2016, so many high-
profile cyberattacks occurred, it's impossible to highlight
all of them. Perhaps the most notable examples were the
Sony and Yahoo attacks, which were highly publicized. A
cybersecurity breach can significantly impact not only the
reputation or brand of a company, but it can also cause
severe financial harm. With digital interconnectedness,
enterprises are obviously exposing their most important
intangible assets. These assets include intellectual property
(such as patents, customer lists, and employee information)
as well as possible information about strategies, business
model, and key metrics. It's imperative that organizations
view cyber threats as a significant danger to the enterprise.

Elite enterprises understand this threat and are focusing
on the risk by taking a direct interest and involvement in
protecting vital assets. This leadership begins by changing
the mind-set of the organization by effectively
communicating and training everyone in the company on
the seriousness of the threat. Cybersecurity needs to be
viewed in the context of enterprise risk, and, thus, it needs
to be fully integrated into the enterprise risk management
process.

To integrate cybersecurity, one needs to know how to frame the argument. The authors P. W. Singer and Allan Friedman capture this well, "The real battle in cybersecurity is not just about high technology. It is also driven by the human factor, the fight over our behavior ... While there are varied advanced threats in cybersecurity, many of the most successful take advantage of good old-fashioned human error ... many IT experts believe that if a network has any kind of sensitive information in it, all users need to be regularly certified in cybersecurity basics. This means everyone, from junior staff all the way up the leadership."[liii] Elite leaders understand this importance and are taking appropriate proactive measures to protect the enterprise to the extent possible. However, as someone knowledgeable in this space once said to me, "With cybersecurity, you are trying to defend the indefensible."

Big Data

In a September 20-21, 2014 *Wall Street Journal* article by Shira Ovide, big data is defined as: "... the flood of digital information generated by web traffic, sensors, networked communications, and internet-connected machines." The vast amounts of information being generated in today's digital economy is regularly mined by elite companies in their quest to make predictions about customer behavior. Data science is an emerging exceptional capability that can't be ignored. This data value chain is a critical tool that can provide a company with a distinct competitive advantage.

Big data and the ability to mine the information effectively has been made possible by several key factors.

First, data collection and storage costs have declined considerably, which makes it cost effective to collect and store large quantities of data. Second, the proliferation of cloud computing has enabled new players to enter the market due to the relative low cost of cloud computing capabilities. And third, the emergence of data scientists who can skillfully accumulate and analyze immense quantities of data has brought this capability to many organizations.

McKinsey Global Institute summarized the potential benefits of big data in their insightful report titled, *Big data: The next frontier for innovation, competition, and productivity.*

Here is an informative except:

There are five broad ways in which using big data can create value. First, big data can unlock significant value by making information transparent and usable at much higher frequency. Second, as organizations create and store more transactional data in digital form, they can collect more accurate and detailed performance information on everything from product inventories to sick days, and therefore expose variability and boost performance.

Leading companies are using data collection and analysis to conduct controlled experiments to make better management decisions; others are using data for basic low-frequency forecasting to high-frequency nowcasting to adjust their business levers just in time. Third, big data allows ever-narrower segmentation of customers and therefore much more precisely tailored products or services.

Fourth, sophisticated analytics can substantially improve decision-making. Finally, big data can be used to improve the development of the next generation of products and services. For instance, manufacturers are using data obtained from sensors embedded in products to create innovative after-sales service offerings such as proactive maintenance (preventive measures that take place before a failure occurs or is even noticed).[liv]

Cloud Computing

Some elite companies are adopting cloud computing technologies to reduce the need for in-house servers and data centers. Cloud computing reduces the number of people in the organization that are required to maintain networks and support computing power. More importantly, it reduces the amount software and hardware that must be purchased which in turn lowers capital expenditures. For an asset-light business model, cloud computing technologies is just one more mechanism available to lower the amount of capital employed. Cloud computing is also a great enabler. When additional capacity is required in an organization, it can essentially be added seamlessly. Cloud computing also provides an enterprise with the ability to scale quickly. Finally, cloud computing has enabled the explosive growth that we have seen in all types internet services.

So, what exactly is cloud computing? According to the authors P. W. Singer and Allan Friedman cloud computing is, "A shift in control of computing resources from the individual or organization to a shared resource run by a third party. By pooling network-enabled resources, cloud computing enables mobility, scalability, flexibility, and efficiency, but increases the dependency on the cloud provider."[lv] Some of the more popular enterprise software run on the cloud include supply chain, human capital, and various financial applications.

An elite company on the vanguard of cloud computing is Netflix. In a *Wall Street Journal* article titled, "Netflix Is Ready to Pull Plug on Its Final Data Center" published August 15-16, 2015, the authors Robert McMillan and Rachael King stated, "Netflix Inc. said it plans to shut down the last of its data centers by the end of the summer which would make it one of the first big companies to run all of its information technology remotely ... The closing of Netflix's last data center has been seven years in the making." Today, cloud computing is commonplace, and it's utilized across the spectrum from start-ups to large, established companies. Amazon and Microsoft are two of the most important market leaders in providing this critical service.

Mobile Computing
Mobile computing has totally transformed how individuals and the enterprises they represent go about conducting their business. The connectivity of mobile devices to the internet has enabled this amazing transformation. The best way to look at mobile computing was captured by McKinsey Global Institute in their insightful and groundbreaking report, *Disruptive technologies: Advances that will transform life, business, and the global economy*. Here is how they framed what they call the mobile internet:

"Ubiquitous connectivity and an explosive proliferation of apps are enabling users to go about their daily routines with new ways of knowing, perceiving, and even interacting with the physical world. The technology of the mobile internet is evolving rapidly ... The mobile internet also has applications across businesses and the public sector, enabling more efficient delivery of many services and creating opportunities to increase workforce productivity."[lvi]

Elite companies recognize and harvest the power of mobile computing. They use apps to improve worker productivity and effectiveness. On the mobile e-commerce side, elite companies are focusing their mobile strategies on the customer. Shoppers are increasingly using mobile computing to order goods and services. From Amazon to Uber to Starbucks, all these elite companies have developed innovative mobile apps for their customers.

Social Media Social media is used effectively by elite companies as a business tool to promote their brand, communicate effectively, seek feedback on their products and services, promote new products and services, and improve the overall customer experience. Social media when used properly can be a powerful mechanism for public relations, advertising, and capturing valuable data. It's also a vital tool to use when dealing with a crisis.

Habit 15: Adopt Habits of Elite Activists
Some of the habits or characteristics that define an elite activist investor include: a history of successful execution on activist campaigns; well capitalized firm, strong

financial position; proven, well tested team; a history of creating shareholder value; consistently doing the right things, the right ways, for the right reasons; taking a long-term view to improve the company; and, exceptional operating capabilities. This habit can be further broken down into the following exceptional capabilities and characteristics:

- Demands best-of-class operating excellence
- Builds a highly optimized and efficient organization
- Transforms good businesses into great businesses
- Creates a learning entity environment that is disciplined and focused with the objective of learning from both successes and failures
- Creates an environment and culture that allows CEO and management to excel and succeed
- Ensures that the all decision making consistently considers the long-term benefit of the business
- Achieves best-of-class operating margins and revenue growth
- Achieves complete strategy alignment between board, management, and investors
- Ensures that best practices are shared across the enterprise
- Leverages scale to the benefit of the enterprise by reducing costs and increasing revenues
- Ensures that management team is focused on developing a culture of high performance
- Reduces complexity throughout the organization
- Reduces or eliminates corporate overhead burden, eliminates bureaucracy

- Ensures that all tactical moves are in complete alignment with the agreed strategy

As evident from the above list, there's much that enterprises can learn from elite activists. These habits, once clearly understood, can be adopted by organizations in their quest to ascend the summit. How can one argue with creating shareholder value, exceptional operational excellence, and building a high performing management team?

Habit 16: Make Every Customer Touch Extraordinary
Southwest Airlines (Southwest) is the only major U.S. carrier to not have gone through Chapter 11 bankruptcy. Why? First, the company has a superior recipe (business model) that is executed flawlessly, and second, it has an extraordinary culture that focuses on customer service. No matter how you measure it, Southwest's performance has been simply elite! In fact, according to an October 1, 2015 *Fortune* article by Shawn Tully, since its listing on the NYSE in 1977 Southwest has delivered, "17.5 percent average annual returns compared with the 11 percent average gain for the broader market over the same span."

Since we have already and extensively covered Southwest's recipe in *CEO Lifelines*, this habit is focused on exceptional service. Southwest simply has a fanatical focus on ensuring that every customer touch is extraordinary. Underpinned by their so-called nonconformist culture, Southwest boasts the industry's best-of-class service levels. The culture of the company's employees—pilots, flight attendants, customer representations at airport, reservation employees, of course, the management team—is focused on making the customer and everyone associated with the company happy.

Another elite company focused on making every customer experience extraordinary is Disney. If fact, Disney's core purpose (or mission) is, *"To make people happy."* Just like an interaction with Southwest, one only must visit a Disney theme park to see overwhelming demonstrable evidence of their focus on making every customer touch simply extraordinary.

Habit 17: Know Your Customer Through Value Selling
Perhaps nothing is more important in business than truly knowing your customer. An effective mechanism that can be used to achieve this deep knowledge of your customer is value selling. Value selling is simply a focused approach on the customer; ideally, your sales force should know more about the customer than the customer knows about him or herself. This mind-set is completely different mind-set from traditional selling. It requires gaining a deep understanding of your customer's challenges and needs so that you can develop innovative solutions that can be sold on value.

To effectively utilize value selling to transform an organization, some critical capabilities must be developed, all underpinned by a customer-centered culture. The exceptional capabilities that need to be developed include the following:

- *Customer Relationship Management (CRM).* An effective CRM system is essential to value selling and developing a deep understanding of the customer. Incredible CRM software packages are available that operate in the cloud. A CRM system provides an enterprise with the tools necessary to effectively manage customer data and customer interaction. CRM automates the sales and marketing process, it automates customer support functions, and it provides a multitude of information and metrics that can help drive sales growth. A powerful CRM system arms the sales team with the necessary information that can drive value selling.

- *Bid Data.* Big data needs to be utilized in conjunction with CRM as part of the value selling process. Effectively mined big data about the customer, the markets, products, and trends is indispensable in building an effective value selling culture in the organization.
- *Extensive Training.* Sales personnel must be extensively trained in value selling to allow an organization to truly realize its potential benefits. A large part of value selling is changing the mind-set of the sales team.
- *Mobile Technologies and Apps.* An effective value selling team must have the right tools to considerably improve their effectiveness, which can be accomplished with mobile technologies and specific apps. These technologies should be implemented to not only reduce the overall administrative burden on the sales team, but to also provide them with a powerful sales tool while with the customer.

SECTION 3

EXCEPTIONAL HABITS OF ELITE BOARDS

Great minds discuss ideas; average minds discuss events; small minds discuss people.
Eleanor Roosevelt[lvii]

S ir Edmund Hillary, a New Zealand Mountaineer, impressed the world when he—along with a Nepalese Sherpa named Tenzing Norgay—became the first to climb the summit of Mount Everest in 1953. Their successful ascent to the highest point on earth—an incredible feat at the time—opened a new chapter in mountaineering.

Hillary's extraordinary achievement was made possible by teamwork, discipline, and exceptional capabilities, a combination that he forged early on through the strong and lasting relationship made with his partner, Tenzing Norgay, and with the entire support team accompanying them. And a mighty team it was, involving more than 400 people, including 362 porters, twenty Sherpa guides and 10,000 pounds of baggage.

It is generally reported that Sir Hillary and his partner both reached the summit at the same time, but according to Norgay it was actually Sir Hillary who was first. Sir Hillary's humility is instructive and consistent with this innate precocious characteristic of many elite leaders.

Just as Sir Hillary and his partner worked effectively as a team to ascend the tallest summit on earth, board of directors must demonstrate such cooperation at a similarly high corporate level. Such collaboration is essential today when the pressures on public boards continues to increase as activist investors demand extraordinary performance. Boards today need to help management see what they can't see or have difficulty seeing clearly. Boards that do this effectively can truly differentiate themselves and in the process help create value for the enterprise and its shareholders. In this section, we will explore the effective habits of elite and visionary boards that truly understand what value creation is all about.

During my four decades of professional experience, I've experienced interactions with a multitude of boards as an advisor, a board member, and as a CEO. I can speak firsthand about the difference in performance between elite boards and everyone else. The most successful ingredients needed to create an elite board include:

- A great culture within the board and the company

- Total alignment between the CEO and the board on strategy and key people decisions
- An excellent blend of skills on the board
- The right behavior at the board level and the executive level driven by humility
- Board members who truly understand their role as a director
- Board members who have a laser focus on value creation
- Collaboration is evident and team spirit is high within the board and the management team
- An exceptional, proven lead director who is selected on abilities and not simply on some political protocol
- Directors who are fully and deeply engaged and take substantive time to understand the business
- An effective and robust succession planning process drives performance and ensures leadership continuity
- A highly effective board evaluation process that holds members accountable

In this section, we will expand on all the above points. Furthermore, we will examine in more detail why elite boards thrive and share their most effective habits.

Habits of Elite Boards

The exceptional habits in this section, like the sections on leaders and enterprises, is broken down into three essential foundational pillars: leadership, strategy, and execution. Boards that focus on these three areas, along with an overall awareness of the luck spread foundational pillar, stand the best chance of sustained, high performance success and to ultimately achieve elite status. The exceptional habits in this section include:

Chapter 8:   11 Leadership Habits of Elite Boards
Chapter 9:   3 Strategy Habits of Elite Boards
Chapter 10: 7 Execution Habits of Elite Boards

CHAPTER 8

11 LEADERSHIP HABITS OF ELITE BOARDS

The task of the leader is to get their people from where they are to where they have not been.
Henry Kissinger[lviii]

E lite Boards exhibit eleven essential leadership habits:

Habit 1: Elevate Technology on the Board Agenda
Habit 2: Deal Effectively with an Activist Investor
Habit 3: Provide Prodigious Lifelines to New CEO
Habit 4: Invest in Your CEO
Habit 5: Hold the Board Accountable
Habit 6: Be Engaged
Habit 7: Have Compliance Report Directly to the Board
Habit 8: Engage Effectively with Investors
Habit 9: View the Board as a Team

Habit 1: Elevate Technology on the Board Agenda

Elite companies and their boards lead the way on effectively utilizing technology to provide a distinct competitive advantage. The importance of technology is evident in many elite companies. GE now has a growing $5 billion software business. Roper has transformed its business dramatically over the years by embracing technology and emphasizing their software business, even changing their name to Roper Technology. Disney, MasterCard, and numerous others have clearly benefited from incorporating the latest technology into their business model.

Elite companies (and their elite boards) have elevated technology as a key area requiring their board's attention. Consequently, many boards are adding a digital director to the board. Boards slow to react to this trend may be missing an opportunity to create additional shareholder value since it is part of their fiduciary responsibility to oversee and understand how technology should be employed in the business. Technology can be so disruptive to the business model that boards must aggressively embrace technology and allocate appropriate resources to protect the future of the enterprise.

The need for adding a digital director or directors to the board and elevating technology to high level of importance on the board agenda was captured well in an article in the August 26, 2013 *Agenda* by Wendy Markus Webb "Digital technologies, mobile and social media have created new business models, new competitive threats and new opportunities for all companies ... This means that boards face an undeniable shift in how their companies establish and maintain strategic competitive position, build awareness, interact with consumers, advertise, sell and deliver their products. Boards must accept the idea that, in today's world, every company is a technology company. Otherwise, they risk putting their companies at a competitive disadvantage."

Habit 2: Deal Effectively with an Activist Investor
Imagine being the CEO and Chairman of an elite company. Your company just announced another record quarter. Growth in revenues, earnings, and free cash flow are the envy of peers. The board of directors is obviously pleased with the performance. Despite all the headaches that come with being a leader of a public company, sustained excellent performance can easily quell the cacophony of noise typical of operating a business in the public arena. Good feeling and inner peace can easily be shattered by an activist investor. When this happens, CEOs and boards of directors face one of their most difficult challenges.

Investor activism is at an all-time high—and no enterprise is immune! Even the most elite organizations are tested by the rising clout of high profile activists such as Carl Icahn (Icahn Enterprises), Nelson Peltz (Trian), William Ackman (Pershing Square), Dan Loeb (Third Point), and Jeffrey Smith (Starboard Value). Even one of the most elite companies in the world, Apple, has been a target of activist investors as well as other well-known companies–DuPont, Netflix, Dow Chemical, Yahoo, Procter & Gamble, Disney, Sotheby's, PepsiCo, Ingersoll Rand, Allergan, Darden, Chesapeake Energy, and eBay to just mention a few.

The bad news for CEOs and boards is that the activists are winning. Before we examine in detail the activist phenomenon and why they are winning, it's important to understand two critical facts. First, activism is now an asset class that has increasing support from institutional investors, and these activists have an ever-growing amount of funds to invest. Second, the number of activist campaigns continue to increase. For example, in 2010 there were approximately 221 high impact activist campaigns, and by the end of 2015 that number increased to approximately 377. It appears that the growth in announced campaigns will continue at a strong pace in the future as well.

About Activist Strategies

After buying a stake in the company, activists simply press for change. Their equity stake is usually not material—typically well under 5 percent—but their influence is often outsized. Usually, activist will champion both financial and strategic changes that they believe will drive share prices higher and thus create shareholder value. Activists normally articulate extremely well their recipe for getting to the ultimate summit of value creation. Martin Lipton, the highly recognized and followed partner of a prestigious law firm, wrote the following about activists in his annual letter on December 2, 2014: [lix]

"Companies today are more vulnerable to activist attacks than ever before. Over the past decade or so, several trends have converged to foster an environment that is rife with opportunities for activists to extract value. These include the steady erosion of takeover defenses, the expansion of the ability of shareholders to pressure directors, the increasingly impatient and short-term mind-set of Wall Street, and a regulatory disclosure regime that is badly in need of modernization to reflect current realities of rapid stock accumulations by activists ..." Lipton also went to say that, "Yesterday's corporate governance crusades have turned an evolutionary corner in the last few years, to morph into the heavyweight attacks of today where entire boards of directors are ousted in proxy fights and a 3 percent shareholder can compel a $100+ billion company to accommodate its demands for spin-offs, buybacks and other major changes."

So, what are the key focus areas of activists? The list, based on recent cases, should not be of a surprise to anyone:

- **Weak, underperforming share price and poor return on invested capital.** Valuation of the company clearly lags peer group or historical values. This focus area usually calls for one or some (or all) of the following actions: significant cost reductions; a change in CEO; a break-up of the company; a spin-off of a division, segment of the company, or sometimes the sale of the entire company. At times, board representation is also pursued by an activist.

- **Market value of the various parts of the company exceed the entire value of the enterprise.** A large discrepancy in value between the sum-of-the-parts and the whole usually calls for a spin-off. In addition, capital allocation policy is often challenged, which can include opposing an announced transaction. The actions that are advocated under this scenario are like the bullet point above, including possible board representation.

- **Excess cash on the balance sheet.** This usually calls for one or some (or all) of the following actions: a one-time large cash dividend, an increase in the dividend rate, and substantial share buy-backs.

- **Governance concerns.** This typically calls for changes in executive compensation, board structure, board composition (skills), board tenure, and various other matters.

So why are activists often successful at improving shareholder value? First, they are very experienced and very smart, and their tactics are usually designed to evade corporate takeover defenses adopted by the company. Second, they are highly skilled at public relations campaigns and garnering institutional support for their cause. They are also masters at controlling the narrative.

Third, activists know how to use the proxy battle weapon very effectively for obtaining board representation. Although not all activist campaigns seek board representation, the ones seeking such representation are highly disruptive and expensive. Proxy fights can, at times, be a major diversion for the management team and the board of directors. Sometimes, the campaign can take a very negative tone and become a public spectacle. These tactics often cause boards and CEOs to negotiate to avoid expensive public battles. However, activists have also shown that they are willing to negotiate during this proxy contest. Fourth, they use the so-called, "wolf-pack" tactic by aligning with like-minded hedge funds.

As you can see, CEOs and boards of directors are up against a formidable challenger. However, elite boards can utilize credible countermeasures. Here are some common-sense countermeasures to use:

- **The most effective weapon, of course, is sustained superior performance.** But, as Apple discovered, that sometimes is not enough.
- **Preparation is highly critical, and it can be a powerful countermeasure.** A comprehensive assessment should be performed by the company and the board to expose potential vulnerabilities. Outside experts such as your investment bankers and lawyers can assist with this endeavor. Once vulnerabilities are clearly identified, a plan should be developed to address them.
- **The company needs to develop a well-articulated communication plan to deal with activists.**
- **Proactive and ongoing engagement with institutional investors can also help, and it should be part of the tool kit in dealing with activists.**

- **Enterprises need to sharpen their strategic focus.** This often requires hiring some outside specialists to assist in a strategic review of the company.

- **CEOs and boards should engage in constructive dialogue with activist to point out vital elements they are missing that could move them on to the next target.** A great example of this dialogue is Netflix. According to a November 26, 2014 article in the *Wall Street Journal* by David Benoit, here is how Netflix effectively handled Carl Icahn's activist activities: "Netflix Inc.'s Reed Hastings earned the respect of Icahn, who in 2012 wanted the online video company to sell itself but the dropped the idea after Hastings showed him its soon-to-debut series "House of Cards." That helped convince Icahn that the company's future was bright."

Habit 3: Provide Prodigious Lifelines to New CEO
Boards of directors have two obligations to ensure CEO success. The first obligation centers on the five lifelines that must be provided to a newly appointed CEO. The second—which is covered in the next section—centers on continuous investment in the development of the CEO.

The five lifelines that board of directors must provide to newly appointed CEOs are vital to the future success of the leader. I believe that it is the board's professional, fiduciary, and moral obligation to take substantive and measurable action to ensure that the new leader is given every tool and weapon possible to increase his or her chance of success. Remember, if the CEO fails it normally means that the board has fallen short on its most important responsibility. Here are the five critical lifelines that must be provided to a newly appointed CEO:

- First, the board must provide unwavering support to the new leader
- A requirement that the new leader accept a position on another company's board of directors after one year on the job
- Require the new leader to attend a high caliber program that is exclusively designed for new CEOs, either just before or after appointment to CEO
- Appointment of a natural mentor, which can be a board member, the retiring CEO, or the even the Chairman (if separate position from CEO)
- Encourage the new leader to develop an outside relationship with a trusted professional confidant

It is important that these five lifelines be augmented by a robust long-term plan that is focused on developing and improving the overall skill set of the CEO. There's clearly a cumulative beneficial effect to the CEO and to the enterprise when a focused and well-structured program to continuously improve the leader's skill set is in place.

Habit 4: Invest in Your CEO
An ongoing investment in the CEO increases the chances that the CEO will succeed and remain in a leadership position. Stability is important because CEOs need time to not only complete their strategic initiatives but develop a group of talented potential successors. So, by investing in the success of the CEO, the board is forging a strong

foundation for the future. Here are some critical investments that should be made by the board to develop a CEO:

- *Staff leadership rides.* As discussed in Chapter 2, staff leadership rides are not only for the development of the global leadership team, but also for the development of the CEO. An additional benefit is that the practice builds strong CEO relationships with his team and the board of directors.

- *Personal assessments, 360 reviews.* The CEO needs constant feedback and professional advice on how to continuously improve. This feedback can be accomplished through personal assessments that are carefully conducted by an outside professional group that specializes in these reviews. Don't delegate this requirement to individuals without a deep knowledge and expertise in this area because the results can fall short and or even be counterproductive.

- *CEO Forums.* Leaders should be encouraged to participate in high caliber CEO Forums. When well done, they allow the CEO to meet with other leaders with the overall objective of sharing and learning.

- *Strong relationship with lead director.* Another important CEO development mechanism is fostering a strong relationship with the lead director. The lead director obviously should be a highly-experienced board member able to provide effective feedback and assist with the development of the CEO.

- ***Ongoing training***. Specific training and development programs should be designed with the assistance of outside professionals.

Habit 5: Hold the Board Accountable

Boards are increasingly being held accountable for results, a reality that is often the consequence of activist investors and highly engaged shareholders. Boards must demonstrate their value to the enterprise just like CEOs and should be held accountable for their underperformance. Numerous mechanisms and metrics can be implemented to measure value creation and fulfillment of fiduciary responsibility.

Boards should implement a robust assessment process for evaluating each board member, each committee, and the overall effectiveness of the board. The board should be measured on such critical responsibilities as succession planning, enterprise risk management, governance, and strategy. Also, the board should be measured on total shareholder return. And probably most importantly, boards should be measured on how they have performed relative to their responsibility of overseeing the CEO. Boards need to build a robust process that ensures these vital elements are properly measured and incorporated in their annual assessment or report card. As part of this process, a mechanism should be implemented whereby board members are asked to step down when they are not performing to the standard established.

Habit 6: Be Engaged

Elite boards take engagement beyond expected traditional duties. Highly engaged boards make a substantial commitment to obtaining a deep knowledge of the company, obtaining a deep knowledge of the management team, and to improving their individual skill set. Let's examine these areas a little closer.

Making a commitment to gaining a deep knowledge of the company is demonstrated in many ways. It means visiting sites (at least annually) to see first-hand how the company operates. It also means new sites are visited every year (sometimes multiple sites are visited in the same time period). A November 17, 2014 *Fortune* article detailed Home Depot's elite site visit practice that requires directors to go on two store walks a year. Obtaining a deep knowledge of the company also means spending time navigating each business unit website, reading and understanding product literature, and watching videos on sites like YouTube. Obtaining a deep knowledge means understanding the industry and the competitors.

Likewise, obtaining a deep knowledge of the management team means attending the annual global leadership meeting so that directors can interact and spend substantial time with the top 100 people in the organization. It means attending at least one quarterly operating review meeting with the top senior team. It means obtaining a deep understanding of the team by sitting through a comprehensive talent-management and succession planning session at least annually and preferably semi-annually. And, it means participating in a leadership staff ride with key executives.

Being an engaged board member also means improving your overall skill set. Elite boards make commitments to improvement that include attending annual outside training. Reading the right material written specifically for boards available through various media channels is another key element.

Habit 7: Have Compliance Report Directly to the Board

Enterprise risk management is a key board responsibility, especially for global companies. Elite boards are increasingly following the lead of highly regulated industries, such as financial services, by changing the reporting lines of the chief compliance officer (CCO) directly to the board of directors.

A Deloitte report, highlighted in a June 1, 2015 *Agenda* article by Melissa J. Anderson shows that "21 percent of companies have a direct reporting relationship between the board and CCO ... Boards that maintain a direct connection with the CCO may put themselves in better graces with regulators if the company falls under government scrutiny. The reporting structure can also help protect boards from shareholder lawsuits that claim a breach of fiduciary duty." This habit can be viewed as an effective mechanism for enhancing transparency and fulfilling one of the board's key functions of overseeing enterprise risk management.

Habit 8: Engage Effectively with Investors

In today's hypercompetitive environment, the pressure on CEOs and boards has never been greater to develop a different mind-set about how they directly and effectively engage with investors, and activists.

Investors are more demanding than ever from insisting on proxy access to requesting a dialogue with key board members concerning the performance and strategic direction of the company. Pressure from activist investors have raised the stakes even higher. How a board (along with the CEO) responds and engages with these investors is vital. Note that one positive benefit of engagement is that it allows the company to educate investors.

Here are some clear guidelines and best practices on engaging with investors. The following comments assume that the CEO is also the Chairman. If these two positions are separate and the Chairman is non-executive, then that individual would represent the board.

- **Preparation is the key.** A company must be well prepared before any meeting is conducted.
- **The right team must be assembled.** The CEO and possibly the lead director should have substantial involvement. Outside advisors may also be required in certain circumstances. A spokesperson needs to be identified which is usually the CEO or possibly the lead director.
- **Listening is key.** The main objective is for the representatives of the company to listen to the investors' questions and concerns.
- **Speed is critical.** Speed is critical from assembling the team, to scripting what will be communicated, to responding to specific requests.
- **The right response.** A thoughtful and well-reasoned response is a must.

Habit 9: View the Board as a Team
Clearly, high performing teams get better results, and high performing boards get the same results. The only way to build a value creating board is by putting together a strong and effective board team. So, the same principles that apply

to building strong teams apply to boards. The four principles—as outlined in General McChrystal's groundbreaking book, *Team of Teams*—include: trust, common purpose, shared consciousness, and empowered execution. Let's examine these crucial elements as they apply to boards.

Trust. Elite boards are made-up of highly talented, successful, and insightful individuals. They bring tremendous skills and perspective—which benefit the enterprise they serve. Elite boards clearly understand the importance of building trust in the boardroom. Trust is so important that it is the cornerstone to creating a high performing and value creating board. Such an intangible attribute is, of course, built over many years of a board's working together. An important and effective mechanism is the "leadership staff ride" program that was mentioned earlier. I have seen wonderful results from this program. Other mechanisms are available as well, including the offsite strategy meeting that allows board members to spend considerable quality time together away from the board room.

Common Purpose. The purpose of the board is to oversee the activities of the company. Such a broad purpose includes specific and vital board expectations and functions such as the following: accountable and responsible for the CEO and succession planning; oversees enterprise risk; oversees strategic planning; oversees executive compensation; ensures a healthy culture underpinned by high ethical standards; ensures there's a strong and nimble governance framework; and are directly accountable to shareholders. Every board member needs to clearly understand this common purpose, and elite boards clearly do.

Shared Consciousness. This is defined in General McChrystal's book as, "... the way transparency and communication can be used in an organization to produce extraordinary outcomes across even large groups." [lx]. Elite boards like elite CEOs must build teams with total transparency and effective communications. Of course, one feeds the other beginning with how the CEO builds teams, which is the foundation the board builds upon. There are numerous mechanisms available for boards to ensure transparency and strong communications, including the following: conduct robust executive sessions; invite all board members at least once a year to committee meetings where they are not a member; chairman communicates periodically with the board on key matters as they occur throughout the year; board material is of the highest quality; best-of-class board assessment tools are effectively utilized; and requiring board members to visit at least annually a different business unit in order to gain firsthand exposure to management and the business.

Empowered Execution. Boards are obviously empowered by the shareholders to oversee the activities of the company. Thus, it's imperative that boards clearly understand their responsibilities and that each element of their responsibility is executed with excellence. This execution is how an elite board is built.

Habit 10: Create a Robust Lead Director Position
When the CEO is also the chairman of the board, it is essential (at least from a governance standpoint) that the

board appoint a strong independent lead director and that the respective duties of the position be clearly defined and understood. These duties should be disclosed in the proxy statement. The duties of the lead independent director would also apply to an independent chairman. Let's examine what the key duties are that should be clearly defined for this vital governance position. The following duties are in no particular order, but they are all important:

- Works in concert with the CEO/Chairman and other members of the Board, and is deeply involved in planning, reviewing, and approving board meeting agendas
- Advises and coordinates closely with the CEO/Chairman on meeting schedules and information sent to directors
- Chairs the executive sessions with the independent directors and develops topics to be discussed during the session
- Is empowered to call meetings of the independent directors as he or she deems appropriate. Presides at board meetings at which the chairman is absent or is unable to chair a meeting due to a possible conflict
- Is fully engaged with the CEO and other board members in ensuring that the board performs at the highest level; i.e. the board is creating value. Value means: the board is completely aligned with the CEO on strategy; the board assessments process is strong and well aligned with the requirements of the Governance Committee and the board, as a team, has a healthy culture; that each board member has

an absolute and clear understanding of their role and responsibility; that a director assessment process is in place and functioning properly; that director succession planning and development is aligned with the company's vision, purpose, values, and long-term strategy

- Provides constructive and unfiltered feedback to the CEO/Chairman on behalf of the board
- When appropriate, is available to communicate with major shareholders

Habit 11: Possess a Deep Knowledge of Board Responsibilities

The enterprise and the board are subject to the rapid pace of change and the turbulent environment in which both must operate, which is why it is imperative for all board members to possess a deep knowledge of these factors relative to best-of-class board responsibilities.

In his annual letter dated December 7, 2015, Martin Lipton— who is a renowned expert of corporate governance matters— provides his perspective on what is expected of boards. Lipton states, "The ever-evolving challenges facing boards of public companies prompts an updated snapshot of what is expected of them—not just the legal rules, but also the aspirational best practices that have almost as much influence on board and company behavior." The letter goes on to outline twenty bullet points of board expectations, but I will only cover the salient points here, segmented into two categories: the traditional role of boards and an updated, current view.

Traditional role of boards. Clearly, boards are responsible for choosing the CEO, monitoring his or her performance, and ensuring that a sound succession plan is in place. The board must also work with the management team to ensure the long-term success of the company. This means that the strategy must be right; it means that risk is appropriately managed; and that the right team is in place that can execute the strategy. The board must also ensure that a strong governance and compliance framework is in place and is working. Moreover, the board needs to ensure that the proper compensation plans are in place and that the board's performance (each individual member, the committees, and board overall) is strong.

Updated view of board responsibilities. In addition to the points that we just covered, boards today must focus more attention on planning for a crisis, ensuring that there's a healthy and strong culture in both the boardroom and the enterprise. They must also deal with the demands of activists and develop a better understanding of shareholder needs and perspectives. Moreover, boards should ensure that lifelines are being built for the future. More than ever, boards must clearly understand what creating shareholder value really means. Finally, boards today have raised the bar on board performance. This expectation means that elite board members must be recruited. With the ongoing escalation in the amount of work and time required to fulfill all the duties and responsibilities, only the right board members with strong skills can meet today's challenges.

CHAPTER 9

3 STRATEGIES OF ELITE BOARDS

The essence of strategy is choosing what not to do.
Michael Porter[lxi]

E lite Boards exhibit three essential strategy habits:

Habit 1: Build a Value-Creating Board
Habit 2: Form a Technology or Innovation Committee
Habit 3: View Digital Technology as a Transformative
Opportunity

Habit 1: Build a Value-Creating Board

Boards are often viewed as nothing more than a required governance mechanism. But the fact is great boards can create value and help the enterprise differentiate itself in the marketplace. My view, underpinned by decades of observing, studying, consulting, running, and participating in board meetings, is that a company's stock price is (or should be) a proxy for the board's performance. Unfortunately, sometimes boards do not fully understand their accountability or their value creation fiduciary responsibility to their shareholders.

The board has three primary, performance-linked responsibilities of the board tied to value creation: the CEOs performance and his/her related succession; supporting the strategy of the enterprise as outlined by the CEO and the management team; and overseeing risk, which includes governance.

Building and sustaining a value-creating board, however, is not easy. To do so, following the recipe elements outlined here is key. First, the right people must be at the board table. The board must be composed of members with a perfect blend of skills, perspective, and diversity. Getting this blend right takes a great deal of planning, deep knowledge, a robust process driven by strong leadership, and a lot of luck. Recent studies have shown that highly diverse and skilled boards perform at a higher level and create value.

Diversity means not only minorities and women, but also having members with different skills such as a digital director to address the digital disruption occurring in the marketplace. Such proactive enterprises are more adaptive and will outperform companies not keeping pace with today's digital explosion.

The next element in building a value-creating board requires boards to possess a deep knowledge of the company, the end-markets they serve, the competitive landscape, and the customers the enterprise serves. Since this responsibility is time consuming and requires great leadership, board members must be willing to commit a substantial amount of time to learn the industry and the company. The governance committee should monitor this learning curve to ensure that board members are fulfilling this key responsibility.

Third, there must be a culture of trust and respect in the board room. Creating a healthy culture takes tremendous skill and years to achieve. A strong and effective succession planning process is an essential element of this respect and trust. Sometimes board members may think they run the company or are responsible for strategy origination. No, the board's role is to oversee and support management and to challenge, protect, and approve decisions made by the enterprise. Board members should never forget their roles.

Fourth, board members must be fully prepared for every meeting (that means doing their "homework"), be fully engaged during the meeting, and not afraid to ask tough questions.

Fifth, the board must be led by either a strong non-executive chairman or a lead director, depending on whether the CEO also holds the chairman's title. Thus, the lead director or the non-executive chairman needs to be someone with a history of strong leadership. At times, directors are put into this leadership role through a perfunctory process, rather than through a generative thinking process. Making this mistake can have unintended consequences. Choosing a leader without going through a thoughtful process is like rolling the dice, and you could end up with a lead director guaranteed to fall short of expectations.

Finally, a strong board performance assessment process must be in place. Non-performing board members must be held accountable and, if necessary, replaced. Elite companies have implemented effective mechanisms to ensure that a robust assessment process is established. One mechanism is to hire an outside independent expert to conduct confidential individual interviews with board members. The normal process of having each director complete an assessment lacks the depth and confidentiality necessary to obtain the type of feedback necessary to elevate the board performance.

Habit 2: Form a Technology or Innovation Committee
In today's digital world, it's essential that boards possess a clear understanding of technology trends and its potential impact on the business. Exceptional boards are forming technology or innovation committees, and these elite companies are leading the way in understanding how technology can benefit enterprises in new and completely innovative ways. In fact, boards have an opportunity today to advocate for embarking on a strategic transformation of the company by fully embracing digital technology. This opportunity is further discussed in the next habit. The transformative and disruptive nature of technological innovation, and the real threat from cybersecurity all demand that boards think in new ways about how global enterprises are managed and governed.

When forming an innovation committee, members must have a strong grounding in technology and a good understanding of market trends. These requirements are necessary, so board members can ask the right questions and focus on the right areas for investment. Also, committee members should be required to attend an annual training class specifically centered on current and emerging technologies and risks. An effective innovation committee can benefit the board and the company in a multitude of ways.

Habit 3: View Digital Technology as a Transformative Opportunity

As stated in the previous habit, elite boards are forming technology or innovation committees. Some elite boards, however, are taking this mind-set to another level by viewing digital technology as a transformative opportunity. As we discussed in several parts of this book, Roper successfully transformed itself from an industrial company to a technology company by adopting this mind-set and, in the process, created substantial shareholder value. I have also highlighted how General Electric is building a relatively large software business. The opportunity is obviously available for many enterprises; it just requires boards and the leadership team to think differently about the company and its competitive position.

In the February 13, 2017 edition of *Agenda*, the author Tim Bridges captures the essence of this emerging and important elite habit. Here are some key excerpts, "Clearly, any business that neglects to consider the promise of digital technology leaves opportunities on the table, meaning it might not be acting in the best interest of shareholders. Digital technology should be understood as a business transformation opportunity that underpins every single process, operation and interaction across the organization."

He goes on to say, "Mastering digital technology today is not about dreaming up the next great app or pursuing a few strategic hires ... It requires a board of directors ready and willing to rethink their own role as one that empowers their organizations and challenges the status quo." And finally, the article points out that "To make the transition ... boards should acknowledge that both people and processes will need to change, and some of these important shifts require board-level direction."

So, how does a company transform itself using digital technology? I will highlight some basic building blocks that should be considered as guidelines by an enterprise in its quest to transform itself. A good place to start is to study enterprises that have successfully achieved this amazing transformative change. Second, the leadership team needs to re-examine its business model and core purpose. Third, boards need to rethink the composition of board members and bring in digital directors as well as directors that have been involved in successful transformations. Fourth, an effective technology committee must also be involved to not only provide insight and perspective to the leadership team, but also to report regularly to the board. Lastly, the board should encourage the leadership team to seek outside partners and experts that can assist with the transformation.

CHAPTER 10

7 EXECUTION HABITS OF ELITE BOARDS

Having just the vision's no solution,
everything depends on execution.
Stephen Sondheim[lxii]

Elite Boards exhibit seven essential execution habits, including:

Habit 1: Succession Planning Beyond the CEO
Habit 2: Optimize the Board of Directors Structure
Habit 3: Excel at Board Succession Planning
Habit 4: Act Like a Private Equity Board
Habit 5: Assess CEO Performance with Facts
Habit 6: Create an Effective Development Plan
Habit 7: Shed Board Seats

Habit 1: Succession Planning Beyond the CEO

Elite leaders and enterprises all understand that a robust leadership-development and talent-management process for succession planning is an exceptional capability that separates the elite from everyone else. A highly effective succession planning process takes considerable resources in both time and money. Elite companies don't view this commitment as a cost but as an opportunity to build a world class organization.

Succession planning—particularly the job of preparing for CEO succession—is also one of the most critical responsibilities of the board of directors. It has never been more relevant than it is today. Although most companies have some form of succession planning in place, the evidence shows that too often these plans fall short because they are too shallow or outdated or simply ineffective.

Elite boards ensure a total focus on building an organization prepared to endure for generations. They clearly understand that extraordinary results are derived from a world class succession planning process and that it underpins the long-term health and viability of the enterprise. So, what are some of exceptional habits of elite boards, beyond CEO succession planning? Here are some key elements:

- Succession planning covers the entire C-suite and at least one layer below, but it is not unusual to see planning mapped out for two layers below the executive leadership group.
- Succession planning must be thoughtful and comprehensive in nature.

- Succession planning must be viewed as a process, and it must be driven by the CEO. The CEO should own talent-management and leadership-development. The board is responsible for overseeing the process and is directly responsible for the CEO, but ultimately the entire process must be owned by the CEO since the future of the company depends on the viability of the plan.

- On an annual basis, the board should conduct an in-depth review of the company's succession plan. The review should be done with the CEO and, at times, might include key senior officers. It is the CEO's job to provide insight on each key seat in the form of a written summary and a verbal report.

- A world class succession plan ensures that the company is never forced to recruit the CEO from the outside. When a company recruits from the outside, it usually means that that the board has fallen short of its most important responsibility. This failure can be avoided by implementing a high quality, sustainable succession plan that ensures a consistent large pool of candidates who have a deep passion for the company's core purpose, its core values, and its business model. The plan also ensures that selected candidates are developed over a period of decades. Some companies have a pool of about 25 potential candidates with the best candidates emerging over time.

- The board and the CEO should have a robust dialogue about the most desirable competencies and

characteristics of a future CEO and use this profile
to measure all potential candidates against it.

- The succession plan must be well organized with
  essential information, such as: Which executives are
  ready immediately to step into a new position;
  which executives will be ready in the near-term
  (one to three years); which high potential key
  employees will be ready in the future (three to five
  years); and perhaps which high potential candidates
  will be ready beyond five years.

- The succession plan includes detailed development
  plans for each potential successor and should
  include such elements as stretch assignments,
  overseas experience, mentoring, and specific
  internal university and external training. Star
  candidates should be provided with indispensable
  experiences, including running a large business, so
  they are well developed for their next key
  assignment.

- The CEO development plan should also ensure that
  the culture of the company is embedded in the DNA
  of each potential future leader.

- Also, built into the plan are key metrics such as the
  number of key seats filled with the right people
  along with a metric-based assessment of each
  candidate.

- The independent directors should meet in executive
  session to discuss the CEO succession plan.

Habit 2: Optimize the Board of Directors Structure
The average board size of large companies is about eleven.
I believe that a board can be more effective and create more
value by optimizing the structure to include perhaps eight
to nine members. Smaller boards tend to be nimble and
highly focused which usually results in better performance.
Currently, some elite companies do operate very effectively
with a smaller board —these include both Apple and
Netflix. Although this structure poses a few staffing
challenges for the board's three key committees, the
benefits of a smaller board can greatly outweigh this
relatively minor concern. A smaller board simply requires
some directors to serve on two committees instead of one,
but the upside is that such a structure increases engagement
and focus. Another benefit is corporate overhead costs.
Smaller boards obviously cost less. So the benefit of less
costs and greater performance is a recipe for value creation.

The Wall Street Journal published an article on this
thought on August 26, 2014, titled "Smaller Boards Get
Bigger Results." Here are some excerpts from the article by
Joann S. Lublin that provides important insight into the
benefits of a smaller board:

> Companies with fewer board members reap
> considerably greater rewards for their investors,
> according to a new study by governance researchers
> GMI Ratings prepared for The Wall Street Journal.
> Small boards at major corporations foster deeper
> debates and more nimble decision-making,
> directors, recruiters and researchers said ... Among
> companies with a market capitalization of at least
> $10 billion, typically those with the smallest boards

produced substantially better shareholder returns over a three-year period between the spring of 2011 and 2014 when compared with companies with the biggest boards, the GMI analysis of nearly 400 companies showed. Companies with small boards outperformed their peers by 8.5 percentage points, while those with large boards underperformed peers by 10.85 percentage points. The smallest board averaged 9.5 members, compared with fourteen for the largest. The average size was 11.2 directors for all companies studied, GMI said ... It's tough to pinpoint precisely why board size affects corporate performance, but smaller boards at large-cap companies like Apple and Netflix Inc. appear to be decisive, cohesive and hands-on. Such boards typically have informal meetings and few committees.[lxiii]

Habit 3: Excel at Board Succession Planning

Succession planning for the board should be viewed with the same lens as succession planning within the enterprise. The main objective is to build a team that wins! Fulfilling this goal is no easy feat, but elite companies have developed the right formula or recipe for building a value-creating board. Here are some of the most important elements that make up that successful recipe.

The governance and nominating committee, along with the chairman and CEO, should design an effective internal sourcing system for board candidates. An effective sourcing system should identify candidates who have the perfect blend of backgrounds. The internal sourcing system should be augmented by outside professional board search firms to help identify high quality candidates.

The required skills of potential board members should be carefully analyzed and dialogued. A matrix of desirable skills should include candidates with diverse backgrounds such as digital, international, innovation, leadership, private equity, and numerous other important skills necessary to build a value-creating board. Prospective board members must possess and demonstrate some key characteristics, such as critical thinking, sound judgment, and insightful perspective. These desired skills should be compared to the board's current gap analysis to determine if a candidate might fill that gap. This gap analysis should also take into consideration the future state of the business and what skills the board will need in the future that align with the strategic direction of the company.

The succession planning process should embrace diversity including women and minority candidates. A highly diverse board benefits the enterprise in a multitude of ways including enhancing the culture and performance of the board and ultimately that of the company they serve.

Succession planning for the board should also be tied to the long-term strategy of the enterprise. It is imperative that the composition of the board has the right blend of skills and backgrounds to serve the future state of the company. The wrong board member impacts the enterprise negatively just as profoundly as the wrong choice for senior executive. Poor board selections can dilute the overall performance of the board and adversely impact the board's culture. Boards need to avoid this misstep by implementing a highly effective and robust board succession process.

Habit 4: Act Like a Private Equity Board

One of many exceptional habits of private equity is the way their boards function. Private equity boards have a sharp focus on key metrics, strategy, specific goals, and leadership execution. They focus on making a company better, that is, taking a good company and transforming it into a great company. They concentrate on value creation through relentless focus on operational execution, meeting and exceeding specified targets, and ensuring that the right leadership is in place.

Although these habits can be found in many public company boards, the main difference from my point of view is the intensity and relentless focus of private equity firms. Such focus is, of course, facilitated by two essential facts. First, private equity boards tend to be much smaller which makes them nimbler and arguably more effective. And second, private equity board members are more hands-on because they are usually heavily invested in the company. I believe that public company boards should adopt many of private equity's highly effective practices such increasing the equity ownership requirement and building a smaller board. Such a relentless focus on key metrics would likely drive elite leadership execution.

Habit 5: Assess CEO Performance with Facts

Nothing is more important for the board than their responsibility to ensure CEO performance. In carrying out this vital responsibility, boards should be composed of directors with tremendous insight, perspective, and critical thinking skills. When boards think about assessing the performance of the CEO, it's crucial that they weigh facts from multiple sources to determine the effectiveness of the CEO. Members should not rely on attribution or anecdotal evidence, but should instead rely on a more substantiated performance assessment based on the following elements being in place:

- A sound process that has yielded strong results over the years
- A CEO self-evaluation memorandum with supporting charts written by the CEO and addressed to the board; the document needs to be both qualitative and quantitative
- Key performance metrics that are agreed to in advance and are clear and focused on performance, such as financial/operational/strategic
- Examination of critical intangible characteristics of the CEO including instinct, leadership abilities, communication skills, and many others
- A feedback mechanism that provides assessment information directly from each board member, and
- A measurement of the reputation and brand of company

Boards should be careful about putting too much reliance on information obtained in the following ways:

- A 360-degree evaluation of the CEO can be helpful if done correctly but it can also include a fair amount of cognitive bias
- Input from directors that is based solely on emotions and attribution as opposed to unimpeachable facts

- Feedback from executives one level below the CEO, from whom the information can be useful feedback but be self-serving if not done correctly
- Analysts' comments should be carefully scrutinized and understood because they only see the company through one lens
- Any anecdotal and attribution comments, no matter the source, must be viewed with skepticism because these comments can be counterproductive and, at times, destructive

An effective and insightful CEO evaluation process is indispensable because any undeserving action taken by the board against the CEO can put the company on a potentially dangerous path from which it may not recover.

Habit 6: Create an Effective Development Plan
Elite boards understand the importance of having each board member involved in a strong and effective development plan. It's imperative that each director be provided with a detailed learning and continuous improvement plan that not only benefits the director but also the enterprise. Some key elements that should be included in an effective development plan are listed below:

- A detailed program that provides significant insight into the business. Directors need a deep understanding of the business, the competitive landscape, and the end-markets. This insight is particularly important for board members without an operations background or members from a totally unrelated industry or have joined the board from the professional services' ranks.

- At least annually, the board should augment the above program with at least an annual visit to one of the operating locations of the business, so the board can see first-hand the operations and interact directly with the management team.
- If possible, board members should attend a global leadership or top 100 meeting annually.
- As part of one of the board meetings, the board should participate in some high level quarterly operating results review meetings with the senior management of the company.
- Each board member should attend, at least bi-annually, an outside training program.
- Each board member should also attend, if possible, a leadership-development program of the company, such as a staff ride.

Habit 7: Shed Board Seats

The amount of time required when serving on a public company board continues to increase due to a number of factors including the significant increase in regulations, the amount of work required in key committees such as audit and compensation, the amount of preparation time before a board meeting, and the need to participate in the offsite strategic planning meetings. As a result, elite boards are tightening corporate governance guidelines to reduce the number of public board seats that members can hold.

While it is difficult to provide specific numbers on how many boards someone should serve on, given the outsized commitment of time required to serve with distinction on a value creating board, perhaps an optimum number is perhaps two to three board seats. It might be possible, however, to serve on as many as four given the right mix of companies. I believe it would be difficult for someone to perform at optimum level while serving on five public company boards. Finally, it should be noted that among my network of other board members, some people take action on their own to reduce the number directorships in response to this new dynamic.

SECTION 4

IMPLEMENTATION TOOL KIT

*Leaders establish the vision for the future
and set the strategy for getting there.*
John P. Kotter[lxiv]

The journey to achieve elite status is arduous but possible by following the management framework outlined in this book. Just as mountaineers rely on a tool kit to help them climb the highest summits, the same principle applies to leaders who want to take their enterprise to the top and be recognized as an elite company. Section 4 provides a tool kit that consists of both checklists and frequently asked questions.

Exceptional habits, as discussed earlier in the book, support three essential foundational pillars: leadership, strategy, and execution. Enterprises, leaders, and boards that focus on these three areas (in addition to an awareness of luck spread, another foundational pillar) have a clear path to achieving elite status. Here are the three sets of exceptional habits required of leaders, enterprises and boards that will be covered in Section 4:

Chapter 11: Checklist—Exceptional Habits of Elite Leaders. In this chapter, all exceptional habits of elite leaders and CEOs are summarized in checklist format as they appear in this book with key salient points added as well. There is a total of thirty-eight habits of elite leaders.

Chapter 12: Checklist—Exceptional Habits of Elite Enterprise. In this chapter, all exceptional habits of elite organizations are summarized in checklist format as they appear in the book with key salient points added as well. There is a total of forty-three habits of elite enterprises.

Chapter 13: Checklist—Exceptional Habits of Elite Boards. In this chapter, all exceptional habits of elite boards are summarized in checklist format as they appear in the book with key salient points added as well. There is a total of twenty-one habits of elite boards.

An additional important tool to implementing the management framework outlined in this book comes in the form of frequently asked questions. The questions are all derived from my leadership experiences, advisory practice, board experiences, and research of elite companies. These FAQs are covered in Chapter 14.

Chapter 14: Frequently Asked Questions—Lifelines Principles and Elite Habits. This chapter provides detailed answers to questions arising from implementing the lifelines leadership framework and the building blocks, which are the exceptional habits.

CHAPTER 11

CHECKLIST—EXCEPTIONAL HABITS OF ELITE LEADERS

To do great things is difficult;
but to command great things is more difficult.
Friedrich Nietzsche[lxv]

Beginning in Section 1, I detailed the top thirty-eight exceptional habits of elite leaders. This checklist provides a quick, bullet point summary of each habit that summarizes the most salient points from these discussions. You should use this checklist as an implementation guide to help you begin the process of incorporating these habits into your daily practice on your journey to becoming an elite leader. The habits included in this chapter include:

- 20 Leadership Habits of Elite Leaders

- 8 Strategy Habits of Elite Leaders

- 10 Execution Habits of Elite Leaders

20 Leadership Habits of Elite Leaders

Habit 1: Manifest Integrity in Every Action, Every Word, and Every Deed

- ☐ Integrity above all will define you as a person and as a leader.
- ☐ Integrity means doing the right things, for the right reasons, in the right way.
- ☐ Integrity and ethical behavior is the cornerstone of building your brand of one.
- ☐ A leader's bond with other people is only as good as the leader's words and actions.
- ☐ A leader must have the moral courage to do the right thing.

Habit 2: Build Your Brand of One

- ☐ Don't be like everybody else.
- ☐ Build your brand of one and differentiate yourself— be authentic.
- ☐ Be reflective and creative and develop a long-term plan for building your brand.
- ☐ Utilize the personal lifelines and the exceptional habits of elite leaders to build your brand.
- ☐ Manifest a deep passion for everything that you do.

Habit 3: Go with Your Instinct—It Will Never Fail You

- ☐ Your innate ability or sixth sense should never be ignored.

☐ Discipline and critical thinking capabilities can help you better understand and strengthen your reliance on instinct.

☐ Major lessons learned on both successes and failures can usually be traced to relying or not relying on your instinct (respectively).

☐ Take proactive actions as a follow through mechanism to rely on your instincts.

Habit 4: Treat All People Equally and With Respect

☐ Treat everyone equally and with respect, no matter their position or standing.

☐ People may forget what you accomplished during your career, but they will certainly never forget how you treated them.

☐ Your behavior must be sincere and authentic; it must come from the heart.

☐ Equal treatment is a critical component of building your brand of one.

Habit 5: Allow for a Period of Inner Reflection and Growth

☐ At least annually, allow for a period of inner reflection; the period allocated needs to be meaningful.

☐ Step back and see the bigger picture, see the landscape through a different lens.

☐ Common sense approach, all underpinned by critical thinking capabilities, is vital to the inner reflection experience.

☐ Inner reflection should result in new perspectives gained and actionable decisions made.

☐ Personal growth should also be an outcome of the inner reflection experience.

Habit 6: Be inquisitive and Develop Critical Thinking Capabilities

☐ It's important to always ask why, why, why? Never assume or take anything for granted.

☐ Learn to value facts that are unimpeachable; validate important matters yourself.

☐ Don't make decisions based on emotions, rumors, innuendoes, or attribution.

☐ Critical thinking improves judgment because it is purposeful and reflective.

☐ Inquisitiveness and critical thinking can provide the ability to see things that others perhaps can't see.

Habit 7: Display a Proactive Mind-set and Bias for Action

☐ Successful leaders are proactive and not reactive; it's important to control events and not let events control you!

☐ Proactive mind-set and a bias for action needs to be underpinned by discipline.

☐ Proactive actions are essential for building a successful and sustainable career.

☐ Discipline keeps you focused on the right things at the right time.

☐ Discipline and integrity form the cornerstone for building your exceptional brand of one.

Habit 8: Deliver on Your Commitments

- ☐ Disciplined people consistently deliver on what they promise; they skillfully manage expectations.
- ☐ Commitments are fulfilled through strong execution capabilities and an unshakeable faith in your abilities.
- ☐ Practice extreme commitment to delivering on expectations.
- ☐ When there's a rare miss, you must have the courage to apologize and learn from the experience.
- ☐ Disciplined people understand the difference between responsibility and accountability.

Habit 9: Maintain an Unwavering Faith and Exhibit Equanimity

- ☐ Always maintain an unwavering faith in your abilities, no matter the circumstance.
- ☐ Be resolute and steadfast in your conviction, so you will prevail.
- ☐ Stay cool, calm, and collected regardless of the situation.
- ☐ Exhibit clear thinking and quiet confidence and confront all challenges.

Habit 10: Learn to Listen and Learn to Stop Doing

- ☐ Stop talking and start listening; you learn more about a person by carefully listening.
- ☐ Your stop-doing list is more important than your to-do list.

☐ Stop doing extraneous things and focus on the critical.

Habit 11: Master the Art of Communication

☐ Articulate your message with passion and authenticity; the message must be pithy.

☐ Effective communication can sometimes be the difference between success and failure.

☐ Great communicators are all wonderful storytellers.

☐ Communicating effectively takes years of practice, discipline, and focus; it's a skill that can be developed.

Habit 12: Deal Effectively with Adversity

☐ A qualitative measure of leadership strength is managing effectively through tremendous adversity.

☐ Adversity can come in many different forms, and it can be segmented into seven major categories.

☐ You can learn a great deal from studying experiences of elite leaders on how they successfully handled adversity.

Habit 13: Know what to Do and What Not to Do

☐ Knowing what to and what not to do are equally important.

☐ Learn to rely on instinct, perspective, critical thinking, and unassailable facts in order to make sound decisions.

☐ When deciding on what not to do, it's important to also develop a stop-doing list.

Habit 14: Think Before You Speak

- ☐ Words really do mean something.
- ☐ It's critical that leaders think before speaking because their words can have an outsized impact on the culture, purpose, and values of the enterprise.
- ☐ Avoid conflicting and confusing messages.
- ☐ Deliver consistency and clarity of message by developing a sound communication plan.

Habit 15: Show That You Are Interested

- ☐ Leaders must consistently demonstrate that they are interested in their people.
- ☐ Interest can be manifested in many ways, but it must always be authentic.
- ☐ Engagement, recognition, and celebration are just a few ways to demonstrate interest.

Habit 16: Be Passionate About Learning and Development

- ☐ Leaders must have a deep passion for learning and continuous self-improvement.
- ☐ It's important for leaders to be proactive, disciplined, and focused in their quest for improvement.
- ☐ Much can be learned from studying elite leaders and their habits on self-improvement.

Habit 17: Demonstrate Gratitude

- ☐ Leaders must be grateful for their teams and the commitment they demonstrate to the enterprise.

- ☐ Willingness to express gratitude is an important habit of a leader.
- ☐ Gratitude must come from the heart, and it must be viewed as authentic.

Habit 18: Adopt the "Buffett" Management Approach

- ☐ Warren Buffett has had an outsized impact on business, and his habits are truly worth learning. These include:
  - o A laser focus on capital allocation, all underpinned by tremendous discipline
  - o Rarely selling acquired companies and holding them with a long-term view
  - o Creating a framework of freedom, responsibility, and accountability that produces results
  - o A distaste for bureaucracy
  - o Avoiding anything that can spike the stock price in the short-term

Habit 19: Adopt the "Jobs" Management Approach

- ☐ Steve Jobs has also had outsized impact on business, and his habits are a must study for leaders: These include:
  - o Passion and an inimitable instinct; he saw things that others simply could not see
  - o Belief in product simplicity and design, with a laser focus on the global supply chain to deliver all the products as efficiently and effectively as possible

- o An innovative business model that disrupted multiple industries
- o Going to extraordinary lengths to deliver or exceed expectations
- o Building a team of all A-Players; he was intolerant of mediocrity
- ☐ Simply stated, he built the best company on the planet

Habit 20: Adopt the "Pessina" Management Approach

- ☐ Stefano Pessina, unlike Buffett and Jobs, is not a household name, but he has consistently demonstrated effective habits of elite leaders. His habits include:
    - o An unblemished track record and building a solid gold reputation underpinned by consistent superior performance
    - o Consistently manifesting an inimitable vision and ability to make it a reality
    - o Always remaining highly focused, disciplined, and proactive, with the adaptability to change
    - o An uncanny ability to successfully complete acquisitions and improve on their performance

8 Strategy Habits of Elite Leaders

Habit 1: Embed an Entrepreneurial Spirit in the Organization

- ☐ Embed entrepreneurial spirit to provide organization with a distinct competitive advantage.
- ☐ Build, retain, and motivate an entrepreneurial management team to drive superior performance.
- ☐ Exhibit entrepreneurial great ability to create change, be flexible, and cultivate a thriving work environment.
- ☐ Do not impose many rules or bury team members in bureaucracy.

Habit 2: Create and Sustain a Startup Mind-set

- ☐ Support being nimble and in a continuous state of innovation; must be adaptable.
- ☐ Empower teams to do great things.
- ☐ Encourage enterprise connection among all team members and practices extreme commitment to the cause.
- ☐ Ensure team members collaborate and are proactive; builds evident trust among team members.
- ☐ Ensure everyone in the company has a deep passion for the core purpose, core values, and business model.

Habit 3: Exhibit a War Mind-set

- ☐ Believe it is best to possess superior power to win battles and, ultimately, the war.

- ☐ Understand military rule that in battle, you do not want a fair fight.
- ☐ Understand that overwhelming power provides a significant competitive advantage.
- ☐ Believe in the power of superb execution through building a cadre of extraordinary people and having an exceptional strategy.

Habit 4: Ensure Your Successor is a Success

- ☐ Take substantive action to ensure that an incoming leader has every chance to succeed.
- ☐ Provide at a minimum the five basic lifelines to a newly appointed leader.
- ☐ Turn over to successor a company with a healthy and distinctive culture.
- ☐ Assemble and turn over to successor an exceptional management team.

Habit 5: Create an Environment that Fosters Creativity and Innovation

- ☐ Ensure creativity and innovation exist in the organization.
- ☐ Create an environment that fosters and rewards creativity and innovation.
- ☐ Be the chief creativity and innovation officer, must lead by example.
- ☐ Hire the best and brightest and create an innovation framework that allows creativity and innovation to flourish.
- ☐ Learn the habits of the most creative and innovative leaders.

Habit 6: Learn Leadership Habits from the Military

☐ Embrace and implement the "staff ride" executive leadership-development program that provides deep insight by military personnel on such important matters as strategy, training, planning, leadership-development, lines of command, purpose, team unity, trust, innovation, learning, the need for overwhelming power.

☐ Use staff ride program to build team unity and company culture.

☐ Gain valuable business lessons from studying decisions that were made by generals and other battlefield commanders.

Habit 7: Develop an Audacious Turnaround Plan

☐ Even elite companies stumble and fall from the summit. Develop an audacious plan when brought in to turn a company around; it's imperative to think big.

☐ Always think big. Enterprises that fail to think big usually end up with a series of plans that span a long horizon with minimal impact.

☐ Use to your advantage the "100-day" plan (honeymoon period) for newly appointed leaders to develop a strategic plan to revive the company.

☐ Use superb execution to make substantive progress in the first 100 days.

Habit 8: Build an Enduring Enterprise

☐ Understand that elite enterprises are built over a long period, usually measured in decades, and that enduring companies will transcend multiple leaders.

☐ Build a prodigious number of lifelines so the enterprise can withstand any unexpected shocks or series of shocks. The lifelines include:

  o Ample cash reserves
  o Highly rated balance sheet
  o Consistent and disciplined investment in people and the company
  o Sustaining a superior culture
  o Leadership-development and talent-management programs
  o A clear core purpose
  o Strong core values
  o Exceptional operational capabilities
  o Investment in innovation and an innovation culture
  o Effective and nimble governance framework
  o Building teams that win
  o A performance culture that creates value at all levels

10 Execution Habits of Elite Leaders

Habit 1: Act Quickly and Decisively

☐ Understand that change in the business environment is occurring at unprecedented speed.

☐ Elite enterprises act quickly and decisively.

☐ Develop instinct, deep business knowledge, and perspective as essential characteristics to help you choose wisely when making quick decisions.

☐ Act quickly and decisively when a crisis or a significant shock develops.

Habit 2: Stand Your Ground When Challenged

☐ Since leaders are constantly challenged from a multitude of sources, it is crucial that leaders stand their ground, particularly if the challenges involve ethics or the enterprise's financial health.

☐ Price reductions challenges, particularly those from customers, should be resisted with steadfast determination since capitulation can take the enterprise down a path that it will likely regret.

☐ If a leader must capitulate, at a minimum there must be some form of *quid pro quo*.

Habit 3: Live the Inverted Pyramid

☐ Use an inverted pyramid management concept that puts the frontline troops first and the C-level executives at the lowest level.

- ☐ Understand that frontline customer-facing employees are crucial to the success of the company.
- ☐ Effective leaders work to clear unnecessary obstacles so that the frontline troops can perform their jobs optimally.

Habit 4: Be the Top Salesperson in the Organization

- ☐ The CEO is the face and voice of the company, and so he or she must be the top salesperson in the organization.
- ☐ Support customer visits that are an integral part of a leader's playbooks.
- ☐ Apply the ability to be the most effective salesperson in closing a deal when needed, but also knows when they are there to sell and when they are there to listen and learn from the customer.
- ☐ Use sales ability with everyone including customers, the board of directors, shareholders, employees, and the many other constituencies.

Habit 5: Focus on Indispensable CEO Metrics

- ☐ Understand the challenges of selecting the most effective measures for managing the business and keep an elite focus on growth in revenues, margins, and free cash flow.
- ☐ Focus on the critical lifeline of the balance sheet.
- ☐ Segment metrics into operating performance and business valuation.

Habit 6: Guard Against Attribution

- ☐ Leaders must guard against blind attribution because it can lead to flawed decisions.
- ☐ Mechanisms must be implemented that guard the facts and dispense with the attribution.
- ☐ Use after-action reviews as a powerful mechanism to provide unfiltered and unbiased feedback on both successes and failures.

Habit 7: Be Intolerant of Mediocrity

- ☐ Leaders need to be intolerant of mediocrity; they must expect the best.
- ☐ Keep an intense focus on hiring the best and brightest.
- ☐ Implement a robust talent-management and leadership-development framework to build a world-class team of A-Players.

Habit 8: Utilize the Quarterly State of the Business Report

- ☐ Sometimes the most basic habits are the most important.
- ☐ CEO should personally write state of the business quarterly report.
- ☐ Keep reports succinct, insightful, and provides a broad perspective.
- ☐ Create a report that is both quantitative and qualitative and one that captures the essence of what is transpiring in the company.

Habit 9: Empower Your Employees

- ☐ Understand the effectiveness of employee empowerment.
- ☐ Work to free people from bureaucratic policies and practices.
- ☐ Push decision making down to individuals and teams.
- ☐ Implement appropriate mechanisms to ensure empowerment is embedded in the organization.

Habit 10: Develop an Obsessive Focus on Survival

- ☐ Leaders must obsess on surviving the so-called Death Zone.
- ☐ Be prepared for unexpected events well before they happen.
- ☐ Build an abundance of lifelines.
- ☐ Skillfully manage risks and uncertainties and effectively scan the environment for brewing storms.

CHAPTER 12

CHECKLIST—EXCEPTIONAL HABITS OF ELITE ENTERPRISES

The quality of a person's life is in direct proportion to their commitment to excellence, regardless of their chosen field of endeavor.
Vince Lombardi[lxvi]

Beginning in Section 2, I detailed the top forty-three exceptional habits of elite enterprise. This checklist provides a quick, bullet point summary of each habit that summarizes the most salient points from these discussions. You should use this checklist as an implementation guide to help you begin the process of incorporating these habits into your daily practice on your journey to becoming an elite enterprise. The habits included in this chapter include:

- 12 Leadership Habits of Elite Enterprises
- 14 Strategy Habits of Elite Enterprises
- 17 Execution Habits of Elite Enterprises

12 Leadership Habits of Elite Enterprises

Habit 1: Appoint a Digital Advisory Board

☐ Understand that an effective digital strategy is indispensable in building an elite enterprise.

☐ Create a digital advisory board with a clear purpose and an appropriate governance framework.

☐ Assess the effectiveness of the advisory board at least annually.

☐ Recruit digital directors and establish alliances with key technology partners.

Habit 2: Don't Make One Large Bet, Make Small Targeted Investments

☐ Understand that it is better to make a series of small bets rather than one large bet; make smaller bets on areas that may seem speculative.

☐ Make key investment decisions with a laser-like focus and discipline.

☐ Expand investment commitments in a building block fashion based on gained experience.

Habit 3: Create a High Energy Annual Shareholders' Meeting

☐ Make the annual shareholders' meeting a celebration, underpinned by high energy; example is Berkshire Hathaway's annual meeting, which is a paragon of excellence.

☐ The meeting should be carefully planned and
scripted by professionals to realize maximum
benefit.

Habit 4: Do Not Be Afraid to Fail, But Fail Fast and Well

☐ Understand that not being afraid to fail is essential
to creativity and innovation.

☐ Understand that failing fast and well is the new
paradigm in innovation because it minimizes the
impact on the organization.

Habit 5: Appoint a Strong Number Two

☐ Develop an exceptional number two leader in the
organization identified from either the COO
position or the CFO position or a business segment
president.

☐ Understand that appointing an indispensable
number two is important for succession planning
and executing effectively the strategic plan.

Habit 6: Excel at Communications

☐ Understand that effective and focused
communication plan is an essential lifeline for an
enterprise.

☐ Develop a well-crafted communication plan and put
it as a top, professionally managed priority.

☐ Understand that a professionally managed plan is
indispensable and can be the difference between
success and failure.

Habit 7: Stop Providing Earnings Guidance

- ☐ Provide only annual earnings guidance and stop providing quarterly guidance.
- ☐ Issue an 8-K explaining any large expectation gap during any given quarter while at the same time reaffirming the annual number.

Habit 8: Elevate the Chief Information Officer Position

- ☐ Put the CIO position at the same level as the CFO.
- ☐ Have the CIO report directly to the CEO.
- ☐ Understand the new digital age requires a new mind-set to deal with the competition.
- ☐ Understand that appointing an effective CIO impacts positively the overall performance of the company and helps to generate more revenues by improving productivity and efficiency.

Habit 9: Focus on Diversity

- ☐ Diversity is an important component to building an elite enterprise.
- ☐ Build diverse teams and understand that such teams are more innovative, creative and positively impact financial performance.
- ☐ Implement key mechanisms that allow diversity to become deeply rooted in the organization.

Habit 10: Appoint and Empower a Global Leadership Team

- ☐ Put a superior team in place to build and sustain an elite company.

☐ Understand talented people have an outsized positive impact on the performance of the company.

☐ Identify, build, and develop a global leadership team.

☐ Build and sustain an effective talent-management and leadership-development system.

☐ Fill the global leadership team with the right people in the right seats.

Habit 11: Stop with the Serial "Adjusted" Earnings

☐ Develop a stop-doing list that includes eliminating the serial adjusted earnings mind-set.

☐ Understand that one-time adjustments must be both truly unusual (non-recurring) and material in amount.

☐ Perform both a qualitative and quantitative analysis when determining if an event is truly a one-time adjustment.

☐ Serial practice of adjusted earnings is slowly undermining generally accepted accounting principles.

Habit 12: Go Private

☐ Understand that public companies are at a disadvantage because of the obligation to disclose competitive information and the quarterly earnings obsession of the market.

☐ Understand that private markets are friendlier and less scrutinized and that the cost of being a public company continues to increase.

☐ Consider private equity as an effective mechanism to take a company private.

14 Strategy Habits of Elite Enterprises

Habit 1: Build A Value Creating Corporate Center

☐ Recognize that value creation process begins with having the right mind-set and that a corporate center must add value to the portfolio of businesses.

☐ Understand that arrogant, bureaucratic, allocation of high overhead costs can be value destroying as are highly centralized decision-making, excess staff and an old-style office design.

☐ Emphasize the value of entrepreneurial, lean staffing, less bureaucracy, and encourage decentralized decision making along with modern office design.

☐ Use a corporate center to showcase its innovative business model, core philosophy, robust strategic planning process, exceptional capabilities such as mergers and acquisitions, disciplined and sound capital allocation, nimble governance, entrepreneurial culture, value creating board, and an optimized cost structure.

Habit 2: Create a Unique and Sustainable Competitive Position

☐ Recognize their unique position must be captured within the business model, including the recipe and the organizational structure.

☐ Build organizational structure to efficiently execute each crucial element of their fully articulated recipe.

☐ Keep recipe to approximately eight to twelve elements.

- ☐ Understand that recipe elements can usually be identified by reading and studying CEO letters to shareholders, annual reports, 10-K filings, and analyst presentations.
- ☐ Learn about competitors and how other elite companies are built by studying their recipes.

Habit 3: Build Formidable Intangible Assets

- ☐ Understand that key intangible assets drive culture and exceptional performance and that human capital is the most important intangible asset.
- ☐ Recognize other critical intangible assets including superior brands, patents, trademarks, and knowledge-based solutions.
- ☐ Build teams that win; it starts with hiring the right people.
- ☐ Build a diverse portfolio of powerful brands that can transform a company and an industry.

Habit 4: Be Audacious with Transformations and Restructurings

- ☐ Avoid being a serial restructurer; be audacious when undertaking a major transformation or restructuring.
- ☐ Develop a thoughtful and well-conceived, long game plan that is audacious and pays off quicker and more effectively than a cautious approach.
- ☐ Study and learn from other elite companies that were successfully transformed or restructured.

Habit 5: Differentiate with Disruptive Innovation

☐ Recognize that innovation is one of the most important lifelines of an organization and that without innovation, a company will eventually wither away and become irrelevant.

☐ Apply technology and innovation throughout the organization to derive a competitive advantage.

☐ Create tremendous shareholder value through transformative innovations.

Habit 6: Use a New Model for Creativity and Innovation

☐ Understand that creating a start-up environment that fosters creativity and innovation is extremely difficult, but that the rewards can be significant.

☐ Some non-tech elite companies have launched programs inside their company to create in-house startups and recognize these new entities infuse an entrepreneurial mind-set in the organization.

☐ Implement effective mechanisms to create and sustain a creative environment.

Habit 7: Properly Segment Platforms

☐ Constantly perform a deep dive on your competitive position by reviewing each business platform.

☐ Use the four-part quadrant tool—elite brands, cherished jewels, emerging starts, and flashing lights—to determine where each business platform fits.

☐ Underpin quadrant analysis with free cash flow evaluation.

Habit 8: Build an Internal Venture Group

☐ Recognize that internal venture groups can expand the reach of the company and accelerate innovation.

☐ Use new ventures to provide an opportunity to be exposed to new business models and open new markets to grow revenues.

☐ Consider the power of incorporating technology sector internal ventures model.

Habit 9: Create the Future with a Powerful Vision Statement

☐ Develop a powerful vision statement.

☐ Recognize that without a clear vision statement, it's extremely difficult to build an elite company.

☐ Include two critical parts in the vision statement: the core ideology and envisioned future.

☐ Separate core ideology into two parts: the core purpose and core values.

☐ Separate envisioned future into two parts: a BHAG and a vivid description.

Habit 10: Build an Enduring Culture that Wins

☐ Create an interconnected winning and enduring culture that immunizes the enterprise against adverse forces.

☐ Build a distinctive culture which is a vital lifeline for an organization.

☐ Ensure the strong culture includes these key elements that address: the way people connect, particularly the leadership; the way people behave and think; the way people embrace the business model and the core ideology; and, the way key processes and communication links function.

Habit 11: Develop a Strong Growth Engine

☐ Understand that growth is the lifeblood of any company.

☐ Build a growth engine through both organic and inorganic means.

☐ Ensure that growth is well balanced and managed.

☐ Recognize that different skill sets are required for organic and inorganic growth.

☐ Adopt Facebook's key business innovation, the "growth team."

Habit 12: Build a Flat and Responsive Organization

☐ Understand that the key component to building an elite company is the way it is organized.

☐ Build an innovative company structure that is both nimble and adaptive.

☐ Create a flat and highly responsive organization to drive improved performance.

☐ Create an organizational framework of accountability and responsibility that has the right people in place.

Habit 13: Excel at Strategy and Execution

- ☐ Understand leaders need to be exceptional at both strategy and execution.
- ☐ Ensure complete alignment between the management team and board on the long-term vision and strategy of the company.
- ☐ Develop a strategy to implement the vision framework and the business model.
- ☐ Drive the execution of strategy through an effective strategic planning process.
- ☐ Achieve exceptional execution by being operationally a best-of-class performer.
- ☐ Recognize that exceptional operational execution of the strategy is the economic engine that can propel the company to greatness.

Habit 14: Re-imagine Your Business Model

- ☐ Has an ability to re-image what the business should look like—including an innovative business model—as the competitive landscape changes.
- ☐ Possesses a truly visionary company's mind-set with the ability to execute business transformations and reinventions.
- ☐ Create a vision framework that can be made a reality with the right team, the right business model, the right core purpose, and a laser focus on execution.

17 Execution Habits of Elite Enterprises

Habit 1: Utilize Zero-Based Budgeting

- ☐ Recognize that zero-based budging is an effective tool for significantly reducing costs; and if used properly, it can be transformative.
- ☐ Understand the power of zero-based budgeting when companies are facing extremely challenging economic times.
- ☐ Develop the required discipline and focus to use zero-based budgeting to achieve notable and sustainable cost reductions.
- ☐ Understand fully zero-based budgeting concepts: managers plan each year's budget as if they were starting from scratch; requires managers to break down spending to the lowest level of detail before spending decisions are made.

Habit 2: Allocate Capital Effectively

- ☐ Understand that capital allocation is one of the most important decisions for both leaders and the board and that return on invested capital must exceed the cost of the capital employed.
- ☐ Recognize the skills required at the senior management level and at the board level to make capital allocation decisions.
- ☐ Understand that enterprises facing high levels of capital investment need to understand that they must be experts at allocating capital.

☐ Recognize that allocating capital without the ability to forecast and project future results with confidence increases the level of risk dramatically.

Habit 3: Simplify the Business

☐ Seek simplicity and understand that simplicity usually wins over complexity almost every time.
☐ Apply simplicity to nearly everything in an organization, from the core purpose to business processes to organizational structure.
☐ Understand simplicity's link to increased productivity, efficiency, and flexibility.

Habit 4: Focus on Free Cash Flow

☐ Recognize that free cash flow should be the primary focus of the enterprise and that free cash flow is the most complete metric because it touches all key aspects of a company.
☐ Use multiple levers to improve free cash flow, including net income, working capital components, and capital expenditures.

Habit 5: Manage Risks and Understand Unknowns

☐ Ensure that risks are segmented from known to unknown.
☐ Manage known risks with an appropriate tool kit that includes the transfer of risk, sharing of risk, acceptance of risk, and minimization of risk.
☐ Manage unknown risks by closely monitoring key external events (scanning the environment).

☐ Use an effective tool for managing risks such as Enterprise Risk Management or ERM.

Habit 6: Implement Effective Mechanisms

☐ Implement effective mechanisms designed to improve the enterprise, provide early warning signs, and keep the organization focused.

☐ Understand that mechanisms are essential because they instill discipline and focus.

☐ Make mechanisms simple, ensure they are strictly adhered to, and enforced without exception.

Habit 7: Be Highly Adaptive

☐ Ensure that people in the organization have an ability to think differently and can easily adapt to change.

☐ Make agility and problem-solving skills part of the enterprise's DNA.

☐ Use the U.S. Military model—particularly Special Forces—as an exemplary for its ability to adapt and think differently.

☐ Build highly effective small teams with ability to adapt and change quickly.

Habit 8: Scan the Environment in Real Time

☐ Scan the environment in real time as a key early warning mechanism, a technique used by adaptive enterprises.

☐ Develop bias for fast action so the company can be proactive and avoid or at least minimize potential threats and risks.

- ☐ Develop an ability to quickly and accurately analyze the data being accumulated.
- ☐ Focus on critical scanned elements including: technology, competitive landscape, geopolitical events, regulatory matters, and other key items that can have a material impact on the company.

Habit 9: Form an Internal University with a Clear Purpose

- ☐ Recognize that corporate universities can be particularly useful when attempting to change the culture.
- ☐ Ensure that corporate universities have a clear purpose; otherwise, they will eventually become less effective and could possibly fail.
- ☐ Use internal universities as a highly effective tool for talent-management and leadership-development.
- ☐ Utilize both internal and external professors to optimize learning.

Habit 10: Adopt Best Practices from Private Equity

- ☐ Recognize that much can be learned from private equity, particularly their relentless focus on operational excellence and astute capital allocation.
- ☐ Emulate private equity firm's focus on value creation.
- ☐ Emulate private equity firm's mind-set that passionately believes that all businesses can be improved.
- ☐ Align owners, management, and the board of directors to have a common purpose.

☐ Holds management teams to a high standard of accountability and responsibility.

Habit 11: Optimize the Tax and Legal Structure

☐ Understand that optimized legal and tax structure have a material impact on the organization both economically and in terms of risk.

☐ Build a legal firewall to protect the company from certain risks that threaten the enterprise.

☐ Create tax planning strategies to optimize the tax structure of the company.

Habit 12: Forecast Accurately

☐ Recognize that the ability to forecast the future accurately is fraught with risk because scenarios can differ dramatically due to macro-economic or geopolitical events; historically, approximately every decade includes some form of major economic disruption.

☐ Understand that the new norm of shock and unpredictable events requires a new way of thinking when preparing annual or long-term plans.

☐ Build key elements into the planning cycle that increase accuracy and reliability. These include the following: fully challenging and vetting every assumption, effectively scanning the environment, using big data analytics in developing assumptions and gathering facts, organizing an effective A- team adapt at preparing scenario analysis and planning models.

☐ Always have a substantive "Plan B".

□ Build a prodigious number of lifelines so that the company can withstand any shock.

Habit 13: Understand Customer Profitability Management

□ Use customer profitability management (CPM) tools to identify relative profitability of each customer and replace intuitive impressions of customer profitability with fact-based information and supporting analysis.

□ Use CPM measure that includes adding value to most profitable customers, making less-profitable customers more profitable, and stopping or at least reducing the erosion of profitability from unprofitable customers.

□ Use a costing system, such as ABC so that profitability of each customer is measured properly.

Habit 14: Utilize Technology to Gain a Competitive Position

□ Smartly use technology to drive growth, secure confidential information, and to provide a competitive advantage.

□ Use key technologies including: artificial intelligence, cybersecurity, big data, cloud computing, mobile computing, and social media.

Habit 15: Adopt Habits of Elite Activists

□ Adopt key habits of elite activists and study their history of creating shareholder value.

☐ Consider implanting some key attributes of elite activists such as: demand best-of-class operating excellence, the ability to transform a good company into a great one, and how they excel at building a high performing management team.

Habit 16: Make Every Customer Touch Extraordinary

☐ Ensure that every touch experience by the customer is extraordinary.

☐ Ensure that the culture of the company and its well-designed processes are major factors in ensuring that the customer experience at every touch is truly special.

☐ Train everyone in the organization to be passionate about making every customer touch important.

Habit 17: Know Your Customer through Value Selling

☐ Truly know the customer; possess a deep understanding of challenges facing the customer.

☐ Master the art of value selling through extensive training of sales personnel and developing a new mind-set.

CHAPTER 13

CHECKLIST—EXCEPTIONAL HABITS OF ELITE BOARDS

If you're going to employ people anyway,
why not make them the differentiator.
Angela Ahrendts[lxvii]

In Section 3, I detailed the top twenty-one exceptional habits of elite boards. This checklist provides a quick, bullet point summary of each habit that summarizes the most salient points from these discussions. You should use this checklist as an implementation guide to help you begin the process of incorporating these habits into your daily practice on your journey to becoming an elite enterprise. The habits included in this chapter include:

- 11 Leadership Habits of Elite Boards

- 3 Strategy Habits of Elite Boards

- 7 Execution Habits of Elite Boards

11 Leadership Habits of Elite Boards

Habit 1: Elevate Technology on the Board Agenda

- ☐ Recognize that the effective use of technology can provide a company with a distinct competitive advantage; some enterprises have been totally transformed by embracing technology.
- ☐ Possess technology savvy and put technology on the board's agenda.
- ☐ Appoint a digital director to the board.
- ☐ Embrace technology. It's the board's responsibility to oversee how technology can be employed in today's hypercompetitive environment.

Habit 2: Deal Effectively with an Activist Investor

- ☐ Understand that no enterprise is immune from the rising clout of activist investors and that these investors are now a separate asset class.
- ☐ Perform comprehensive assessments to expose potential vulnerabilities resulting from activist investors and understand that the most effective weapon against activism is sustained performance.
- ☐ Communicate through a well-articulated communication plan, including one to deal with activists.
- ☐ Deal with institutional investors and activists through proactive and ongoing engagement tool kit.
- ☐ CEOs and boards engage in constructive dialogue with activists.

Habit 3: Provide Prodigious Lifelines to New CEO

☐ Provide the new CEO with every opportunity to succeed. It's the board's professional, fiduciary, and moral obligation to take these substantive and measurable actions.

☐ Provide five basic lifelines to new CEOs and continuously invests in their development:
   o Unwavering support
   o Requires and assists with obtaining a seat on the board of another company
   o Enrolls the new leader in a high caliber program designed for new CEOs
   o Appoints a mentor, but it must be a good and natural fit,
   o Encourages the CEO to develop a professional relationship with an outside trusted advisor, someone who can be a sounding board, another perspective

Habit 4: Invest in Your CEO

☐ Invest in the development of the CEO in a focused and substantive way. Some of these ongoing investments include:
   o Staff leadership ride program
   o Personal assessments and 360-degree reviews
   o Attending CEO forums
   o Developing a strong relationship with the lead director

o   Regular ongoing training programs specifically designed to assist with the development of the CEO

Habit 5: Hold the Board Accountable

☐ Boards are held accountable for results; this accountability is being driven mainly by activist investors and highly engaged institutional shareholders.

☐ Demonstrate clearly that shareholder value is being created.

☐ Implement a strong assessment process for evaluating each board member, each committee, and the entire board itself for effectiveness.

☐ Performance is measured on total shareholder return and how they have performed relative to overseeing the CEO and succession planning.

☐ Implement a mechanism as part of governance framework that requires board members to step down when they are not performing.

Habit 6: Be Engaged

☐ Insist on engagement beyond traditional duties and expectations.

☐ Make a substantial commitment to obtaining a deep knowledge of the company and the management team.

☐ Show commitment to improving their own skill set by attending outside training and staying current on a broad spectrum of subjects including technology.

Habit 7: Have Compliance Report Directly to the Board

☐ Recognize that enterprise risk management is a key board responsibility.

☐ Take substantive action to ensure that governance framework is properly managed due to ever-increasing regulations.

☐ Enhance transparency and focus by having the chief compliance officer report to the board.

Habit 8: Engage Effectively with Investors

☐ Develop a new mind-set to respond to more demanding investors.

☐ Respond and engage well with investors (when appropriate) along with the CEO.

☐ Follow key guidelines for engagement:
  o Prepare before any engagement
  o Assemble the right team to provide perspective and advice
  o Ensure the company representative(s) is a good listener and communicator
  o Understand speed is critical in dealing with investor actions
  o Possess a thoughtful and well-reasoned, scripted response to activists and investors

Habit 9: View the Board as a Team

☐ Build a value creating board underpinned by creation of a strong and effective team using same principles for building a strong management team.

☐ Recognize that strong teams are built through trust, common purpose, shared consciousness, and empowered execution.

Habit 10: Create a Robust Lead Director Position

☐ Appoint a strong independent lead director who is a proven leader whom everyone respects.
☐ Disclose clearly the duties of the lead director in the proxy statement. Duties should be robust.
☐ Include these key duties of a lead director:
  o Work in concert with the CEO/Chairman and the board
  o Coordinate board activities and agenda
  o Chair the executive session and provide feedback to CEO
  o Fully engage and focus on value creation, strong governance, and a healthy board culture
  o Empower to call meetings of the independent directors

Habit 11: Possess a Deep Knowledge of Board Responsibilities

☐ Board members must each possess a deep knowledge of his or her responsibilities.
☐ Include these traditional board roles:
  o Choose the CEO, monitor his or her performance, and succession planning
  o Ensure the strategy of the company is right

- o Ensure there is a strong enterprise risk management focus and strong governance framework
- ☐ Include these updated responsibilities:
    - o Focus on crisis management
    - o Deal with activist investors
    - o Ensure that a prodigious number of lifelines are being built over a long horizon
    - o Clearly understand what creating shareholder value really means

3 Strategy Habits of Elite Boards

Habit 1: Build a Value Creating Board

- ☐ Understand that great boards can create value and help the enterprise differentiate itself in the marketplace.
- ☐ Focus on these three primary responsibilities that are directly linked to value creation: the CEO's performance and succession planning; agreeing to the strategy of the company; and overseeing risk, including governance. Although the board has other critical duties, none are more important than these three.
- ☐ Build a value creating board by ensuring
  - o the right board members are at the table and that they possess the right skills;
  - o board members have a deep knowledge of business;
  - o a culture of trust and respect exists in the boardroom;
  - o board members are fully prepared for every meeting;
  - o board is led by an exceptional leader; and
  - o a strong board performance process is in place and functioning properly.

Habit 2: Form a Technology or Innovation Committee

- ☐ Understand that technology is rapidly changing how business is conducted and that elite boards are establishing technology and innovation committees

in their quest to add value and gain a competitive
advantage.

☐ Ensure that committee members must have a strong
grounding in technology and a deep understanding
of market trends.

Habit 3: View Digital Technology as a Transformative Opportunity

☐ Boards are viewing digital technology as a
transformative opportunity.

☐ Require boards and the leadership team to think
differently about the company and its competitive
position.

☐ A digital technology transformation impacts all
major processes and operations of the company.

☐ Begin transformative journey by first studying
enterprises that have successfully achieved this
amazing change.

☐ Commence transformative journey by taking key
steps that include
   o re-examination of business model and core
     purpose;
   o rethinking the composition of board
     members;
   o appointing an effective technology
     committee; and
   o seeking outside partners and experts.

7 Execution Habits of Elite Boards

Habit 1: Succession Planning Beyond the CEO

☐ Recognize that succession planning has never been more important and more relevant than it is today.

☐ Implement an exceptional leadership-development and talent-management process to underpin the succession planning process.

☐ Ensure a total focus on building an organization that will endure for generations.

☐ Include these key elements to ensure a world-class succession planning process:

    o The succession planning process covers the entire C-suite and at least one layer below

    o Succession planning is thoughtful and comprehensive

    o The process needs to be driven by the CEO

    o At least annually, a comprehensive review of succession planning is conducted with the board

    o A best-of-class plan that ensures the company never goes outside for a CEO

☐ Ensure that the world-class succession plan also includes the following elements:

    o A profile for the CEO position must be developed and dialogued

    o A well-organized plan that provides essential information about each key person

    o A plan that includes detailed development plans for each person

- o A plan that ensures the culture of the company is embedded in each key person
- o Key metrics are built into the plan

Habit 2: Optimize the Board of Directors Structure

- ☐ Optimize board structure to around eight to nine members and move away from the average board size of about eleven members; smaller boards can be more effective.
- ☐ Recognize that smaller boards tend to be nimbler, more decisive, and more highly focused, which usually translates to better performance and greater shareholder value.
- ☐ Understand that a smaller board does present a few challenges, particularly with filling the three key committees, but that the benefits greatly outweigh the negatives.

Habit 3: Excel at Board Succession Planning

- ☐ View succession planning with same lens and importance as succession planning for the company; main objective is to build a board team that wins by creating shareholder value.
- ☐ Ensure governance and nominating committee has an effective process for sourcing high quality candidates.
- ☐ Utilize a skill matrix tool to analyze any gaps that need to be filled.
- ☐ Board skills need to mirror strategic direction of the company.

☐ Board candidates possess a broad array of skills and characteristics.

☐ Succession planning process embraces diversity.

Habit 4: Act Like a Private Equity Board

☐ Recognize that private equity boards are highly effective because they have a sharp focus on key metrics, strategy, specific goals, and leadership execution and that these firms are skilled at taking a good company and turning it into something greater.

☐ Mirror the relentless focus of private equity on operational execution, meeting or exceeding targets, and ensuring that the right leadership team is in place.

☐ Become more hands-on like private equity entities that operate with a much smaller board of directors, which results in a more engaged commitment to the company.

☐ Become more personally invested like private equity entities where all board members are financially committed to the company.

Habit 5: Assess CEO Performance with Facts

☐ Recognize that nothing is more important for the board of directors to do than overseeing the CEO.

☐ Weigh all the facts when assessing the performance of the CEO.

☐ Do not rely on attribution or anecdotal comments.

☐ Boards should rely heavily on:
  o Sound processes

- o A CEO self-evaluation memorandum that is both qualitative and quantitative
- o Key performance metrics that are agreed in advance
- o Assessment of critical personal characteristics
- o Measurement of reputation of the company
- o Relevant information that is based solely on facts
- ☐ Boards should not rely on too heavily on:
  - o 360-degree evaluations because they include a fair amount of cognitive biases
  - o Feedback from executives that is self-serving
  - o Anecdotal attribution from various sources
  - o Any other source of feedback that only sees the company from a narrow lens

Habit 6: Create an Effective Development Plan

- ☐ Provide each director with a detailed learning and continuous improvement plan.
- ☐ Ensure that directors have a deep knowledge of and significant insight into the company they serve.
- ☐ Ensure that development program includes visits to operating sites to better understand operations and be more exposed to the management team.
- ☐ Ensure that periodically, board members attend a top 100 meeting.
- ☐ Participate in at least one quarterly operating review meeting with the senior team.
- ☐ Attend a staff ride leadership-development program.

☐ Attend an outside directors training program.

Habit 7: Shed Board Seats

☐ Recognize that the amount of time required to serve on a public company board continues to escalate due to significant number of ever increasing regulations.

☐ Ensure directors are more engaged to meet the challenge of greater board responsibilities.

☐ Think carefully about the number of boards directors should serve on, but consider that the trend is clearly moving toward fewer commitments, not more. Elite directors understand this change and are acting on their own and are reducing the number boards they sit on.

CHAPTER 14

FREQUENTLY ASKED QUESTIONS ABOUT LIFELINES PRINCIPLES AND ELITE HABITS

Management is doing things right;
leadership is doing the right things.
Peter Drucker[lxviii]

This chapter of the book is organized in a question-and-answer format to address specific matters raised through my advisory practice, particularly as they relate to the lifelines leadership framework principles and the exceptional habits building blocks. In addition, during my career—particularly in the past decade—I have been asked a multitude of questions by clients, employees, shareholders, professional peers, board members, politicians, friends, and family about building and sustaining an elite enterprise. These questions have stayed with me because of their importance. Although most of these questions have already been answered to a certain degree in both this book and *CEO Lifelines: Nine Commitments Every Leader Must Make*, they are included in this chapter to provide more context and, hopefully, a deeper explanation.

Each question in this chapter will be answered in the most complete and comprehensive manner possible. The objective is to provide readers with a reference section on some key lifelines principles and habits and specifically as they relate to building and sustaining an enduring elite company. You should use this chapter as an implementation guide to help you begin the process of incorporating these lifelines principles and elite habits into your daily practice on your journey to becoming an elite enterprise. Please note that the questions posed are in no particular order.

Q1: How should a leader view both books?

CEO Lifelines: Nine Commitments Every Leader Must Make is an integrated and innovative leadership framework for visionary leaders that are committed to building a successful and sustainable career, while simultaneously building and sustaining an enduring enterprise. I call this the *lifelines leadership framework*. Essentially, the lifelines leadership framework is a blueprint for excellence at both the leadership level and at the organization level. These are high-level principles that need to be used to build and sustain an enterprise. On the other hand, *CEO Lifelines— Climb On: Exceptional Habits of Elite Companies* comprises the exceptional habits that are the essential and necessary building blocks to executing and making the lifelines leadership framework principles a reality.

Both the lifelines leadership framework and the exceptional habits are underpinned by the foundational pillars: leadership, strategy, execution, and luck. As explained in this book and in question three below, the foundational pillars must be expanded into the lifelines leadership framework and then implemented through the exceptional habits.

Q2: Can you explain why you use the lifeline metaphor in both books?

Lifelines are a safety device used in the construction industry and in mountaineering (called a belay). In the extreme, lifelines can be the difference between life and death. That is, terminating the quest or climbing on. Even under normal circumstances, lifelines are essential to have even for the strongest and most elite mountaineers. It is no different in business. Lifelines are a useful narrative device that illustrate the individual and organizational challenges all leaders face in their climb to the summit. Lifelines can also be a powerful resource that can be effectively utilized to seize opportunities as they present themselves during a major crisis or ongoing turbulent times.

Enterprises that build a prodigious number of lifelines (over many decades) are more likely to not only survive global economic shocks—such as the great recession and the European sovereign debt crisis—but they will also likely outperform organizations that are less prepared. Abundant lifelines provide flexibility, strength, and the ability to recover from an unforeseen economic shock or series of shocks.

Q3: Can you explain what you mean by the "elite management framework," and how long does it take to implement the high-level lifelines principles and the building blocks (habits)?

As explained throughout this book, the elite management framework is the holy grail to building and sustaining an elite enterprise. The management framework includes the foundational pillars, the lifelines leadership framework, and the exceptional habits.

First, the foundational pillars, which include strategy; execution; leadership, and luck. I believe that an elite company cannot be built and sustained without developing an exceptional strategy, possessing exceptional execution capabilities, building a world class leadership team, and having a keen awareness on the need to stay on the right side of the luck spread. These foundational pillars then need to be expanded into the lifelines leadership framework, which includes three personal lifelines and six enterprise lifelines. The lifelines leadership framework consists of high-level principles for achieving elite status; and the exceptional habits of elite leaders, elite boards, and elite enterprises translate these principles into specific building blocks that are essential for building and sustaining an elite company.

With respect to how long it takes to implement the elite management framework, the simple answer is that there is no set timeline. The horizon is dependent on numerous variables, particularly: an in-depth assessment of existing lifelines, commitment of the leadership team and the board to the transformation of the company, and the strength of existing habits of the enterprise, its leaders, and the board of directors. Having said that, much can be accomplished and put in place in a three-to-five-year period provided there's vigorous implementation, focus, and execution of all the elements. However, as stated in Chapter 1, it normally takes decades for companies to achieve elite status. Although some companies such as Facebook have done it faster, there are no shortcuts to the summit. This is true of mountaineers as well.

Q4: How do you instill an innovation culture in a company?

Innovation was a key focus of mine when I was CEO, and that mind-set continues today in my role as a management consultant and as an independent board member. I believe that innovation needs to be broadly viewed as not only new products and services, but it also needs to incorporate the science, research, information technology, generative thinking, business processes, and the business model necessary to manage and drive the enterprise. The best way to view innovation is that it must touch every part of an enterprise. For example, the way the company is organized can be a major innovation and so are the underlying processes that drive the company. Innovation must be the lifeblood of an organization, and it must provide a distinctive, competitive advantage. Wonderful examples of how innovation is done right can be found at Apple, Goggle's (Alphabet) Advanced Technology and Projects group, and MasterCard Labs. There are also wonderful examples at other companies such as 3M, Disney, and UPS.

When I was CEO, I wanted innovation to drive our solutions-based approach to the customer. My objective was simple: sell more value to the customer by providing knowledge-based solutions that were underpinned by technology, science, and generative thinking. I viewed this objective as a win-win scenario. This initiative focused on making our company an indispensable partner to our customers. I saw a quote from Dr. Zhang Xiaogan,

President of Anshan Iron and Steel Group in China, that captured my sentiment and what I was striving to accomplish by implementing what we called our innovation network. Here is what he said:

> *Innovation has a cultural dimension too, so Anshan Steel has taken steps to nurture a culture in which innovation can thrive. This includes building relationships with external research institutions; engaging clients in research and development; creating a corporate environment in which risk-taking is encouraged and mistakes are tolerated and recognizing and rewarding individual initiative.*

In order for innovation to be successful, the right culture needs to be established in the organization. In Walter Isaacson's wonderful book, *the INNOVATORS*, he essentially provides what I call the *innovation recipe* for a company to be successful. He writes, "The key to innovation ... was realizing that there was no conflict between nurturing individual geniuses and promoting collaborative teamwork. It was not either-or. Indeed, throughout the digital age, the two approaches went together. Creative geniuses ... generated innovative ideas. Practical engineers ... partnered closely with them to turn concepts into contraptions. And collaborative teams of technicians and entrepreneurs worked to turn the invention into a practical product. When part of this ecosystem was lacking ... great concepts ended up being consigned to history's basement. And when great teams lacked passionate visionaries ... innovation slowly withered."[lxix]

Also, all the lifelines leadership framework and the exceptional habits outlined in the book need to be implemented so that innovation takes hold. To build a successful innovation culture, the following framework should be established:

☐ An innovation mind-set must be created in the organization. Everyone must clearly understand that innovation touches all parts of the organization, from the business model to business processes to developing new products.

☐ On-the-edge investments should be made to explore new ways of doing business and discovering new products and processes. These investments should be in the form of small bets; stay away from making one or several large bets.

☐ Open innovation, collaboration, joint ventures, strategic alliances, and even acquisitions need to be used as key mechanisms for developing and acquiring innovation.

☐ All existing technology should be cataloged; and key managers, engineers, scientist, and technicians should be trained on what is already available.

☐ All current research and development projects, along with engineering projects, process reinventions, and transformation initiatives must be closely reviewed to determine alignment with the company's mission statement and core values.

☐ All employees in the organization should be trained on the importance of innovation, and they should be encouraged to bring forth ideas, from basic improvements to disruptive technologies. Recognition of employee contributions need to be part of this culture.

☐ Key people should be trained to scan the outside environment for existing technology that can be adapted and used to bring knowledge-based solutions to solve customer problems.

☐ Continuous feedback should be received from the customer as to what solutions they are looking for. Often customers can provide leads and ideas on improvements to existing technology.

☐ Celebrate, recognize, and reward innovation.

☐ Crowdsourcing should be utilized in order to tap into a global network of research scientists, entrepreneurs, and inventors. Research and development initiatives should be approached in multiple ways. Some should be done internally. Some should be outsourced to universities that are part of the established network. Some should be outsourced to independent labs that specialize in certain basic sciences. Use a network of partners that consists of universities, research labs, joint venture partners, tech startups, independent researchers, and even government agencies.

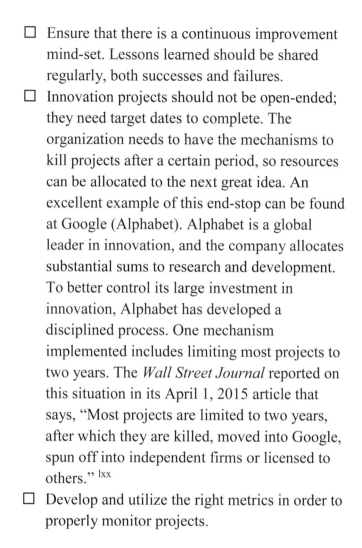

☐ Ensure that there is a continuous improvement mind-set. Lessons learned should be shared regularly, both successes and failures.

☐ Innovation projects should not be open-ended; they need target dates to complete. The organization needs to have the mechanisms to kill projects after a certain period, so resources can be allocated to the next great idea. An excellent example of this end-stop can be found at Google (Alphabet). Alphabet is a global leader in innovation, and the company allocates substantial sums to research and development. To better control its large investment in innovation, Alphabet has developed a disciplined process. One mechanism implemented includes limiting most projects to two years. The *Wall Street Journal* reported on this situation in its April 1, 2015 article that says, "Most projects are limited to two years, after which they are killed, moved into Google, spun off into independent firms or licensed to others." [lxx]

☐ Develop and utilize the right metrics in order to properly monitor projects.

Q5: If you had to pick one, and only one, what metric would you use to determine if a business is successful?
The best metric to use is free cash flow and growth in free cash flow. That is, cash flow from operations, less cash outflow for both capital expenditures and dividends. If dividends are truly discretionary (which often is not the

case), then they can be excluded from the free cash flow calculation.

Free cash flow represents the true discretionary cash available to the business for paying down debt, making acquisitions, repurchasing shares, and for other strategic uses. Enterprises that generate sustainable prodigious amounts of growing free cash flow are truly elite. They have the most vital lifeline available to a business.

Q6: If you had to pick one mechanism, what would you implement to drive and help achieve a company's free cash flow objectives?

The best mechanism to implement is a cash flow discipline called *cash return on investment*. The company that is exemplary and is "best-of-class" in utilizing this metric is Roper Technologies. Here is what their CEO said about this discipline in the 2014 annual report to shareholders, "We measure this through a metric called Cash Return on Investment (CRI), which has been a powerful value creation tool for us for many years. High CRI businesses are much nimbler and often have structural competitive advantages over their competitors. Roper businesses work to improve CRI annually, by generating more cash flow while maintaining or reducing asset levels. Through a combination of internal improvements and disciplined capital deployment, Roper has increased CRI dramatically since 2004, while our shareholders have enjoyed a total return of 445 percent during that period."[lxxi]

In 2014, Roper Technologies generated an astounding $803 million in free cash flow, which represents approximately 23 percent of their revenues. However,

Roper calculates their free cash flow without deducting dividends which is not unusual. I believe that you should include dividends in the free cash flow calculation if they are not truly discretionary. Thus, if you adjust for their $80 million in dividends in 2014, their free cash calculated as cash flow from operations minus capital expenditures and minus dividends is still a very healthy $723 million or 20 percent of revenues. This is still truly an exceptional performance and why Roper is an elite company.

Q7: Dividends and stock repurchases are the two most common ways of returning capital to shareholders; which of the two is most effective and why?
There's a tremendous amount of work published on both dividends and stock repurchases, so I'm not going to reiterate all the pluses and minus of each. I'm going to approach this subject from a different perspective. Before I provide my view on this topic, it's important to understand that every company's circumstance is different, so what I'm going to outline may not apply to everyone.

I believe that a company should use both mechanisms but in a very disciplined and focused way. First, let's review share repurchases. Under normal circumstances, I believe that stock repurchases should be used only to deal with dilution from stock based compensation so that the number of outstanding shares do not materially increase. There are, of course, circumstances where it is appropriate to repurchase a substantial number of shares, but that's only in special situations. For example, if there's a temporary and substantial decline in the value of the shares. However, I believe that most the time, share repurchases that are done on a large scale can be counterproductive. Since capital is a scarce and precious resource, the cash should be used instead to grow the business and possibly even the dividend.

With respect to dividends, I believe that this mechanism is the best over a long horizon to return capital to shareholders. There are numerous reasons for this, but the most important will be covered in the next paragraph.

Dividends and, more importantly, consistent dividends which increase every year, can make a notable contribution to the overall total shareholder return (TSR) metric, which is made up of the increase in stock price and the dividend. TSR is one the most important metrics for public companies, and a consistently increasing dividend rate is obviously an integral component of that metric. This contribution is annual, and for elite companies that pay an ever-increasing dividend, the dividend makes a large contribution to the TSR over a long horizon. On the other hand, stock repurchases tend to provide a one-time boost to the share price, which is often ephemeral.

Companies that have been able to consistently increase their dividend every year for—say at least 25 consecutive years—belong to a small, privileged class. These companies tend to be high performers. These companies demonstrate high earnings power and are revered by investors that value dividends that are safe and consistently increase. This builds long-term shareholder loyalty.

Q8: Can you provide guidance on what you mean by choosing the "right" people?

Nothing is more important than having the right people on the team, particularly the leadership group—just ask any successful CEO or any elite mountaineer. If leaders fall short on building an elite team, they will certainly be destined to mediocrity or irrelevance. So, how does a leader build a team of the right people? Although the specifics can vary and do vary from enterprise to enterprise, certain critical traits can assist a leader in identifying the right people. Let's examine each one of those traits a little closer.

First, the right people are the ones who fit with the core values and mission of the enterprise. If they are not deeply passionate about each of the core values and the purpose of the company, they will certainly fail in the organization. Second, the right people do not need to be micromanaged, and they do not need to be buried in meaningless bureaucracy. Under this trait, the right people are the ones who are self-motivated, passionate, disciplined, and of the highest integrity. Third, the right people are accountable, responsible, and always deliver on their commitments. They are substantive, they do not point to others, and they take full responsibility when things go wrong. They also give credit to their teams when things go right. And finally, the right people enhance the culture of the company; they are collaborative and are fierce competitors. They have unwavering faith in their abilities. They function effectively as team members.

Q9: What are the key negative markers that one should look for to indicate that a company may be heading to challenging times?

When you follow companies, many markers are available that investors can discover by simply reading the SEC public filings, press releases, reviewing investor presentations, and listening to quarterly earnings call. For someone who is not an expert in analyzing companies, here are three markers that are easy and interrelated to identify which may indicate that a company may be going into a period of turbulence:

☐ **Struggling with sales and operating margin declines for years or for many consecutive quarters.** Sales and margin declines lead to lower free cash flows which over a cumulative period of time will put significant stress on a company's liquidity, balance sheet, and performance metrics, all of which will have dire consequences to the stock price. If a company seems to be stuck in a sustainable period of decline, it's a good bet that there are some significant problems inside the enterprise. Although it is usually impossible to ascertain exactly what is going on inside a company, it's often a good bet that you may find the next two elements which correlate to this decline.

☐ **Multiple management teams over a relatively short horizon.** Pay close attention to 8-K filings because this is where you will see the significant changes in management. Companies that are constantly changing management, particularly the CEO, are likely setting themselves up for some very challenging times. I have seen some public companies change CEOs so often that it is unthinkable to believe that they will find their way anytime soon. Sometimes boards overact and make significant senior management changes when a cacophony of voices is clamoring about the stock price. Everyone knows how Steve Jobs was first treated when he was asked to separate from Apple. Although the CEO needs to be held accountable by the board, it is also important for the board to make sure that they have all facts before acting and that they are not relying too much on attribution. Once a CEO change is made, the change could have unintended consequences and could set-off a chain of events that ultimately puts the company on a dangerous path of decline.

☐ **Varying strategies.** With changing leadership, usually the strategy of the company will vary from the past. This difference may not be a bad thing and could actually be positive. But, when it comes with ever-changing leadership, then the varying strategies will most likely have an adverse effect on the performance of the company.

Q10: What are the key positive markers one should look for that indicate a troubled company may have successfully turned itself around?

The first elements that are critical to look for are an improvement in free cash flow, increasing gross and operating margins, and revenue growth. Once there is ample evidence that this turnaround is happening, then you move on to the repair of the balance sheet. Evidence that

the balance sheet is being repaired or has been repaired
should include many of the following items:

- ☐ Debt repayment and improved debt-to-capital
  ratio
- ☐ Improvement in key ratios to which the rating
  agencies pay close attention
- ☐ A rating upgrade and/or at least an improving
  outlook opinion from the agencies
- ☐ Lower borrowing costs
- ☐ Capital raised through an equity offering and/or
  debt offering
- ☐ Growing shareholders' equity
- ☐ Growing cash balance

A strong balance sheet is vital to the long-term viability of
the enterprise. It is a true lifeline!

**Q11: A great deal has been written about zero-based
budgeting and cost cutting in general. So, how should
leaders approach this in their organization?**
Although cost-cutting is specifically its own habit, there are
some additional salient points to make. With the rise of
activism and the ongoing struggle for growth due to less
than robust global economic environment, a focus on
expenses needs to be relentless no matter how well a leader
perceives their organization do be doing. Leaders who do
not have a proactive and relentless focus on productivity
and efficiency will most likely find themselves in a future
situation where someone else takes the initiative for them.

Leaders need to have a laser focus on costs, which means that they need to do a "deep dive" on their cost structure. No expense should be spared. I believe a great place to start is with the global supply chain and the SG&A category. The global supply chain should be all encompassing including such elements as procurement, warehousing, transportation, logistics, manufacturing, product standardization, and numerous other items that touch the product and/or service from beginning to end. With respect to SG&A, all costs need to be closely examined and justified. Technology and innovation needs to underpin both cost reduction initiatives because it can have a large positive impact on improving productivity and efficiency.

Q12: What are the precocious characteristics that an aspiring CEO candidate needs to possess?

The CEO position is obviously the most important job in the company. The scrutiny on CEOs today by boards, investors, employees, and numerous other parties is something that only a few people are capable of managing effectively. When developing a pool of potential successors to the CEO, these aspiring future leaders must possess some key characteristics. These characteristics need to be vetted through many years of exposure because it is the only way to truly determine if the candidate possesses them. Therefore, I believe that the CEO must come from within because of this critical vetting process.

When boards of directors bring a new CEO in from the outside, they can possibly miss this important and indispensable part of the puzzle. So I will outline what I believe to be the most important key characteristics that high potential successor to the CEO needs to possess to become appointed leader of the company. However, it's important to understand that certain characteristics are a given and should already be innate—such as passion, instinct, and empathy. It's also a given that CEO candidates already possess high intellect, a history of accomplishment, and a history of indispensable experiences. Here are the additional key characteristics:

- ☐ Possesses the highest moral and ethical character. Individual must manifest this quality in every word, every deed, and every action.
- ☐ Has a dedication to personal responsibility and accountability, all underpinned by disciplined action.
- ☐ Commands an ability to communicate effectively at all levels and ability to effectively lead teams.
- ☐ Owns a deep understanding of the business, its people, customers, suppliers, and competitors.
- ☐ Expresses great insight, perspective, and sound judgment. He or she is a critical thinker.
- ☐ Exhibits the ability to think outside the box, ability to drive change, ability to adapt, and ability to scan the environment to better understand both near-term and long-term macro-environment elements that can have a profound effect on the business.
- ☐ Is grounded in reality, is humble, and can relate well to people.

Aspiring candidates must consistently manifest these characteristics throughout their careers. This is a pre-requisite to even being considered a potential CEO candidate.

Q13: Is the Chief Operating Officer (COO) position obsolete, or is there a place in the c-suite for this senior position?

The position of COO is not obsolete, but the role has evolved and changed, particularly over the past decade. There's no fast rule on whether you should or should not have a COO in the organization. Every company is different, and every circumstance is different. Organizational structure, macro competitive environment, strategic direction of the company, the composition of the team and its skill-set are all factors that will influence whether a need exists for a COO.

There is a role for a COO, but not in all circumstances and in all companies. The CEO and the board need to dialogue the possible role of a COO because the COO position is a very powerful one, and it will have a dramatic impact on both the culture of the company and how it operates. The COO position will have the most impact on the CEO because he or she will no longer directly manage the business unit leaders; that responsibility will fall to the COO. However, on the other side, it frees the CEO to focus on strategy, the board, key customers, investors, acquisitions, succession planning, and numerous other vital responsibilities.

Another obvious advantage of having a COO position filled by a highly competent individual is that it provides the company with a key back-up to the CEO. Also, as advocated in one of the habits, it's important for companies to appoint a strong number two.

Q14: How do elite boards deal with company strategy?
One of the key responsibilities of the board is to oversee the strategic planning process. One thing boards and executives must clearly understand, it is not the board's duty to create strategy. The board should challenge assumptions and specific objectives, but they cannot and should not define the strategy. The strategy must be developed by the CEO with help of his or her executive team.

The strategic planning process should focus principally on growth, profitability, free cash flow, capital allocation, the business model, the portfolio of businesses, the competitive landscape, macro-economic cycles, and geopolitical matters, all underpinned by the need to build a high performing and sustainable elite company.

Elite boards approach the strategic planning process from two perspectives. First, they require the CEO and the senior management team to develop and then present the strategy to the board. During this process, which is usually done at an offsite location, elite boards will ask insightful questions, offer their perspective, and conduct a robust dialogue to ensure that the key assumptions are realistic and consistent with the capabilities of the executive team and the entire organization. Through this deliberate and robust process, the board helps shape the thinking and ultimately the key elements of the strategic plan. Second, elite boards then sign on to what is agreed. There must be full agreement between the board and the executive team, so there are no misunderstandings. Complete alignment between the board and executives binds everyone to the strategic plan, which helps avoid future conflicts. As part of this alignment, it's important to agree on what metrics will be used to monitor performance relative to the strategic plan and how executive compensation will be connected to the plan. Also, other qualitative measures need to be agreed in advance. It is imperative that success is clearly defined, and that the board and the senior management team are fully aligned on the definition.

Q15: How do elite boards assess prospective candidates?

As explained in this book, board succession planning is a critical habit, and it needs to be approached with the same focus and discipline as succession planning in the business. Finding the right board member is essential to building and sustaining a value-creating elite board. This means that identifying the right prospective team members requires a strong process, hands-on approach (cannot outsource to a recruiter), and patience. An effective and highly potent succession-planning process for board members should rely mostly on internally developed candidates, augmented by board search firms. I believe that you need a perfect blend of the two but with a strong bias towards candidates who are well known and have a history of performance and teamwork.

The governance and nominating committee, who is responsible for overseeing board recruitment, needs to develop a process that is exemplary. This ideal is important because a highly effective board succession-planning process can be a paragon for the entire organization, and it can be infectious. This ideal is important also because when an elite board is built, exceptional habits will positively influence the CEO and the entire organization.

When a board candidate is brought in for interviews, a similarly robust process is used by elite companies, which means the process must be disciplined, well organized, and well managed. The process should also include directors who are skilled in interviewing. Also, an effective process includes a healthy dialogue between the committee, the CEO/Chairman, and the entire board. Appropriate metrics should be utilized to ensure that the process consistently produces elite board members who align well with the culture of the board and the strategic direction of the company.

Q16: How do elite boards handle executive sessions?
Executive board sessions are one of the most important governance practices. Executive sessions allow each outside board member to offer their perspective on the CEO and the company in a thoughtful and structured way. The lead director is responsible for overseeing this great governance practice. It's also the lead director's responsibility to communicate in a cogent manner the sentiment of the board. This feedback can be highly effective to the CEO and the executive team.

Here are some general guidelines for creating a strong and effective executive session:

- ☐ Each board executive session should be conducted after every board meeting, if possible.
- ☐ Each board member should be allowed to provide their insight and perspective.
- ☐ The lead director needs to control the process to ensure a good outcome.
- ☐ The lead director needs to summarize in a cogent manner the sentiment of the board and the key points need to be immediately communicated to the CEO.
- ☐ The lead director should ensure that there is proper follow-up on key items.
- ☐ The culture of the board needs to be such that every member feels free to voice a thoughtful opinion. There must be trust and respect within the team.

Q17: Can you provide a good example of a learning entity?

The best example is the U.S. Military and particularly special operations. Since the elite practices of the military are covered in many parts of this book, I will comment on another good example of a learning entity—the Chinese government.

The Chinese government dispatches students and official throughout the world with the objective of learning best practices. They strive to learn innovative and effective business models from elite organizations and then adopt many of their best practices at home with objective of continuously improving their economy and their home-grown enterprises. Recently, one area that the Chinese have been successful is the tech sector. China now boasts some prominent technology firms that didn't exist ten years ago, such as Lenovo, Alibaba, and Tencent, to name a few.

Q18: Can you provide more insight and perspective on what you mean by a global supply chain?
An exceptional global supply chain can provide a company with a distinctive competitive advantage. This subject is covered in both books, but I will augment what has been said with a summary of the strategic benefits of building and executing an effective and innovative global supply chain. The most critical benefits include:

- ☐ Elimination or significant reduction of production disruptions
- ☐ Elimination or reduction of excess inventory
- ☐ Ensuring product availability
- ☐ Elimination or reduction of premium freight charges
- ☐ Reduction of the cost of sourcing
- ☐ Leveraging the supplier base for innovation
- ☐ Building strategic relationships with key suppliers
- ☐ Reduction of the cycle time, particularly when speed is vital
- ☐ Improvement of the return on invested capital

Information Technology (IT) is crucial to building a highly effective global supply chain. Here some key technologies that innovative organizations are using in their supply chain:

- [ ] Integrated ERP System is the foundational technology necessary to efficiently and effectively manage the overall global supply chain as well as the entire business.
- [ ] Big data analytics are utilized to provide insight and valuable information that can be utilized to improve the overall supply chain.
- [ ] Cybersecurity, cloud computing, and mobile computing are all being utilized effectively, and each can play a key role in the overall management and effectiveness of the global supply chain.

In addition to IT, elite companies also form strategic alliances with suppliers to further strengthen their position. One of the most successful and innovative strategic alliances that I have come across is the Renault-Nissan partnership. The French and Japanese strategic alliance was formed back in 1990s when Nissan was facing some challenging times. The alliance was established for product development, sourcing and procurement, and even production. From a legal standpoint, both companies retained their own board of directors, and their shares are traded separately. However, the parties did execute cross shareholding that ultimately favored Renault.

Q19: Can you provide more insight into the ten most important personal rules by which all CEOs and leaders need to live by?

The ten personal rules by which all CEOs and leaders need to live by are all covered in some form throughout both books, but it is important to list them all in one place. Also, these rules assume that everyone is intensely focused on adopting the habits of elite leaders. Here is the list:

☐ Walk the talk and set the tone for the organization by manifesting integrity in every action, every word, and every deed.

☐ Go with your instinct, your sixth sense; it will never fail you.

☐ Learn to listen—there's so much to learn from others.

☐ Learn to stop doing, which can be more important than a to-do list.

☐ Manage in good times as you would in bad times.

☐ Prepare daily for your ascent to the summit with discipline.

☐ Engage everyone in the organization in robust dialogue and validate anecdotal comments and attribution with unimpeachable facts whenever possible.

☐ Consistently display a proactive mind-set.

☐ Be humble and maintain an unwavering faith that you will prevail no matter what the circumstances.

☐ Manifest passion, commitment, optimism, and wisdom in all actions and decisions.

Q20: What are the most important considerations for a leader in achieving people excellence?

It's impossible to build and sustain an elite company without first having elite leaders that focus on talent-management and leadership-development. Thus, people excellence requires skill, focus, discipline, and the habit of being intolerant of mediocrity. Elite leaders focus on certain elements when building an A-team, which form an integrated framework for people excellence:

- ☐ Selecting A-Players, developing them, and retaining them is the most important responsibility of a leader.
- ☐ Understanding that when it comes to talent, we are not all created equal. Exceptional people will have an outsized positive impact on the performance of the company.
- ☐ When in doubt about a prospective candidate, don't hire. Hire only when you've found a great candidate.
- ☐ Recruiting from the outside for talent, particularly for senior level positions, is fraught with risk. If possible, promote from within the organization.
- ☐ People excellence begins by developing essential personal leadership characteristics that the right people on the team need to possess.
- ☐ An innovative hiring process is essential, and it must be underpinned with people who possess strong interviewing skills.
- ☐ A powerful internal talent-management and leadership-development process must provide the enterprise with people who possess the right skills.
- ☐ People decisions must be consistent and disciplined. Leaders need to be intolerant of mediocrity.
- ☐ Hiring and developing people that possess the personal characteristics that are well aligned with the mission and values of the company.

☐ Standard processes, predictive tools, and metrics must be established and utilized to drive improved performance.

Q21: Can you provide more insight as to why there is some confusion over creating an appropriate core philosophy?

The core philosophy has two elements: a core purpose (or mission) and core values. The core purpose, which is also commonly referred to as a mission statement, is an organization's most fundamental reason for being whereas the core values are a handful of guiding principles.

The purpose or mission of an organization needs to capture the fundamental reason for its existence. If we explore, for example, Google's core purpose, *"To organize the world's information and make it universally accessible and useful"* we clearly see the fundamental reason for its existence. This statement is powerful and effective because it is simple, clear, and everyone in the organization most likely understands the mission of the company. Another exceptional core purpose is Disney's, *"To make people happy"* which is very simple but powerful. If you are a Disney employee, you should have no confusion as to what your purpose is. Their core purpose is absolute.

My experience with mission statements or core purposes is that organizations make them too long, too complicated, and too confusing. I conducted an unscientific scan of a dozen different websites and noted that about half of the organizations did not have a clear mission statement like Disney's. The most common error that I noted is that they are too long, which made it difficult to immediately see the organization's reason for being. Here are some guidelines that will assist in developing your core purpose:

- ☐ Needs to be authentic
- ☐ Must be succinct
- ☐ Must reflect the actions and culture of the company and its employees
- ☐ Must be communicated constantly and reinforced
- ☐ Everyone in the organization must be passionate about the core purpose

On the other hand, the core values of organizations in my sample of twelve disclosed better results. However, I noted two main shortcomings in my review. First, many organizations have too many core values. The recommended approach is to use between three and five. I personally like three, but five core values are acceptable. In my sample, I noted that some organizations had up to nine. The other shortcoming, I noted, is that the core values are too long. Instead of concise and clear core values, many were too long, and it was difficult, at times, to discern exactly what the core values were. Here is a core value from my business to make my point: *"Integrity and trust in all engagements."* I have also seen core values that use just one word. For example, a friend uses three words to describe the core values for his company and they are, *"respect, innovation, and passion."* Here are some guidelines that will assist in developing your core values:

- ☐ Need to be deeply ingrained principles that guide all actions
- ☐ Must be authentic

☐ Everyone in the organization must be passionate about the values
☐ Must be vigorously maintained and promoted
☐ Must be embedded into the fabric of the company
☐ Poorly implemented core values can damage a company's culture and purpose
☐ Properly implemented values should, at times, cause pain. The pain comes from strict adherence, no matter the circumstance

Q22: What's the difference between a vision and a mission?

Examining websites over the years and working with clients in my practice, I noted at times that there is confusion around vision and mission. As explained, the mission is the company's core purpose, its reason for being. Vision is something much broader, and it includes four key components or elements. These four items come directly from the ground-breaking article in *Harvard Business Review*, September-October 1994, by Jim Collins and Jerry Porras. The four items include core purpose, core values, big hairy audacious goal (BHAG), and vivid description. We have reviewed the core purpose and core values, so let's examine the other two elements: BHAG and vivid description.

A BHAG is an audacious long-term goal, such as: we will become a $100 billion-dollar company by 2035, or we will build the world's most admired brand by 2040. Here are some guidelines in establishing a BHAG:

☐ Requires a 10-to-30-year period to complete
☐ Must be clear and compelling

- ☐ Serves as a unifying focal point of effort and acts as catalyst for the team
- ☐ It has a clear finish line so that the company knows when it has achieved the goal
- ☐ Setting the goal requires thinking beyond the current capabilities of the company and the current macro environment
- ☐ It engages people; it reaches out and grabs them
- ☐ It is tangible, energizing, highly focused. People get it immediately.
- ☐ Forces the team to be visionary
- ☐ It should not be a sure bet, but the company must believe that it can reach the goal
- ☐ It should require an extraordinary effort to achieve

The vivid description is simply a vibrant and engaging description that specifically spells out what it will be like to achieve the BHAG. It's painting a picture of the BHAG into succinct words, so that everyone in the organization can easily understand and articulate. The vivid description is usually one or two paragraphs.

Q23: What is the most effective way to implement a vision framework?

What I have discovered through my advisory practice is that most companies do not have a complete vision framework. To recap, a vision framework consists of two parts with each part having two elements. The first part is the core philosophy or ideology which includes the core purpose and the core values. The second part is the envisioned future which includes the BHAG and the vivid description. The most effective way to develop a strong

vision framework is through an offsite workshop. The
workshop usually spans two long days with some
additional follow-up. The workshop participants should
number anywhere between ten to twenty people. Every
company is different. I advocate for participation by all key
people in the organization because they must fully embrace
and be passionate about the vision framework.

During the workshop, we first focus on the core purpose
and the core values. Sometimes the core purpose alone can
take an entire day and even possibly longer. Once the core
purpose and core values are agreed upon, I ask the team to
reflect on them for the remainder of the day and overnight.
Then, the next day before we begin the second part of the
vision framework, we review the core ideology one more
time. Once this ideology is agreed upon, we finally move
on to the envisioned future.

With the core ideology in place, the envisioned future is
much easier to prepare. I have the group participate various
exercises in that gets them closer to the envisioned future.
Once all the results from the exercises are reviewed and
summarized, we focus on refining both the BHAG and the
vivid description. When we define the BHAG, I'm a big
proponent of using a very specific target BHAG, one that
can be clearly measured and understood by everyone in the
organization. For example, we will be the most admired
brand in the U.S. for our product or service by 2035.
Brands can be measured, and the rankings of top brands are
common. Another more specific target could be that we
will be $1 billion in revenues by 2035, or we will operate in
fifty countries by 2035. Like the core ideology, I ask the

team to reflect on the envisioned future and report back to me.

After the two-day workshop, I ask the team to further reflect on everything before finalizing the vision framework and communicating it to the entire organization. Frequently, we have follow-up meetings and calls before the vision framework is cast in stone. I advocate patience with this process because it is obviously highly important for the future of the company.

Q24: Can you provide more insight on why an innovative business model is vital to creating an elite organization?
An innovative business model provides a distinctive, competitive advantage. Since the business model has two components—the *recipe* and the *organizational structure*—enterprises that create an innovative model around both components can create substantial shareholder value. The recipe represents all the critical and unique practices of the company, and the organizational structure is used to execute these practices in the most effective and efficient way possible.

In both this book and *CEO Lifelines: Nine Commitments Every Leader Must Make*, I highlight an exceptional company called Roper. I identify what I believe to be Roper's unique activities that have driven their extraordinary performance over the past decade. Roper's recipe should be used as a best-of-class example on how to create your own recipe. In this book, I highlight both Nucor's and Aldi's recipes which are also excellent. Both Michael Porter and Jim Collins highlight Southwest Airlines in their work as an exceptional example of a well-

developed recipe that provides a competitive advantage.
We can learn a great deal from studying these innovative
recipes.

I recommend that you select a company that you believe
to be a superior performer. Then, read their 10-K SEC
filings, annual reports (particularly the CEO and chairman
letter), and investor presentations. From this information,
you should be able to identify the unique activities of the
company. Although you may not get every one of them,
you should be able to discern the majority of them. These
publications will give you great insight into the company
and, more importantly, provide a framework for how you
should develop your own recipe.

Now let's move on to the second part of an innovative
business model, the organizational structure. At a very high
level, there are three organizational structures:
decentralized, centralized, and matrix (hybrid). Remember,
no two organizational structures are alike. Numerous
variations exist of each model. What is important is that the
structure is organized around the unique activities or recipe
of the company, and that the structure aligns well with its
culture and management style of its leader. It's important to
revisit what the great Steve Jobs once said, *"I discovered
that the best innovation is sometimes the company, the way
you organize a company."* There is a reason that one of the
greatest CEOs of all time was so focused on the
organizational structure; he knew that it would provide a
competitive advantage. You should know this fact as well.

Q25: Culture is often difficult to explain and understand; can you define culture in a simple statement?

Broadly viewed, culture is simply the way people connect with each other; the way people behave and think; the way the leadership team behaves, thinks, and communicates; the way everyone commits to the core philosophy and business model of the organization; and the way discipline is instilled in the organization through a nimble and effective governance system.

It is important to remember that once established, a company's culture is extremely difficult to change. In most companies, culture just happens—no one plans it. As discussed earlier, an effective mechanism to positively influence culture is an internal university. Culture should be at the top of the list for all leaders. A healthy and strong culture can also attract top talent to a company.

Q26: Can you provide an example of building a global business on an asset light infrastructure?

In this book, I discuss how companies should build a global business based on a variable cost model. This exceptional capability is necessary when a truly asset light business model is not practical or is impossible due to the heavy investment in infrastructure that is required to scale the business. Examples of a heavy capital investment model are companies like FedEx and UPS; both need to invest billions of dollars in infrastructure. There are many elements to designing your business around a variable cost model. For example, it is vital that people, assets, and capital employed are minimized quickly when the company experiences a downturn and scaled quickly when there is a major expansion. It's also imperative that standards be developed for key items, such as capital expenditures. However, most or all of this upheaval can be avoided with an asset light model. So, let's examine this model a little closer.

One of the best and successful examples of this model is Uber, the car services company. Uber has built an impressive and innovative business model with minimal capital investment. Uber's global network of drivers are responsible for investing in vehicles. Contrast this idea to limousine services companies whereby they invest in vehicles, large garages, and maintenance facilities. Uber avoids this large and relatively inflexible overhead which allows them to scale their business at a rapid rate. However, Uber's model has been under constant attack by regulators and others challenging, among many things, the relationship of the drivers to the company. There are groups trying to prove a nexus that the drivers are actually employees. Uber is obviously and aggressively defending itself, and it will be interesting to see how this plays out in the courts over many years.

Another excellent and successful example of an asset light business model can be found in the hospitality industry. Many of the large hotel companies own few properties. The generate their revenues from management services. Probably the best example of this model can be found at InterContinental hotel, which is a large British company. According to the *Economist* magazine, Intercontinental Hotel owns just eight properties out of a total portfolio of 4,942. This model is simply smart business.

Q27: What is the best way to develop the business model?

What I typically discover with most companies that I work with is that they have no clear documented business model, which includes the recipe and the organizational structure. The companies have evolved over time, and both elements exist, but they are not codified, and, in many cases, the companies have no clear consensus on what all the key parts are.

Like the vision framework, I advocate for a similar type workshop to work first on the recipe. The organizational structure needs to follow the recipe. Once I explain and provide examples of effective recipes, workshop participants get it quickly and usually become energized. Defining the recipe elements (between 8 and 12) is usually a very interesting undertaking. It forces companies to define what they are or what they should be because the recipe is all about developing a unique position in the marketplace.

With respect to the organizational structure, the workshop is more challenging due to the complex nature of structuring a company. To overcome these natural complexities, I simplify the overall objectives of the workshop by focusing mainly on identifying the top seven processes or systems that drive the organization and on the role of the corporate center. Then we proceed with a high-level design that takes into consideration the recipe elements, the underlying top seven processes, and the role

of the corporate center. However, due to the complex
nature of organizational structures, it's impossible to outline
all the considerations that need to be considered in a
workshop and particularly in this answer. In fact, entire
books have been written about organizational structure, and
they should be consulted for additional insight. I also
recommend that one of top management consulting
companies be retained to assist with the structure, if
financially feasible for a company.

**Q28: What were your strategic objectives with the
OneCompany initiative that is outlined in *CEO
Lifelines: Nine Commitments Every Leader Must Make*?**
The OneCompany concept has been around for a long-time,
and it has been used by numerous companies to optimize
their respective organization and to also unify their culture.
My objective was similar. The OneCompany initiative that
I championed was complex, and it required five key
building blocks, which were all interconnected. The five
interconnected building blocks included the following:

- ☐ Connections between operating groups that
  accelerated the development of markets across the
  globe
- ☐ Connections between groups that fostered
  innovation and a creative thinking culture
- ☐ Connections that facilitated a move from a
  service/product focus to an integrated solution focus
- ☐ Connections that promoted the speed of change
- ☐ Connections that created a distinctive culture

We discovered that the most effective way to implement an integrated OneCompany initiative is to utilize a hybrid or matrix organizational structure. This structure was optimal for our company to accomplish all of the above. More specifically, our structure clearly spelled out key responsibilities of each business segment and the corporate center, and they included the following elements:

☐ First, each business segment operated separately and was responsible for all its daily activities including operations, innovation, marketing/sales, sales/distribution channels, site management, and so forth.

☐ Second, the corporate center had three primary roles, each distinctively different. One role is what I call *business strategic services* which included strategy development, capital allocation, and board of directors. Another role is what I call *business segment support services* including human resources, compliance and governance, risk management, internal audit, financial reporting, treasury, and taxes. The third and final role included what I call *business segment operations support services* including global supply chain, environmental, health, and safety management, and sometimes research and development.

Q29: Conglomerates are being transformed into more focused businesses through spin-offs, divestitures, and acquisitions. Is the conglomerate model obsolete?
Highly diversified conglomerates like GE have been around for a long time, and they came into prominence in the 1960s. In recent years, activist investors have changed the landscape by demanding more focus, more commonality, and better performance. The list of enterprises that have announced a break-up over the last couple of years is impressive. They include GE, ITT, Danaher, Johnson Controls, and Hewlett-Packard to name a few. Even GE announced an audacious transformation, as we reviewed earlier. Also, many others like United Technologies and DuPont have spun-off large segments. Some companies, however, have resisted and bucked this trend with the most notable being Honeywell. Honeywell believes in its business model and continues along its path of a successful highly diversified conglomerates.

As I have explained in both this book and *CEO Lifelines: Nine Commitments Every Leader Must Make*, an effective and innovative business model can provide a competitive advantage. Thus, the focus should not be solely on the how the company is structured, but it also needs to be on the recipe. Remember, the business model has two interconnected parts: the organizational structure and the recipe. Also, it is important to remember that no two business models are alike. Every company has its own distinct business model. Before the organizational structure can be designed or reinvented, it's important to first get the recipe correct. The recipe will then dictate the type of organizational structure. Unfortunately, and too often, business articles tend to focus too much on such things as conglomerates when they should be focusing on the recipe part of the business model.

Q30: CEO unplanned exits are never easy. How should a CEO handle an unplanned separation?
Unplanned exits are a reality for an increasing number of CEOs. Separations are never easy, but CEOs can do some practical things before and after the fact to ease the transition. I'll use my own story to illustrate how an unplanned separation should be handled.

My story begins with my separation, in February 2012, from a $3 billion diversified global industrial company. I had joined the company thirty-two years earlier as an entry-level auditor and eventually worked my way to president and ultimately to CEO and Chairman. As a poor Italian immigrant, I am the embodiment of what is known as "living the American Dream." My dream came to an end after fifty months of leading the company through its most challenging period in history. I also served approximately four months as CEO-elect from August 2007 to December 2007. Perhaps I shouldn't have been surprised. The average tenure of a Fortune 500 CEO is fifty-four months, which is exactly the period I served counting the months as CEO elect. Nearly 80 percent of S&P 500 CEOs companies depart before retirement.

The economy following the 2008 US financial meltdown and later the European sovereign debt crisis led to sharp declines in construction and steel, the company's two key markets. In addition to navigating unprecedented economic turbulence, I was simultaneously overseeing a comprehensive business transformation strategy centered

on *globalization, innovation* and *optimization*. In the fifth
year of that crucial transformation, the company's board
decided it was best to bring in a new set of eyes to
complete the process, so we amicably separated.

As CEOs, we must always remember that we are
accountable for what happens no matter what the
circumstances are or the economic environment. The
ultimate responsibility always resides with the CEO. It's a
real no-excuse job!

When you're a sitting CEO, the world comes to you.
The day when you become the "former" CEO, it's a
different story. Board opportunities, for example. When I
was the CEO, hardly a month went by without an overture
to join an outside board. Given my work and travel
schedule, I didn't feel I had the time to consider such
opportunities. I thought I served the company best by not
diluting my energies with outside board duties. I thought
that board opportunities would always be available.

I was wrong on both counts. First, CEOs should not be
wary of serving on outside boards on the theory that such
involvement distracts from their primary responsibilities.
Research has shown that CEOs involved in outside boards
have a higher return on assets than CEOs who do not. In
fact, the research shows businesses serving intensely
competitive markets whose CEOs served on outside boards
see concrete benefits from such participation. These CEOs
had returns on assets that were 15 percent higher than their
counterparts whose CEOs did not serve on outside boards.

Now that I had the desire, time, and energy for board
assignments, the opportunities melted away. The recruiters
who had so enthusiastically courted me just a month earlier

now were, for the most part, unresponsive. That's the reality. It's more difficult for former CEOs to find board seats, so I recommend that CEOs who have an interest in outside boards and whose organizations permit it—4 percent of Fortune 500 companies don't—occupy such seats before it's too late. As stated in the habits of elite boards, CEOs should be required to serve on the board of another company because that service is a vital lifeline.

It's difficult, but not impossible, for a former CEO to be invited to serve on boards. After a period of proactive outreach through my vast network of connections, I eventually joined the boards of several excellent companies.

Unplanned exits can weigh heavily on a CEO's mind-set. It's tempting for separated CEOs to lick their wounds in private. Understandable, but counterproductive. For me, the secret was a path of inner reflection and illumination, followed by a strategic plan. I found the most effective antidote to the emotions of an unplanned exit is to immediately engage in new adventures. I believe that it's important to not make one large bet immediately after a separation. It is more important to first try many little things to see what is the best fit. One of my early initiatives was writing *CEO Lifelines*. I know in my heart that the book is immeasurably better for its author having gone through the ordeal of experiencing an unplanned exit.

An unplanned exit is one of the biggest jolts life can deliver a CEO, but it can also be a wakeup call. There is a life after losing a CEO position. New adventures await those people who are willing to give up an old identity to make room for something new. Thus, my advice is to climb on!

Q31: What are the best questions to ask a candidate interviewing for a high-level position?

As a rule, I don't believe in recruiting from the outside for high level management positions. This thought is based on many decades of experience. Unfortunately, circumstances sometimes force a leader to look to the outside to fill a critical position. This situation usually occurs when the company has an unexpected event, and no one is ready in the organization to step up to fill the vacancy. When this situation happens, three elements need to be in place in order to increase the probability of hiring the right candidate.

First, there needs to be a robust and well-designed hiring process. Second, people doing the interviewing need to be skilled at hiring. And the final element, the right blend of questions need to be asked of prospective candidates. Google is known to have one of the best processes, exceptional teams that know how to interview, and they ask insightful questions. Google is clearly on the vanguard of this vital skill, and elite leaders can learn a great deal from them. Here are some key questions and statements that should be considered during the interviewing process:

☐ When you were young, what did you dream about as far as a career or goal? Tell me why that was important to you.

- ☐ Tell me about your failures and successes, and what did you learn from them? What changes, if any, did you make?
- ☐ Tell me what type of leader you would be under a turnaround situation where the company is in a state of difficulty and turbulence? Would you be a different leader if you were running a healthy and growing company?
- ☐ What are some of your favorite business books and why?
- ☐ What innate characteristics do you possess that differentiate you from other candidates?
- ☐ Tell me a story about your life, starting when you were young until today. Be as succinct and articulate as possible.
- ☐ What are you most passionate about outside of your career?
- ☐ What are some the most important rules by which a leader should live by?

Q32: What was your most satisfying achievement during your long professional career?

This question is difficult to answer because there's much that I'm proud of. My career has spanned four decades (and still going), and I usually segment it into the period before becoming a CEO, when I was a CEO, and then the period after being CEO. Since most people usually associate success with metrics, I would have to say specifically the year 2008, and then the three-year period from 2007 to 2009 as the events that stick in my mind as to my most satisfying achievements.

During this span of three years, we achieved extraordinary record financial results, record cash flows, record stock price, sold a commodity manufacturing business for $300 million in cash right before the great recession, expanded all the businesses across the globe, focused on new innovations, built a robust business in China and India, and achieved numerous other strategic objectives as well.

Q33: What did you observe or experience during your long professional career that you found disappointing?
Again, this question is difficult to answer, but I would have to say two things. The first item as a general statement is the behavior of some people. More specifically: people making promises and then not delivering on their commitments, people not being loyal and supportive at the most critical time of need, people relying on attribution and anecdotes as opposed to unassailable facts, and people not being disciplined in all respects.

The other major disappointment is when leaders are appointed, promoted, or dismissed mainly through a less-than-optimal process. I'm a strong believer in process, justice, and facts. Unfortunately, during my long business career I have witnessed some situations where critical decisions were made, to a certain degree, on knowledge attained from attribution, anecdotal evidence, superficial facts, and emotions. As opposed to following a robust process that includes, among other things, truly understanding and valuing unassailable facts, taking into consideration accurate qualitative and quantitative information that spans a lengthy period of time, and then making appropriate judgments based on those unimpeachable facts. These judgments need to be made by people who have many years of insightful perspective, that is, elite leaders who possess strong precocious characteristics.

At the enterprise level, the CEO needs to ensure that appropriate processes and mechanisms are in place so that vital facts drive critical decision making. Likewise, at the board level, the lead director needs to ensure that the board, working through its various committees, also has in place appropriate and effective processes and mechanisms that can be relied upon to bring the facts forward. Emotions and attribution have no place in either scenario and should be discounted or ignored.

Q34: What is the recipe for restoring America's economic greatness, and does that recipe translate well to the business environment?

Throughout my travels, I have been asked this question often, and it unexpectedly came from people overseas. I believe that many of the points highlighted in this response offer valuable insight and possible recipe elements on how to restore a company that is in a state of decline.

Many have commented and written in recent years that America's best days are behind it. They point to a multitude of valid and substantive reasons for the decline. Some of these same pundits have boldly stated that the twenty-first century is the Asian Century and particularly China's time to rise to prominence. Many people are forecasting that China will ultimately displace the United States as the number one economy in the world. I don't dispute that the

Chinese economy may some day in the future ultimately displace the U.S. in size given their projected GDP growth and because the population of China is about four times that of the U.S. What I do dispute and want to make the point is that the U.S. can remain the best most innovative and value creating economy in the world—provided we change the mind-set of the nation. However, the downfall of the U.S. can become a self-fulfilling prophecy if we allow it to happen. There is a solution, or better yet, a recipe, which is outlined in the following paragraphs. Before we examine the recipe, let me support my hypothesis that the U.S. economy can continue to be the best (not necessarily the largest) in the world and that it is truly inimitable.

I have traveled the world, and I have seen first-hand how many of the world's economies work. I can state with total confidence and without hubris that the U.S. economy is without a peer. Further, U.S. companies normally have the best management teams, and innovation at American companies is unmatched. We also have the most productive workforce on the globe. We are entrepreneurial, and no model anywhere can replicate the U.S. capitalist system. And finally, the U.S. has most the world's top universities.

The only thing that stands between reclaiming our greatness is our mind-set and politicians with all their misguided regulations and policies. If we can correct the wrong path that we are on by changing our mind-set and electing leaders who think differently and put the interest of the United States first, we can take this nation to new heights—to the ultimate summit.

Walt Disney once said, *"All our dreams can come true, if we have the courage to pursue them."* For the U.S. to deal effectively with the emergence of strong global competition, great leadership, and the courage to think differently will be imperative. Moreover, the change needs to be audacious in scope and bold in execution. I see two interlinked parts: It is no different in the business environment, particularly when a company is in a state of decline. To reverse a company's fall, it will likewise take great leadership, the courage to think differently and be adaptive, an audacious turnaround plan, a superb strategy, and exceptional execution. Now let's review the two interlinked parts.

First, we need to establish a true partnership between the government, the people, and business. These three entities need to be viewed as one team. This alignment is critical to the long-term economic viability and health of our nation. It needs to be built on mutual trust, common purpose, shared consciousness, and empowerment—the key attributes identified by General McChrystal. Having seen this type of team effort first-hand in my travels overseas, aligning the interests of citizens with the business community and government can provide a powerful competitive advantage to the United States. Yet it can only come about through extraordinary leadership that is willing to boldly change the course. Again, looking at this situation from the lens of a business in decline, the management team, the board, and key seats in the organization all need to work as a team. They need to embrace the four elements identified by General McChrystal.

The second critical element is that a strategic road map needs to be developed for the country that incorporates policy reforms, economic reforms, educational reforms, and goals that are aligned with the long-term interest of the nation. Having a sound strategic road map executed by the partnership already mentioned is the best solution to dealing with any global economic threat. This road map needs to include energy independence, infrastructure development, substantive reduction in regulations, fiscal discipline and debt reduction, and corporate tax reform. It also needs to deal with the poor state of our public school system. It is imperative that the nation addresses these elements if we are to remain competitive and great. Again, looking at this situation through the lens of a company in decline, it's no different. A strategic road map needs to be developed; the business model recipe needs to be clearly defined—both of which are essential in restoring the health of a business.

The countermeasures to address emerging global economic threats is clear. Great leadership; the courage to lead and think differently; an audacious road map; and a partnership of government, people, and business can reverse the U.S.'s decline, and, ultimately, position the country once again for growth and economic prosperity. The strategic road map should be measured against key performance metrics. Moreover, the American people should be given a comprehensive report card each year as part of the President's State of the Union address, detailing the progress being made and where the nation is falling short. History has clearly shown that greatness can only be achieved when a country perfectly blends strong economic growth and military strength with an enlightened and aligned population that is supportive of its leadership. Many of these recipe elements can also be utilized by companies that need to restore their position and reverse their decline.

The American miracle can be recaptured and reenergized. America, we need to once again aim for the stars and reclaim our global leadership. Let's preserve and cherish the nation built by our visionary Founding Fathers and protected by the brave men and women of our Armed Forces. We owe it to them!

CHAPTER 15

CONCLUSION—

THE JOURNEY NEVER ENDS

Every mountain top is within reach
if you just keep climbing.
Barry Finlay[lxxii]

It's important for readers to understand that the journey to achieve elite status never ends! It's also vital that readers clearly understand that it is the culmination of climbing a multitude of summits over a long horizon that ultimately leads to elite status.

In order to successfully climb a multitude of summits over many years and ultimately adding your company to the ranks of the elite, it's paramount that you implement the foundational pillars and the lifelines leadership framework principles, and that you develop the building blocks of exceptional habits discussed in this book. Doing these things is how an enduring enterprise is created. Even if you are lucky enough to reach that ultimate summit where the air is thin, it will take considerable determination, focus, and discipline to sustain it for generations.

During the quest to join the relatively small group of elite enterprises, you will certainly face challenges, missteps, and unforeseen events that can slow or temporarily impair progress or even terminate the quest. What is important is that the organization, its leaders, and the board of directors be steadfast in their objective of climbing the summit. They must have unwavering faith in their abilities that they will overcome all major obstacles because they will encounter the fierce competitive forces determined to overtake them on the summit. At the top is where enterprises can be the most vulnerable.

Once the summit is ultimately reached by an enterprise, it is equally important to sustain elite status—which arguably will be even more difficult. Sustainment will likewise take considerable discipline, a strong will to succeed, and superior leadership. It is imperative that the enterprise, the leadership, and the board avoid the trap of hubris or complacency because it will likely undermine— or possibly even end—the quest.

The takeaway message from this book is that achieving elite status is difficult, but sustaining it for a long horizon is even more challenging. I truly believe that most enterprises have the potential to reach and sustain elite status by following the holy grail road map outlined in *Chapter 1, What Makes Companies Elite?* So, what is most important is to persevere and keep climbing!

Thus, the unrelenting drive necessary to both achieve and sustain elite status during severe challenges can be simply summarized as—Climb on!

Godspeed!

APPENDIX

MY LIST OF ELITE COMPANIES

The summit is what drives us,
but the climb itself is what matters.
Conrad Anker[lxxiii]

C learly many elite companies in the Fortune 500 garner much media attention including, such names as Apple, Priceline Group, Gilead Sciences, and Celgene. In fact, every one of these elite companies ranked in the top twenty in total return to shareholders for the ten-year period from 2005 to 2015, as reported by *Fortune* magazine in their June 15, 2016 edition. Although not all of my elite companies achieved the same ten-year relative total return to shareholders, these companies nonetheless make my list of elite companies because they exhibit consistent superior habits.

Most—or perhaps all—of the exceptional habits outlined in this book can apply to every type of organization—no matter what part of the economy. With a few exceptions—such as financial services—my list of elite companies broadly covers most of the key market segments of the economy. Here is my list of elite twenty-five companies, as they have climbed their respective summits in an exemplary fashion. My list is segmented into two parts. The first list includes Fortune 500 companies which made the top twenty list for total return to shareholders for the period from 2005 to 2015; this list includes a total of fifteen companies. The second list is mix of ten companies which are also Fortune 500 companies. Although these ten companies are not in the top twenty total return categories, they are elite companies nonetheless because of their long-term sustained superior performance.

Top 25 Elite Companies

Superior Total Return to Shareholders (Total of 15 Companies):

- Priceline Group
- Netflix
- Amazon
- Apple
- XPO Logistics
- Salesforce.Com
- Alaska Air Group
- Gilead Sciences
- Alliance Data Systems
- L Brands
- Westrock
- Celgene
- TJX
- LKQ
- Tractor Supply

Top 25 Elite Companies—Exceptional Consistent Performance (Total of 10 Companies):

- Google (Alphabet)
- Facebook
- Disney
- Berkshire Hathaway
- Southwest Airlines
- Nike
- Starbucks
- Danaher
- Honeywell
- 3M

It's difficult to argue with these two lists of exceptional companies—they are all paragons to emulate. Although other names from the Fortune 500 can and should be added to the lists—like MasterCard, Visa, Home Depot, and Moody's—the important take-away from all the names is that they cross multiple industries and end-markets. Thus, I believe the companies that make a deliberate choice to become truly elite and are able to adopt the habits outlined in this book with superior execution, focus, and discipline will undoubtedly increase their chances of ascending to the summit of elite. Elite status is not confined to a certain group of companies. To the contrary, greatness first and foremost is a matter of conscious choice.

ABOUT THE AUTHOR

Salvatore D. Fazzolari is the founder and CEO of Salvatore Fazzolari Advisors LLC. He has broad based professional experience spanning four decades in management, advisory, board member, author, mentor, speaker, and entrepreneur. He is fluent in Italian and has expansive experience in both industrial and consumer markets, including rail, energy, steel, metals, construction, defense, building products, coatings, specialty chemicals, global engineering, and headwear. Salvatore also has experience in private equity, software as a service, academia, and government.

Salvatore is currently a board member of RPM International Inc. (NYSE: RPM), a world leader in specialty coatings, sealants, building products, and related services serving both industrial and consumer markets, OrangeHook, Inc., a software as a service company focusing on identity solutions, Gannett Fleming Affiliates Inc., a private global engineering company, Bollman Hat

Company, a private world leading designer, manufacturer, and distributor of men's, women's, and children's headwear and accessories. He is also an Advisory Board Member of Current Capital LLC, a private equity firm located in New York City. He is also a member of Senior Advisory Council of AEA Investors LP, a private equity firm located in New York City. Salvatore is the former chairman, president, and CEO of Harsco Corporation.

He has published *CEO Lifelines: Nine Commitments Every Leader Must Make* (2014), an article in *Management Accounting* magazine (1988), and had a short essay published in Dr. Richard A. D'Aveni's book *Strategic Capitalism: The New Economic Strategy for Winning the Capitalist Cold War* (2012). Salvatore is currently working on a third book on Italian cuisine and culture. He is also acknowledged by Jim Collins in two books: *Great by Choice* and *How the Mighty Fall*.

He has extensive public speaking experience at universities, investor conferences, companies, and national conferences.

INDEX

REFERENCES

ⁱ Walter Isaacson, *Steve Jobs*, Page 457 Simon & Schuster, New York, November 2011

ⁱⁱ http://www.businessinsider.com/larry-page-at-ted-2014-

ⁱⁱⁱ *The Climb: Tragic Ambitions on Everest*

^{iv} Jim Collins, Great by Choice, page 182

^v Ed Viesturs with David Roberts, *Life and Death on the World's Most Dangerous Mountain*, Pages 1-2, Random House, New York, 2009

^{vi} "Aristotle," BrainyQuote, http://www.brainyquote.com /quotes/quotes/a/aristotle145967.html.

^{vii} Collins, *Great by Choice*, 178.

^{viii} Phil Rosenzweig, *The Halo Effect*, Pages 158-159, Free Press, New York, 2007

^{ix} Phil Rosenzweig, *The Halo Effect*, Pages 203-205, Free Press, New York, 2007

^x "Albert Einstein," BrainyQuote, http://www.brainyquote.com/quotes/quotes/a/alberteins148 778.html

^{xi} http://adventure.nationalgeographic.com /adventure/adventurers-of-the-year/2012/gerlinde-kaltenbrunner/

xii Warren Bennis,
https://www.brainyquote.com/quotes/quotes/w/warrenbenn
121713.html

xiii http://www.greatthoughtstreasury.com/m-h-
mckee/quote/integrity-one-several-paths-it-distinguishes-
itself-others-because-it-right-path-and

xiv Donald T. Phillips and Adm. James M. Loy, USCG
(Ret.), The Architecture of Leadership, Page 3, Naval
Institute Press, Annapolis, Maryland, 2008

xv http://www.brainyquote.com
/quotes/quotes/m/mayaangelo392897.html

xvi http://www.brainyquote.com
/quotes/quotes/a/abrahamlin137180.html

xvii http://www.brainyquote.com
/quotes/quotes/m/marioandre130613.html

xviii Wall Street Journal, May 24-25, 2014, page A11

xix Walter Isaacson, *Steve Jobs*, Page 457, Simon &
Schuster, New York, November 2011

xx Louis V. Gerstner Jr., *Who Says Elephants Can't Dance?*
(New York: HarperCollins, 2002, cover jacket.

xxi http://www.brainyquote.com
/quotes/quotes/j/johnfkenn105511.html

xxii https://www.brainyquote.com/quotes/quotes/m/michaelpo
r381644.html

xxiii http://www.brainyquote.com
/quotes/quotes/t/toryburch439022.html

xxiv http://fortune.com/2014/10/06/hp-ceo-meg-whitman-interview/

xxv Retired United States Army General John Abizaid.

xxvi http://cdn.media.ir.thewaltdisneycompany.com /2015/annual/proxy-2015.pdf

xxvii Fortune 3/15/15

xxviii Phil Rosenzweig, *The Halo Effect*, Page 172, Free Press, New York, 2007

xxix https://www.brainyquote.com/ quotes/quotes/n/naveenjain416008.html

xxx http://fortune.com/2015/06/04/fortune-500-ceo-survey/

xxxi Phil Rosenzweig, *The Halo Effect*, Pages xi, 54, and 49, Free Press, New York, 2007

xxxii "Nelson Mandela," BrainyQuote, http://www.brainyquote.com/quotes/quotes/n/nelsonmand1 78785.html?src=t_great

xxxiii https://www.aei.org/publication/fortune-500-firms-in-1955-vs-2015-only-12-remain-thanks-to-the-creative-destruction-that-fuels-economic-growth/

xxxiv Jim Collins, *How the Mighty Fall and Why Some Companies Never Give In*, HarperCollins, New York, 2009, pages 20-21

xxxv https://www.brainyquote.com/quotes/quotes/w/winstonc
hu101477.html

xxxvi Fortune Magazine, page 92, 3/1/15

xxxvii googleblog.blogspot.com/2015/08/google-
alphabet.html

xxxviii http://www.brainyquote.com/quotes/quotes/e/edwinlan
d193302.html

xxxix Eric Schmidt & Jonathan Rosenberg, *How Google
Works*, pages 238-239

xl http://www.mckinsey.com/insights/corporate_finance
/the_misguided_practice_of_earnings_guidance, March
2006

xli https://www.brainyquote.com/quotes/quotes/m/michaelpo
r381643.html

xlii The Boston Consulting Group, May 2013, page 2

xliii Fortune Jan 2015, page 58

xliv https://www.brainyquote.com/quotes/quotes/v/vincelomb
a385070.html

xlv Walter Isaacson, *the Innovators*, page 277

xlvi Jim Collins, *Turning Goals into Results, The Power of
Catalytic Mechanisms*, Harvard Business Review, July-
August 1999, page 2

[xlvii] *How Google Works*, Eric Schmidt & Jonathan Rosenberg, Grand Central Publishing, New York, 2014, Page 223

[xlviii] *How Google Works*, Eric Schmidt & Jonathan Rosenberg, Grand Central Publishing, New York, 2014, Pages 114-122

[xlix] http://www.brainyquote.com/quotes/quotes/s/stephenhaw378304.html

[l] General Stanley McChrystal, *Team of Teams*, Penguin Publishing Group, New York, NY, pages 99-100

[li] http://www.imanet.org/docs/default-source/thought_leadership/management_control_systems/customer_profitability_management.pdf?sfvrsn=2

[lii] P. W. Singer and Allan Friedman, *Cybersecurity and Cyberwar*, Oxford University Press, 2014, New York, p. 13-14

[liii] P. W. Singer and Allan Friedman, *Cybersecurity and Cyberwar*, Oxford University Press, 2014, New York, p. 65

[liv] http://www.mckinsey.com/insights/business_technology/big_data_the_next_frontier_for_innovation

[lv] P. W. Singer and Allan Friedman, *Cybersecurity and Cyberwar*, Oxford University Press, 2014, New York, p. 294

lvi http://strategiprocessen.stratresearch.se/Documents/Strate
giprocessen/MGI_Disruptive_technologies_Executive_sum
mary_May2013.pdf

lvii http://www.brainyquote.com/quotes/quotes/e/eleanorroo3
85439.html.

lviii http://www.inc.com/lolly-daskal/the-100-best-leadership-
quotes-of-all-time.html

lix http://blogs.law.harvard.edu/corpgov/2014/12/02/some-
thoughts-for-board-of-directors-in-2015-/#printable

lx General Stanley McChrystal, *Team of Teams*, Penguin
Publishing Group, New York, NY, pages 6-7

lxi https://www.brainyquote.com/quotes/quotes/m/michaelpo
r379016.html

lxii http://www.goodreads.com/quotes/188414-having-just-
the-vision-s-no-solution-everything-depends-on-execution

lxiii http://www.wsj.com/articles/smaller-boards-get-bigger-
returns-1409078628

lxiv https://www.brainyquote.com/quotes/quotes/j/johnpkott1
66628.html

lxv http://www.inc.com/lolly-daskal/the-100-best-
leadership-quotes-of-all-time.html

lxvi http://www.brainyquote.com
/quotes/quotes/v/vincelomba121318.html

lxvii http://fortune.com/2015/09/10/angela-ahrendts-apple/

lxviii http://www.brainyquote.com
/quotes/quotes/p/peterdruck131069.html

lxix Walter Isaacson, *the Innovators*, Page 134, Simon &
Schuster, New York, October 2014

lxx Wall Street Journal, April 1, 2015, Page B6

lxxi Roper Technologies, 2014 Annual Report, Letter to
Shareholders.

lxxii http://www.goodreads.com/quotes/tag/climbing

lxxiii https://www.brainyquote.com
/quotes/quotes/c/conradanke760588.html